Understanding World Christianity

Understanding World Christianity

Russia

Scott M. Kenworthy
Alexander S. Agadjanian

Fortress Press
Minneapolis

UNDERSTANDING WORLD CHRISTIANITY

Russia

Cover image: Gabrielle Grassl / Burning candles in a russian orthodox church at Christmas Eve stock photo / iStock
Cover design: Joe Reinke

Print ISBN: 978-1-4514-7250-9
eBook ISBN: 978-1-5064-6917-1

To our students: past, present, and future

Contents

Acknowledgments

We would like to express our gratitude to various colleagues who have read portions of the manuscript and given invaluable feedback, especially the faculty of Miami University's Havighurst Center for Russian and Post-Soviet Studies, including Stephen Norris, Zara Torlone, Vincent Artman, Ben Sutcliffe, Venelin Ganev, and Ann Wainscott. Francesca Silano deserves special thanks for reading the entire manuscript. Scott Kenworthy would also like to thank Miami University Howe Center for Writing Excellence for their writing retreats, where he was able to make significant progress on this manuscript, and his fall 2019 "Introduction to Russian, East European, and Eurasian Studies" class at Miami University for the comments they provided on the manuscript. Scott would like to thank Oana and Paul especially for their patience and support during the writing process, and to Oana for frequent conversations over the material. Alex is grateful for many colleagues, friends, and family who helped complete the scholarly knowledge with first-hand living experience of Russian Christianity.

Note on Transliteration
and Translation

Transliteration of names and terms from the Cyrillic alphabet to the Latin always presents problems. We have chosen to follow the standard Library of Congress style with the exception of names that have already entered into common usage in English (Leo Tolstoy, Nicholas II, etc.), as well as replacing the "-ii" at the ending of names with "-y" (in the text, not the notes). We have also dropped the final soft sign.

Unless otherwise noted, all translations from Russian are our own.

Introduction

For those in the English-speaking world who grew up during the Cold War, Russia was the Soviet Union, and the Soviet Union was the land of Godless communism and militant atheism. When the Soviet Union collapsed in 1991, many American evangelicals rushed in to convert the "atheists," more often than not completely unaware that Russia had just celebrated the millennium of its Christianization. Christianity has experienced a remarkable revival in Russia since the collapse of communism, but not necessarily in the ways either Russian or American Christians in the early 1990s envisioned that might happen. The period after the collapse of the Soviet Union was one of missed opportunities, when Russia, Europe, and the United States might have drawn closer together on shared values of democracy and the broad legacy of Christianity. Instead, the West continued to view Russia through a Cold War lens, while Russia in turn developed in the direction of a resurgent nationalism and authoritarianism that is now wedded to a conservative Christian discourse. Paradoxically, while Americans at the end of the 1980s associated Russia with atheism, by 2020, many Russians associate their own country and culture with preserving traditional Christian values and the West with having abandoned those values in favor of secularism and decadence. Once again Russia and the United States see one another as adversaries, but at least in religious terms, the poles have flipped. Such a rapid reversal is bound to be confusing, and in part this book aims to help clear up some of that confusion.

It is estimated that there are over one hundred million people in today's Russia who declare themselves to be Christian. According to one recent estimate, Russia has the fourth largest Christian population in the world, and by far the largest in Europe.[1] Yet in books about Christianity, Russia hardly features. In courses and surveys of the history of Christianity, Russia is usually passed over with the briefest of treatments. Not only are specialists in the history of Christianity trained with little reference to Russia; students of Russian studies frequently do not take into account the country's religious history and culture. As a consequence, Russian Christianity is characterized with very broad, and frequently erroneous, stereotypes. Although the specialist literature has been growing in the past two decades, there are no general introductions in English to the beliefs and practices of Russian Christianity, its history, theology, and contemporary place in Russian society. This book seeks to fill that gap.

There are many elements necessary to understand the reversals and transformations of recent decades, but the most important one is Russia's historical experience in the past century. After the Russian Revolution of 1917, the victorious Bolshevik Party transformed the Russian Empire into the Soviet Union, among other things the world's first experiment in

---

1. Pew Research Center, "Global Christianity: A Report on the Size and Distribution of the World's Christian Population," December 19, 2011, https://tinyurl.com/y6696ns3.

state-sponsored atheism. After decades of fierce persecution and decades more of forced compromise as a price for survival, Russian Orthodoxy, the country's dominant faith, was broken and demoralized, yet it survived. After the collapse of the Soviet Union in 1991, Russia did not follow the path of some post-communist lands like East Germany or the Czech Republic, where religious identities remained as they were under communism. Instead, the proportion of the population identifying as Christian in Russia has risen dramatically in the past three decades.

Western media tends to portray Russian Orthodoxy, and indeed Russia itself, in monolithic terms that obscure the realities on the ground. In particular, Western observers have long viewed the Russian Orthodox Church as the "handmaiden of the state," giving unqualified support and legitimacy to the state in exchange for the state granting religious monopoly to the Church. Russian Orthodoxy is a complex tapestry woven of many different strands. There is a vast array of expressions, from formal theology and official articulations of Orthodox belief and practice to the popular, lived, folk Orthodoxy of ordinary believers. There are divergent currents, from more open, "liberal" expressions of Orthodoxy to more "conservative," nationalist, traditionalist expressions—and a wide range in between. Russian Orthodoxy is no more epitomized by the proclamations of Patriarch Kirill and the ecclesiastical hierarchy than the Russian nation is represented by the policies of President Vladimir Putin and the Kremlin, though this is often missed by Western media. Through its examination of Russian Orthodox beliefs and practices, historical experience, and current realities, this book aims to help the reader understand not only the entire tapestry of Russian Orthodoxy, but also the diverse patterns within it.

The vast majority of Russians identify as Orthodox Christians, and the Russian Orthodox Church is the largest within the family of Orthodox Churches (which also includes Greek, Romanian, Serbian, and other members). Yet this is a form of Christianity largely unfamiliar to Western readers. For these reasons, this book focuses most heavily on Russian Orthodoxy. It is particularly important for an English-speaking audience to understand Orthodoxy for understanding Russia historically and today. Therefore, although some chapters of this book will incorporate non-Orthodox Christians into the discussion, other chapters, such as those on biography and theology, concentrate exclusively on Russian Orthodoxy.

This is not to deny or neglect the importance of other Christian groups. Over the centuries, Russia has been home to diverse forms of Christianity and indeed a vast array of religious traditions. The majority of non-Orthodox Christians lived in parts of the Russian Empire that are no longer part of Russia, such as Poland, Finland, and the Baltic states. Western Christian migrants, both Roman Catholic and Protestant from Germany and elsewhere, lived in Russia and also attracted some Russian converts. There were many new groups of Pentecostals, Evangelicals, and Jehovah's Witnesses who recruited Russians throughout the twentieth and twenty-first centuries. They also include indigenous forms of Christianity that broke from Russian Orthodoxy or were inspired by Western Christianity. Though not the focal point of this book, these other forms of Christianity are also considered in the narrative.

This book is divided into six chapters, in adherence to the structure of all the books in the Understanding World Christianity series. We begin with a consideration of what is Orthodox Christianity in general for the English-language reader who may be unfamiliar with this form of Christianity, as well as an examination of what is distinctive about Russian Orthodoxy within the broader family of Orthodox Christianity. The second chapter takes the reader on a journey through Russia, exploring how Russian Christianity acquired different characteristics in different regions of Russia through its interactions with religious others in given regions or the unique geography of each region. Chapter 3 provides a broad overview of the historical trajectory of Russian Christianity, while chapter 4 illustrates the experience of the past century through the lives of representative individuals. Chapter 5 examines the development of modern Russian theology. The final chapter analyzes the place of Christianity in contemporary Russian society and politics. Readers interested in particular topics may choose to read selected chapters, which can generally stand alone. However, the material covered in the first half of the book lays the foundation for what follows; the second half of the book builds on, and presupposes familiarity with, the first half.

This book has been very much a collaborative effort throughout. Both of us have spent our professional careers researching religion in modern Russia, and this book grows out of our experience of both researching and teaching this material, but we approach it from different perspectives. One of us is from the United States, the other from Russia; one has focused his research on the history of modern Russian Orthodoxy, the other has researched religion in contemporary Russia from sociological and ethnographic perspectives. Although each of us has been primarily responsible for particular portions of the book, we have worked closely together on the entire text and are both responsible for the whole.

The aim is to illuminate contemporary Christianity in Russia, but for such a task it is vital to understand how Russian Christianity's historical experience shaped its present form.

The authors hope this book can be read with equal profit by the general public seeking to understand Russian Christianity, as well as by students and scholars approaching the subject either from the vantage of world Christianity or Russian area studies.

1

Russian Christianity: Denominational Identities

After spending most of the twentieth century in the world's first state-sponsored experiment in secularism and atheism, Russia has experienced an unprecedented revival of religious identification since the collapse of the Soviet Union in 1991. Two-thirds of the population identified as non-believers and one-third as Russian Orthodox under communism, but that proportion has reversed in the decades since communism's collapse. A Pew survey of 2015–2016 found that 71 percent of Russians identify as Orthodox Christians, more than double the 31 percent at the time of the collapse of the Soviet Union. The next largest group were the non-affiliated at 15 percent, which includes non-believers (down from 61 percent in 1991). Muslims are the largest non-Orthodox religious group (at about 10 percent), with "other" religious affiliations coming in at 4 percent, and Protestants and Catholics accounting for less than 1 percent of the Russian population today.[1]

What this religious identification means is not straightforward, however, since it has not correlated with levels of religious practice, which have not risen significantly over the same time period. This puzzle of the rise of religious identity without a corresponding rise in religious practice—what it means and how it came about—lie at the heart of this book.

The overwhelming majority of Russian Christians today, as throughout Russia's history, belong to the Russian Orthodox Church. This book focuses especially on Russian Orthodoxy because it remains the form of Christianity with which the overwhelming majority of Russians identify. Moreover, because Eastern Orthodox Christianity is generally less familiar to an English-speaking audience, this chapter sets out the basic beliefs and practices of Orthodoxy that characterize not only Russian Orthodox Christians, but also other Slavic as well as Greek, Romanian, and Arab co-religionists.

What Is Orthodoxy?

What does "orthodox" mean for Russian Orthodox Christians? The Oxford English Dictionary defines the adjective *orthodox* as "following or conforming to the traditional or generally accepted rules or beliefs of a religion, philosophy, or practice," and popularly has the connotation of being conventional or

---

1. Pew Research Center, "Religious Belief and National Belonging in Central and Eastern Europe" (May 10, 2017), https://tinyurl.com/y45myggp. This study indicates that in virtually all Orthodox-majority countries of Eastern Europe, there has been a significant rise in the number of people identifying themselves as Orthodox Christians between 1991 and 2015, by contrast with Catholic countries of Eastern Europe, let alone Protestant and Catholic countries in Western Europe. See also Pew Research Center, "Russians Return to Religion, but Not to Church" (February 10, 2014), https://tinyurl.com/q5r8xvb.

rigid. The term *orthodox* is used to characterize certain religious groups, such as Orthodox Jews, who adhere to Jewish traditions more strictly than others, or Protestant theological trends characterized as "neo-orthodoxy." When contrasted with the term *heresy*, "orthodoxy" means correct belief or doctrine. Some of these connotations are more helpful than others when it comes to understanding Orthodox Christianity. The term itself derives from the Greek roots *orthos*, meaning straight, true, or correct (as in *ortho*dontist). The second component, *doxa*, meant commonly accepted belief in ancient Greek, but was also used in the Greek translation of the Old Testament to translate the Hebrew word for "glory" (as in *dox*ology). These two significances come together in the Orthodox Christian understanding, where Orthodoxy means simultaneously the right beliefs about God and the right way to glorify or worship God. Indeed the Orthodox affirm the notion of *lex orandi, lex credendi*—that which is prayed is that which is believed; the rule of prayer is the rule of faith. The emphasis on "orthodoxy" as "right glory" is captured in Russian and other Slavic languages, where Orthodoxy is translated as *pravoslavie*, where *pravo* signifies "right" or "correct" and *slava* means "glory."[2]

Orthodox Christianity is frequently referred to as "Eastern" or "Greek" Orthodoxy to distinguish it from Roman Catholicism (which was Latin and Western at the time of the schism between Eastern and Western Christianity dated to 1054). It is

2. There are many fine general introductions to Orthodox Christianity in English. An excellent place to start is A. Edward Siecienski, *Orthodox Christianity: A Very Short Introduction* (Oxford: Oxford University Press, 2019). The classic is Timothy Ware, *The Orthodox Church* (London: Penguin, 2015); a short presentation that captures the Orthodox ethos is Gillian Crow, *Orthodoxy for Today* (London: SPCK, 2008); more advanced and comprehensive is John Anthony McGuckin, *The Orthodox Church: An Introduction to Its History, Doctrine, and Spiritual Culture* (Oxford: Wiley-Blackwell, 2011).

somewhat of a historical accident that Catholics and Orthodox took those respective titles, since the Roman Catholic Church would certainly claim to be "orthodox" (as in right teaching), and the Orthodox Church claims to be "catholic" (or the universal faith).

Eastern Orthodoxy is simultaneously one Christian confession and a family of churches. As a single Christian confession, it is united by the same faith, the same creed, and the same worship. As such, it claims some 250 to 300 million adherents worldwide, making it the second largest Christian confession in the world today after the Roman Catholic Church. Although there are more Protestants in total, there are more Orthodox Christians than any particular Protestant tradition (Baptist, Anglican, Lutheran, or Reformed, each of which claims 80 to 100 million).[3] Today the Orthodox world consists of the ancient patriarchates of Constantinople, Alexandria, Antioch, and Jerusalem (see below), and a series of administratively independent or "autocephalous" (literally, "self-headed") national churches in countries such as Russia, Romania, Greece, Serbia, and Bulgaria, other nations where Orthodoxy is the dominant confession, as well as those where Orthodoxy is a minority religion, such as Poland and Estonia.

The highest-ranking prelate since the schism with Rome in 1054 is the Ecumenical Patriarch of Constantinople, who resides in Istanbul, Turkey; his primacy is one of honor, however, and in principle he has no rights to intervene in the internal matters of other autocephalous churches. The other ancient historical patriarchates (Alexandria, Antioch, and Jerusalem) have relatively small followings, so their role is

---

3. Pew Research Center, "Global Christianity: A Report on the Size and Distribution of the World's Christian Population" (December 19, 2011), https://tinyurl.com/rop5dez.

largely symbolic. Of the predominantly Orthodox nations, Russia is by far the largest, claiming over one hundred million believers or 40 percent of the world's Orthodox population (followed by Ukraine with thirty-five million, Romania with 18.5 million, and Greece with ten million).[4] Moreover, with one hundred million Orthodox Christians, Russia is the country with the fourth largest Christian population in the world (after the United States, Brazil, and Mexico), a fact almost completely unknown to Western Christians and overlooked even by scholars of World Christianity until now.[5] This is a fact of growing significance, as Russia asserts its role on the world stage as a preserver of traditional Christian values over against the West; Russia's presentation of itself in this light is not only for internal consumption, but also has influence in other parts of the world, especially the broader Orthodox world.[6]

In addition to the "Eastern" Orthodox family of churches, there is a closely related family of "Oriental" Orthodox Churches with an estimated 80 to 90 million adherents worldwide. These two branches parted ways over christological debates in the fifth century, but remain close in ethos, practice, and belief. The Oriental Orthodox include the Ethiopian, Coptic (Egyptian), Armenian, and Syrian churches. The Armenian Apostolic Church is particularly important for its historical connections with Russia. Even today there are an estimated one to two million Armenians in Russia, and most of them

---

4. Pew Research Center, "Global Christianity: A Report on the Size and Distribution of the World's Christian Population" (December 19, 2011). See the Table on Christian Population in Numbers by Country, https://tinyurl.com/udx2hp7.

5. Pew Research Center, "The Countries with the 10 Largest Christian Populations and the 10 Largest Muslim Populations" (April 1, 2019), https://tinyurl.com/tscs6ng.

6. See, for example, Pew Research Center, "Religious Belief and National Belonging in Central and Eastern Europe," part 7, Views on role of Russia in the region, and the Soviet Union, https://tinyurl.com/wmbdzge.

would claim their adherence to the tradition of Armenian Christianity, so we can assume that this is the largest minority of "heritage Christians" in Russia today.[7]

As a member of the family of Eastern Orthodox Churches, the Russian Orthodox Church shares the same faith, structure, worship, and other key features with the rest of Orthodox Christianity. Although the remainder of this book will explore the distinctive features and experience of Russian Orthodoxy, it is important first to understand the common features of Eastern Orthodoxy. The main features of Eastern Orthodoxy took shape in the first millennium of Christian history, and therefore we will look first at the formation of Orthodoxy before the conversion of Russia.[8]

Characteristics of the Orthodox Church

Although the title of this chapter refers to "denominational identities," in fact the Orthodox Church (like the Roman Catholic Church) rejects "denominationalism," a Protestant notion that asserts that different Christian bodies are all equally legitimate churches despite having different names, worship, and organization. The Orthodox would still adhere strictly to the creed that there is one Church that is truly and fully the Church. There is no consensus within Orthodoxy, however, as to what this implies about other Christians.

The Eastern Orthodox Church, like the Oriental Orthodox and Roman Catholic Churches, traces its history to the foundation of Christianity by Christ's apostles. The central features of

---

7. Alexander Agadjanian, ed., *Armenian Christianity Today: Identity Politics and Popular Practices* (London: Routledge, 2014).

8. For a monumental history of the first Christian millennium by a leading Orthodox scholar, see John Anthony McGuckin, *The Path of Christianity: The First Thousand Years* (Downers Grove, IL: IVP Academic, 2017).

Orthodoxy that took shape in early Christianity—distinguishing "orthodoxy," or true Christian teaching, from "heresy," or those teachings that strayed from or distorted the message of Christ's apostles—have always remained central to Eastern Christianity. The central characteristics of the Church that made it "orthodox" were apostolic succession, the apostolic tradition, the rule of faith, the catholicity of the Church, and its canon of Scripture. Early Christian writers such as Irenaeus of Lyon (d. ca. 202) argued that the apostles, when they made converts in new cities, would appoint a person to head that community before continuing their missionary journey elsewhere. The heads of these communities, known as the *episkopoi* (literally "overseers"), or bishops, would in turn appoint their successors. The notion of apostolic succession was that one could be confident that these bishops were passing on what had been entrusted to them by their predecessors back to the apostles.

The apostolic tradition (Greek *paradosis*, literally "that which is handed down") that was passed down within the church was the complete body of teachings and practices that makes up Christianity. At the center of this was the "rule of faith," an early creedal statement that declared that Christians believe in one God who created both heaven and earth; in "one Christ Jesus, the Son of God, who became incarnate for our salvation" and therefore was both divine and human; in the Holy Spirit, who foretold of Christ's coming to the Hebrew prophets and guides and sanctifies believers; and in the future resurrection and union of believers with God.[9] By "catholicity," or universality, early Christians maintained that the same gospel was proclaimed by Christian communities throughout the world, whether in Rome, Antioch, Ephesus, or other cities. This

---

9. Irenaeus of Lyon, *Against Heresies* 2.1–2, https://tinyurl.com/r6v5ued.

concept contradicted those labeled "heretics," who followed the opinions of individual teachers in isolated geographical regions; the notion of heresy was precisely to make one's own choice and follow the opinions of an individual rather than the consensus of the Christian body as a whole.

In the second century, though the writings that would eventually make up the New Testament had all been written, there was no agreed-upon canon of Christian Scripture. Given the plethora of early Christian texts circulating, only those were considered as Christian Scripture that were already in widespread use in the churches (and therefore "catholic") and proclaimed the same message that was passed on in the apostolic tradition and rule of faith. In other words, the rule of faith, apostolic tradition, catholicity, and Scripture were all pieces of a whole that could not be separated from one another. The sixteenth-century Reformation debates posited tradition as a separate body of teachings that derived from the Church's magisterium, either to be accepted (by Catholics) or rejected (by Protestants). The early Christian understanding, which remains the Orthodox one, was that tradition is the entire life of the Church, the whole complex of beliefs and practices passed down from Christ's apostles and their successors.

The above quoted rule of faith, which was elaborated in later creeds (especially the Nicene Creed of 325 CE), should serve as a reminder that most Christians through most of history—Eastern Orthodox, Roman Catholic, and Protestant—have shared the same core beliefs in a trinitarian God, the second person of which, the Son of God, became incarnate as Jesus Christ and whose life, death, and resurrection is salvific for humanity. What divides Christians are not what early Christian defenders of "orthodoxy" considered essential elements of the faith, but other matters: the question of how humans access salvation (faith versus works), the sources of reliable or infallible religious teaching (scripture versus tradition), the structure of the church and its authority, and differences in worship.

What distinguishes Eastern Orthodoxy on these matters from Western forms of Christianity? In what follows we will summarize these key differences.

Religious Authority: Scripture, Tradition, Councils

For the Orthodox, the Scriptures are the Word of God, and therefore all of the great Church Fathers and later theologians devoted their energies to commenting on and interpreting Scripture. The Orthodox canon of the New Testament is the same as that of other Christians. The Orthodox Old Testament, like that of the early Christians, derives from the third- to second-century BCE Greek translation of the Jewish Scriptures (the Septuagint), which contained more books than was later accepted in the canon of the Hebrew Bible; the Orthodox Old Testament, like the Catholic, contains more books than Protestant Bibles, which are based on the Hebrew canon. Precisely because it is the Word of God, the Bible is pregnant with meaning and can be interpreted at multiple levels—and the literal level is not necessarily the most important, especially in reading the Old Testament.

In terms of religious authority, the Orthodox would not agree with Roman Catholics that the earthly head of the church such as the pope could be infallible, since any individual human, no matter the office he occupies, can err. Nor would they agree with the Protestant notion of *sola Scriptura*, that the Bible stands alone as the only infallible source of religious teaching, for although the Bible is infallible, interpretations of it are not. Scripture must be inter-

9

preted—and interpreted within the Church, within the context of tradition, if the interpretation is not going to be just individual opinion. Moreover, key questions such as the nature of God and Christ are not explicitly articulated in Scripture, and the debates on these issues that raged in the early centuries of Christianity were precisely over different ways of interpreting the Bible. Ultimately, these issues could only be decided by the whole Church, and the mechanism for reaching consensus was the ecumenical (or universal) council, which brought together all the bishops as representing the whole body of the church. Moreover, even councils of bishops could err, so they only became considered ecumenical and binding after the fact, when they were received by the Church as a whole.

The Orthodox recognize seven Councils: the Councils of Nicea (325 CE) and Constantinople (381 CE) that resolved the questions of the trinitarian nature of God and produced the Nicene-Constantinopolitan Creed (sometimes referred to simply as the Nicene Creed), recited in every Orthodox liturgy; the Councils of Ephesus (431 CE) and Chalcedon (451 CE), and the Second (553 CE) and Third (680 CE) Councils of Constantinople, which resolved the christological controversies; and the Second Council of Nicea (787 CE) that ended the iconoclastic controversy and defended the use of imagery in Christian worship. Church Councils therefore have the highest doctrinal authority in Orthodoxy. In contrast to Protestants and Catholics, "infallible" authority belongs to the Church as a whole, especially as arrived at in a conciliar fashion. The notion that the essential nature of the church is conciliar was reflected in the old Slavic translation of the Nicene Creed, which translated the word *catholic* in the statement about the church (as "one, Holy, Catholic, and Apostolic") as *sobornaia*, or conciliar, which led to further fruitful reflection on the nature of the church later in Russian theology. (See the theology chapter.)

Although there have not been any Ecumenical Councils since the eighth century, subsequent theological disputes and practical problems have been addressed by "local" councils (those of particular patriarchates or national churches), some of which have taken on near universal acceptance in Orthodoxy, others of which have been crucial for deciding local issues. The Council is therefore the only ultimate means of deciding contested issues in Orthodoxy as a whole.

In the early twentieth century the need to convene a pan-Orthodox Council was put on the agenda, but due to the troubled historical circumstances of the century and deep disagreement, it took about one hundred years for the Council to be convened on the island of Crete (Greece) in 2016. The Council adopted a few major documents to unify the positions and practices of the independent, autocephalous churches. However, the Council partly failed because several churches, including the Russian, pulled out at the last moment and did not participate, mostly because of competing claims to leadership among the Orthodox between the Patriarchates of Moscow and Constantinople.

For the Orthodox, then, only councils can define doctrine and the nature of the Church. In order to administer the Church on an ongoing basis, the Church developed a hierarchical structure. The basic tripartite structure of the Christian clergy of bishops, presbyters or priests, and deacons already emerged in the early centuries of Christianity and still characterizes churches that retained that structure (Orthodox, Catholic, and Anglican/Episcopalian). Over time, the bishops of regionally important cities garnered more authority in practical, administrative, and disciplinary matters. This was particularly true of the largest and most important cities of the Roman Empire: Rome, Constantinople (after its founding as a second capital of the Roman Empire in the fourth century), Alexandria in Egypt, and Antioch in Syria. The bishops of these cities were understood as having a special authority in their respective geographical region. By the sixth and seventh centuries, the model that became accepted was that of the *Pentarchy*, that the church was governed by five bishops, known as popes (in Rome and Alexandria) or patriarchs (in the other three), in the following order of preeminence: Rome, Constantinople, Alexandria, Antioch, and Jerusalem, with the last added for its symbolic role as the "mother Church."

The basic structure of the Orthodox Church was inherited from the first millennium of Christianity, which ascribed the highest authority to church councils, and defined the regular administration of the church regionally, with large swaths of the Roman Empire being administered by the bishops of the major cities (the Pentarchy). The Christians living in the eastern part of the Mediterranean in the early centuries—especially Greece, Asia Minor (today's Turkey), Syria and Palestine, and Egypt—constitute the core of what later made up the Eastern and Oriental Orthodox Churches. Although much of this territory was conquered by the Arabs and later the Turks between the seventh and fifteenth centuries, Eastern Christianity spread north with the conversion of the Slavs first in the Balkans (in the ninth century) and the Eastern Slavs (in the tenth century). Although the ancient Patriarchates of Alexandria, Antioch, and Jerusalem declined in importance after the rise of Islam, Constantinople was strengthened as even the Slavs remained under it for centuries.[10] After the fall of Con-

10. The Serbs and Bulgarians were independent and had their own patriarchates for brief periods in the Middle Ages.

stantinople in 1453, Orthodox Christians in the Muslim Ottoman Empire were subordinated to Constantinople in religious and even civil affairs.

From the middle of the fifteenth century until the nineteenth century, only the Russian Church was autocephalous. In the nineteenth century the Greek, Serbian, Romanian, and Bulgarian churches became autocephalous as part of the struggle for national independence, and only in the twentieth century were their churches restored or elevated to patriarchates (Serbia in 1920, Romania in 1925, and Bulgaria in 1953). Therefore, the division of the Orthodox world into national autocephalous churches headed by patriarchs is relatively recent, though it serves as a powerful precedent for new independent nations such as Ukraine. (On the Ukrainian case see more in chapter 6.)[11]

Schism between East and West

It is worth noting that the first four churches of the Pentarchy were accorded these positions of preeminence because of their status as important cities in the Roman Empire, while only Jerusalem was added for religious reasons—as the "mother Church"—and only in the fifth place. In other words, though the East acknowledged the primary status of Rome, it did so because of its status as the imperial center, not on religious grounds as Roman Catholics would. Each of these heads was understood as having a particular geographical sphere in which they exercised their authority. At the same time as this model was developing in the East, Rome was developing its

---

11. On ecclesiastical structure, see the last section of Hilarion Alfeyev, *Orthodox Christianity*, vol. 1, *The History and Canonical Structure of the Orthodox Church* (Crestwood, NY: St. Vladimir's Seminary Press, 2015).

own conceptions that granted it preeminence over the whole Church with a unique status above all other sees. Since by this time the Roman Empire had collapsed in the West, a cultural drift began by which Eastern and Western conceptions of church authority diverged. This divergence happened gradually and in separate geographical realms, and was therefore unnoticed by either side until both became firmly entrenched in their respective models over the course of centuries. When confrontation finally did come in the eleventh century, the differences had become too entrenched to be reconciled.

The schism between Eastern and Western Christianity is dated to the year 1054, when the bishops of Rome and Constantinople excommunicated one another. But the schism was a process that proceeded over centuries before and after that formal break in communion between the two. Multiple differences developed between Eastern and Western Christianity. The Western Church adhered to the notion that there were three sacred languages—Hebrew, Greek, and Latin—which meant in practice that the Scriptures and worship were only permitted in Latin rather than the vernacular, which would remain the case in the Roman Catholic Church until the Second Vatican Council in the 1960s. The Eastern tradition from the beginning had been to accept multiple languages for Scripture and worship: in addition to Greek, Eastern Christians also worshipped in Syriac, Coptic (an Egyptian language), various Ethiopian languages, Armenian, Georgian, and others. This tradition would continue, especially in the ninth century during the conversion of the Slavs, when the Greek missionary brothers Cyril and Methodius devised an alphabet and translated the Gospels and liturgical texts into Slavic so that it was comprehensible to the new converts. This alphabet was later adapted to what we call the Cyrillic (named after St. Cyril), and is still used today in Russia and other Orthodox Slavic countries, both in the church and in general use (with further modifications).

Other differences between Christian East and West emerged as well. In the early church, both married and celibate men were ordained to all ranks of the clergy. Later in the Western Church, all clergy were to be celibate (although this only became decreed and enforced by the twelfth century). In the Eastern Church, bishops have been required to be celibate since the seventh century, and later tradition required them also to take monastic vows. Priests and deacons, however, could be (and usually are) married men. This is still the practice of the Orthodox Church. Other minor differences also emerged in worship and practices.

The only significant theological dispute between Eastern and Western Christianity in the eleventh century concerned the *filioque*, a clause that was added in the West to the Nicene-Constantinopolitan creed that was rejected in the East. The original creed stated belief in "the Holy Spirit, the Lord and Giver of Life, who proceeds from the Father, and who, together with the Father and the Son, is worshipped and glorified." In the sixth century, some Latin-speaking churches added the clause to state that the Holy Spirit "proceeds from the Father *and the Son*" (*filioque* in Latin). Though it was only in the eleventh century that it was finally added to the creed in Rome, it became a point of controversy when the Roman Church condemned the Eastern Church for leaving it out. The Eastern Church rejected the filioque on the grounds that it was both wrong theologically and also a sign of Rome's attempt to unilaterally exert illegitimate authority, since the Ecumenical Councils that shaped the creed also stated that the creed could only be altered by another ecumenical council. By this point, the Western Church asserted the authority of the papacy over that of councils, which the East regarded as an unacceptable innovation.

In short, by the eleventh century there was a range of differences between Eastern and Western Christianity that fueled polemics of each side against the other, although the most significant and ultimately irreconcilable difference was in the conception of church authority, especially the bishop of Rome's claims to supremacy in the church. In addition to the ritual, administrative, and theological differences, there were also political circumstances that exacerbated the division. The sack of Constantinople by Western crusaders in 1204, more than anything, solidified the division. Other theological differences emerged after the eleventh century, for example, after the doctrine of purgatory developed in the Western Church in the twelfth century, which was not accepted in the East. The differences between Eastern and Western Christianity would only become more pronounced in the centuries between 1054 and the Protestant Reformation in the early sixteenth century. The Orthodox would agree with many of the criticisms that the Protestant Reformers leveled against the Catholic Church, but at the same time would maintain that the Protestants, in rejecting the excesses of the medieval Catholic Church, went too far by also rejecting elements that had been key parts of the Christian tradition from the beginning.[12]

---

12. On the schism between East and West, see A. Edward Siecienski, *The Papacy and the Orthodox: Sources and History of a Debate* (Oxford: Oxford University Press, 2017); Andrew Louth, *Greek East and Latin West: The Church AD 681–1071* (Crestwood, NY: St. Vladimir's Seminary Press, 2007).

Church and State

Another profound difference that developed between Eastern and Western Christianity was the relationship between church and state. In the West, the Roman Empire collapsed in the fifth century during the so-called "barbarian" invasions, and except for brief moments, it was never again unified under a single political ruler. In response to the first sack of Rome, Augustine of Hippo (354–430) wrote his monumental *City of God*, which profoundly shaped Western Christian conceptions of politics. Augustine contrasted the City of God with the Earthly City, positing a disjunction between them and the superiority of the one—the Church as representing the City of God—over the state as belonging to the fallen world. Moreover, the collapse of the Empire in the West heightened the significance of the papacy, which became the only authority that could claim to unify all of what is today Western Europe.

In the East, by contrast, the Empire did not collapse for another thousand years, until Constantinople was finally conquered by the Ottomans in 1453. Though Western historians refer to this Eastern Empire as Byzantine, its inhabitants continued to call it the Roman Empire and saw no break in continuity. This unified political rule meant that instead of a sense of disjunction that prevailed in the West between the religious and the secular, the church and the state, the East conceived of the earthly kingdom as reflecting the heavenly kingdom and of the church and the state as acting harmoniously together. This conception was enshrined by the Emperor Justinian (r. 527–565) in the notion of the *symphony* of church and state, according to which church and state were separate institutionally yet worked together for the welfare of society, with the state being concerned with earthly affairs and the church with the heavenly. Byzantium was not a theocracy, because the clergy did not exercise political power (as the popes did in the West, at least in Italy), nor did the emperors have formal power over the church. The notion of *caesaropapism*—that the emperor was the head of the church and enjoyed the same authority over the Eastern Church that the popes did in the West—is a false Western caricature of the Eastern reality. The emperors in Byzantium—like the tsars in Russia in later centuries—were considered the protectors of the church; they presided over councils and were involved in the appointment of patriarchs. But the emperor never had the right to define doctrine or other exclusively religious prerogatives, and attempts to do so were repeatedly resisted.

At the same time, the ostensibly separate and equal spheres of church and state meant historically, in both Byzantium and Russia, that the church was in practice frequently subordinated to the interests of the state. Nevertheless, the symphonic ideal of church-state relations has been touted as the Orthodox model, and is still one that captivates the imagination of many in the Orthodox world, especially in Russia, where it is considered an alternative to the Western model of church-state separation. At his enthronement in 2009, Patriarch Kirill stated that although Russia was a democracy and therefore a formal symphony was not possible, nevertheless church and state leaders should strive for the "spirit of symphony" in church-state relations.[13]

---

13. From the Moscow Patriarchate's official account of Patriarch Kirill's enthronement (in Russian), February 2, 2009, https://tinyurl.com/yxfkhdb4.

Distinctive Features of Orthodox Theology

The first point about the Orthodox approach to theology is the way they understand the nature of theology itself.[14] The Orthodox rarely attempted to write the type of comprehensive, systematic presentation of Christian doctrine in the way that Western Christians, from Thomas Aquinas to John Calvin to Karl Barth and beyond, have attempted to do. In the Orthodox view, such an effort amounts to a reduction of theology to a rational, philosophical system. They believe that the mystery of God ultimately transcends human reason and the systems it constructs. Keenly aware of the limitations of reason to comprehend God, positive theology (what can be affirmed about God) in Orthodoxy is always balanced by the apophatic or "negative" theological tradition—that is, saying what God is not, as a reminder that words and concepts only approximate God. The purpose of theology is not to produce a rationally satisfactory account of the world, but rather to serve as a guide to deeper personal knowledge or experience of God. Theology for the Orthodox is likened to a map: to reach one's destination, it is absolutely necessary to have an accurate map, but having a perfectly accurate and detailed map is not the ultimate goal, and reading the map should never be mistaken with taking the journey. They therefore take theological articulation very seriously, and many issues have been subject to centuries of intense theological debate. At the same time, producing a

14. Accessible introductions to Orthodox theology include Andrew Louth, *Introducing Eastern Orthodox Theology* (Downers Grove, IL: IVP Academic, 2013); Hilarion Alfeyev, *The Mystery of Faith: An Introduction to the Teaching and Spirituality of the Orthodox Church* (London: Darton, Longman & Todd, 2002). For fuller treatments, see Hilarion Alfeyev, *Orthodox Christianity*, vol. 2, *Doctrine and Teaching of the Orthodox Church* (Yonkers, NY: St. Vladimir's Seminary Press, 2012); Mary Cunningham and Elizabeth Theokritoff, eds., *The Cambridge Companion to Orthodox Christian Theology* (Cambridge: Cambridge University Press, 2010).

comprehensive theological system was never an end in itself, since the goal is ultimately knowing God through prayer and communion, not through reason.[15]

Together with the Roman Catholic and most Protestant churches, the Orthodox affirm belief in a trinitarian God and in Jesus Christ as fully human and fully divine. Christians differ on other points. One of the key debates that divided Protestants and Catholics during the Reformation was in understanding how human beings access salvation (grace/faith versus works). The Orthodox understand these dynamics differently, and that difference also has a historical explanation. The framework in which these questions were understood in Western Christianity—for Catholics and Protestants alike—was defined by Augustine of Hippo. In the East, by contrast, a series of writers shaped the view, while Augustine had virtually no impact.

In the Augustinian conception of the fall, human beings are so tarnished by the "original sin"—which includes the guilt that every person inherits from Adam's sin—that everyone deserves eternal condemnation. Human nature and will are so corrupted that humans are incapable of choosing the good. Salvation, therefore, comes entirely as a free gift from God and depends entirely upon God's grace, to be accepted with faith, and not upon anything merited by human effort. Therefore God chooses (or "predestines") some, though not all, for salvation. This view was modified in later Catholic tradition, which allowed room for free will and the accumulation of merit through "good works," understood as concrete good deeds. The Augustinian conception was revived by Luther and Calvin during the Reformation and dominates most Protestant

---

15. See, for example, Patriarch Bartholomew, *Encountering the Mystery: Understanding Orthodox Christianity Today* (New York: Doubleday, 2008), chap. 3; Kallistos Ware, *The Orthodox Way* (Crestwood, NY: St. Vladimir's Seminary Press, 1995).

approaches. Even those that modify the Augustinian conception nevertheless accept the basic framework that he set forth, so the very nature of the debate is still shaped by this framework. Above all, in the Western Christian traditions, the term that is most emphasized is *justification*, which is understood primarily in juridical terms: though sinners, God chooses to regard those who have faith in Christ as "justified" by overlooking their sin, even though they remain sinners.

Eastern Christians understood these questions differently, and this understanding has had profound implications for their conceptions of human nature, salvation, and the spiritual life. The Eastern Church Fathers understood the primary consequence of the fall to be death (Gen 2:17; Rom 5:12). The fall introduced suffering, sickness, and the struggle for existence (Gen 3:14–19), as a consequence of which all of Adam and Eve's descendants inevitably sin. They are, however, guilty for their own sin—there is no notion of inherited guilt. Christ, through his sinlessness and perfect obedience (in contrast to Adam's disobedience), and through his resurrection from the dead, has conquered sin and death and reversed the consequences of the fall. Those united with Christ through faith and baptism share in his victory over sin and death. The Eastern Church Fathers emphasized that human beings are created in the image and likeness of God, which is not erased despite the fall, meaning especially that human beings retain the capacity for free will. Being fallen means that human beings are incapable of repairing the breach between humanity and God on their own; Christ's incarnation, death, and resurrection are absolutely necessary for salvation. But God's offer of salvation is for all and must be freely chosen and accepted by human beings.

The entire set of issues surrounding the notions of grace and faith versus free will and "works" in salvation was never debated in the Eastern Church the way it was throughout the history of the Western Church. Rather, the process was always understood as synergy or cooperation: salvation is a process of the human will cooperating with God's grace. Salvation is like cultivating a garden: without tilling the soil, pulling the weeds, and watering the seeds (human effort), the garden will not grow properly, but the garden cannot grow at all without sunlight (God's grace).

Moreover, this cooperation of human and divine will is understood ontologically rather than juridically. "Doing God's will" in Orthodox spirituality is less about obeying a certain set of external commandments. Rather, following God's will means conforming one's will to the divine will, so that the divine will actually operates within one and transforms one to become more godlike or holy. The Eastern Fathers, like Athanasius of Alexandria in the fourth century, declared that the Son of God "was incarnate that we might be made god."[16] Christ, by uniting his divinity to humanity, opens the possibility for humanity to unite to divinity in him. The ultimate goal is for humans to become by grace what Christ is by nature—that is, to become deified—though this oneness with God does not erase the distinction between creature and creator, nor does it signify a union that loses distinctions of persons. Believers are incorporated into the "body of Christ" that is the church, which means that believers are no longer part of Adam's fallen humanity, but rather of Christ's deified humanity. This is the goal and purpose of the sacraments and spiritual practices such as prayer and fasting. Salvation as deification is not an event but a process that begins in this life and is fulfilled in the life to come.

16. Athanasius of Alexandria, *On the Incarnation*, trans. John Behr (Yonkers, NY: St. Vladimir's Seminary Press, 2011), 107.

Spirituality and Worship

There are two primary approaches to the spiritual life in Orthodoxy, both of which are regarded as indispensable and complementary: corporate, liturgical worship and sacramental participation, on the one hand, and private prayer and spiritual discipline on the other.[17] All corporate worship conducted in church is liturgical, following elaborate guidelines for the services. The Orthodox place great value on adhering to tradition so that worship is not fundamentally different today than it was a thousand years ago. The clergy dress in intricately decorated vestments and use incense, the faithful light candles, and everything in the service (except for the sermon) is sung or chanted—including Scripture readings. No musical instruments are used in church; everything is sung by a choir, since the human voice is the only instrument created by God. Orthodox worship is also very physical: the faithful frequently make the sign of the cross and bow, venerate icons and crosses by kissing them, and during some services, especially during Great Lent, the faithful prostrate themselves in church as part of the ritual. Everything in Orthodox worship is meant to be beautiful, a feast for all of the senses—because believers worshipping at the altar are meant to reflect the angels and saints in heaven around the throne of God.[18]

The most important worship service is the Divine Liturgy, which is celebrated every Sunday throughout the year as well

---

17. Introductions to Orthodox spirituality include John McGuckin, *Standing in God's Holy Fire: The Byzantine Tradition* (London: Darton, Longman & Todd, 2001); and John Chryssavgis, *Light through Darkness: The Orthodox Tradition* (London: Darton, Longman & Todd, 2004).
18. On Orthodox worship, see Hugh Wybrew, *Orthodox Liturgy: The Development of the Eucharistic Liturgy in the Byzantine Rite* (London: SPCK, 2013); Hilarion Alfeyev, *Orthodox Christianity*, vol. 4, *The Worship and Liturgical Life of the Orthodox Church* (Yonkers, NY: St. Vladimir's Seminary Press, 2016).

as on major feast days, and even more often in some monasteries and cathedrals. The standard liturgy performed in all Orthodox Churches is that attributed to the theologian and bishop John Chrysostom (d. 407 CE). The basic structure of the Divine Liturgy is similar to the Catholic mass or the Eucharistic service in the Lutheran or Anglican churches, with two main focal points: the Liturgy of the Word, culminating in the reading of the Gospel, and the Liturgy of the Faithful, culminating in the Eucharist. In the Russian Church it is in the special liturgical language of Church Slavonic, a modified version of how Cyril and Methodius translated it in the ninth century. It is, therefore, an archaic language, and not necessarily readily comprehensible to modern Russian speakers. It is used for all the services, prayers, and Scripture readings in church (though not the sermon spoken by the priest). For over a century, some Russian Orthodox have advocated the adoption of modern Russian for the liturgy, though there does not seem to be widespread support for such a change.[19]

In addition to the Eucharistic Divine Liturgy, the Orthodox Church has a cycle of daily worship that in effect consecrates each day, with Vespers as the evening prayer and Matins as the morning prayer, in addition to other services. All of these services are conducted daily in a monastery. In an ordinary parish, this cycle of worship is ordinarily limited to the celebration of Vespers (or the "All-Night Vigil" in the Russian tradition) on evenings before the divine liturgy, that is, on Saturday evening and the eve of great feasts, with liturgy following on Sunday or feast day mornings.

Orthodox worship sanctifies time not only through the daily cycle of prayer, but also through an annual cycle of feasts that

19. Brian P. Bennett, *Religion and Language in Post-Soviet Russia* (New York: Routledge, 2011).

commemorate the key moments in the life of Christ and the Virgin Mary as well as the saints, together with preparatory fasts. There are both fixed and variable parts of the services, and the latter vary according to the cycle of the liturgical year or the saint being celebrated. This hymnography consists of profound theological truths conveyed in beautiful poetic form. The center of the liturgical year is Easter, known as *Pascha* (derived from the Hebrew *pesach* for Passover) in most Orthodox languages, including Russian, the feast of feasts celebrated with a joyous midnight service.

The Orthodox Churches retained the calendar of the Roman Empire (known as the Julian calendar) even after the adoption in the sixteenth century of the Gregorian calendar in the West. The difference between them is thirteen days, so that December 25 on the Julian calendar falls on January 7 according to the Gregorian. In the early twentieth century, some Orthodox Churches followed the Patriarchate of Constantinople in adopting a reformed calendar. The result is that some Orthodox (such as the Greeks and Romanians) celebrate Christmas together with Western Christians, whereas others, including the Russians, celebrate Christmas according to the Julian calendar. Virtually all of the Orthodox celebrate Easter together, and this date varies so that it can fall on the same date as Western Easter or as much as a month later. Some Orthodox regard the calendar as an important religious issue.

There are "rules of prayer" meant to be said by every believer privately each day. In addition to daily prayer, every believer is encouraged to practice asceticism, spiritual disciplines to curb sinful inclinations and train the will. Asceticism derives from the Greek *askesis*, a term initially related to sports for exercise and training, which are also necessary for spiritual growth. In principle, prayer is less about asking God to fulfill one's wants; rather, it is about worshiping God and expressing thanksgiving for God's blessings, asking for mercy and forgiveness for one's sins, and calling down God's blessings for other people.[20]

A key form of spiritual discipline is fasting. Fasting in the Orthodox tradition means both eating less and restricting what one eats, above all to refrain from animal products. Wednesdays and Fridays throughout the year are fast days, as well as entire periods such as the forty days before Easter and Christmas. Although by no means all Orthodox Christians observe the fasts strictly, many will be aware that it is a fast and make an attempt at least to observe it partially. According to surveys performed by the Levada Center in 1998, 79 percent of Russians did not change their habits during Great Lent (the fast before Easter); that number had fallen to 69 percent in 2013 and has varied in subsequent years. Although the number of those who completely followed the fast is low (2 to 4 percent), the number of those who intended to fast at least partially rose significantly from 11 to 21 percent over the same time period.[21]

Monasticism has been a central expression of Orthodox spirituality since its emergence in the third and fourth centuries, and has continued to play a vital role throughout the history of Russian Orthodoxy.[22] Monasticism is a vocation to which some Christians are called, though they are generally not considered "superior" Christians to those who remain in the world. In tak-

20. On the contemporary practice of Orthodox prayer, including Russian cases, see Sonja Luehrmann, ed., *Praying with the Senses: Contemporary Orthodox Christian Spirituality in Practice* (Bloomington: Indiana University Press, 2018).
21. See the Levada Center's data at https://tinyurl.com/wspjsj7 and https://tinyurl.com/ub5uvtm.
22. See Scott M. Kenworthy, "Russian Orthodox Monasticism from 988 to 1917" and "The Eastern Traditions Today: Russian and Romanian Monasticism," in *The Oxford Handbook of Christian Monasticism*, ed. Bernice Kaczynski (Oxford: Oxford University Press, 2020), pp. 478–94 and 590–605.

ing vows of poverty, chastity, and obedience, monks and nuns choose to forego career and family, wealth and sex, in order to devote themselves to God. Their lives are centered on prayer, which is complemented by labor (monasteries strive to be self-sufficient communities) and study. Because the entire community is devoted to prayer, monasteries are perceived by the church at large as spiritual havens with solemn liturgies and experienced spiritual guides. They represent an alternative, or a complement, to the parish with its focus on the regular sacraments and local community. As such, pilgrims are attracted to monasteries for spiritual nourishment, perhaps just for a day or two, or possibly for more extended retreats.

The most distinctive practice of private prayer is the "prayer of the heart." Although one worships God with the words of prayer, God is experienced most directly in silence (Greek *hesychia*). This type of prayer is especially to be followed by those who have devoted their lives to prayer, namely the monks and nuns. St. Paul's injunction to "pray without ceasing" led to the development of short prayers that could be repeated in any circumstance, particularly the "Jesus Prayer": "Lord Jesus Christ, Son of God, have mercy on me." By saying this simple prayer attentively, one could still distracting thoughts and impulses. Then, in the stillness of the heart that has been purified by spiritual discipline, the Orthodox believe that one can have communion with God that transcends words. The reality of this union with God was given theological articulation during the Hesychastic controversies in fourteenth-century Byzantium, especially by Gregory Palamas (1296–1359), whose theology was subject to revived interest in the twentieth century.[23]

---

23. John Meyendorff, *St. Gregory Palamas and Orthodox Spirituality* (Crestwood, NY: St. Vladimir's Seminary Press, 1974).

The Sacraments and Religious Arts

Since the seventeenth century, under the influence of Roman Catholicism, Orthodox catechisms and manuals stated that the Orthodox have seven sacraments and that the Orthodox doctrine of the Eucharist was, like the Catholics, one of transubstantiation—namely that the bread and wine become in essence the real body and blood of Christ while keeping the appearance of bread and wine. Some prominent Orthodox theologians of the twentieth century, however, challenged these notions as not reflecting the teachings of the early Church Fathers and the spirit of Orthodoxy. The term for the sacraments in Orthodox languages is *the mysteries*: in the sacraments the church takes ordinary elements of the world, such as bread and wine in the Eucharist or water in baptism, and offers them to God; by the power of the Holy Spirit these elements are transformed, transfigured, to become vehicles of God's grace. By contrast with Roman Catholics, the Orthodox have not been concerned to provide rational explanation for how the sacraments work, accepting that they are mysteries; but by contrast with many Protestants, the Orthodox believe that something real does take place in the sacrament.

For the Orthodox, the Fall concerned not only human beings, but affected all of creation, which has been "groaning in travail" since, but redemption means that "creation itself will be set free from its bondage to decay and obtain the glorious liberty of the children of God" (Rom 8:21–22 RSV). In the Orthodox understanding, just as the disobedience of humans led to the introduction of death, disease, and corruption in all of creation, so believers who have been sanctified are to act as priests of creation, offering creation back to God so that the Holy Spirit can fill it with divine grace and transfigure creation

itself. Some modern Orthodox theologians, especially Patriarch Bartholomew of Constantinople, have taken this view of
creation to develop a fruitful ecological theology by which
humanity's "dominion" over the earth (Gen 1:28) is to be
expressed not by exploiting creation but by exercising proper
stewardship for it.[24]

The most important sacraments are baptism and the
Eucharist.[25] Central to the Orthodox understanding of baptism
is the language in St. Paul's Epistles: in baptism the believer
dies to the fallen, sinful, Adamic humanity and rises to new
humanity in Christ (Rom 6). This is symbolized in the traditional Orthodox practice of baptism by full immersion: entry
into the water is the death to sin, and rising from the water is
rising to new life in Christ. Baptism incorporates the believer
into the body of Christ, which is the Church, the new humanity
that has Christ as its head rather than the old, fallen humanity
under Adam. Baptism is completed in chrismation, which is
anointing with oil that is believed to confer the gift of the Holy
Spirit. It is the sacramental equivalent of Roman Catholic confirmation, except that it is performed immediately after baptism, even for children, which is then followed by one's first
communion. All baptized members of the church, including
children, can receive communion.

The Eucharist is the sacrament of sacraments in Orthodoxy.
The Orthodox believe that when Christians offer the bread and
wine in thanksgiving, it becomes the body and blood of Christ.
The Orthodox do not insist that the bread and wine cease to

24. John Chryssavgis, *Creation as Sacrament: Reflections on Ecology and Spirituality* (Lon-
don: T&T Clark, 2019).
25. On Orthodox sacramental theology, see especially the works of Alexander
Schmemann, beginning with *For the Life of the World: Sacraments and Orthodoxy*
(Crestwood, NY: St. Vladimir's Seminary Press, 1995); and Hilarion Alfeyev,
Orthodox Christianity, vol. 5, *Sacraments and Other Rites* (Crestwood, NY: St.
Vladimir's Seminary Press, 2019).

be bread and wine, but just as Christ is God and human at the same time, the Eucharist can simultaneously be both bread and wine and the body and blood of Christ. All the Eastern Church Fathers affirmed that the Eucharist is a spiritual reality. In the Eucharist, believers partake of the body of Christ (the Eucharist) and thereby become the body of Christ (the Church). Receiving the Eucharist is a primary means of deification: one's physical body is united to Christ's body as a way of transforming it in preparation for the resurrection at the end of time. But precisely because the Eucharist is seen as such a spiritually powerful action, believers are expected to prepare for it by a regular confession of sins, done before a witness—in the sacramental context, before the priest who then says a prayer of absolution. For this reason, it became customary for many centuries in Orthodoxy that ordinary laypeople rarely went to communion and had to prepare for it by a lengthy and rigorous process of fasting and confession, usually once a year during Great Lent. In the twentieth century, however, Orthodox theologians such as Alexander Schmemann urged a liturgical renewal that encouraged frequent communion as a way of making Eucharistic participation a central act of Christian life.

Another distinctive feature of Orthodox worship is its architecture and iconography.[26] Orthodox churches, especially Russian ones, may look grand on the outside, but the interior is generally characterized by an intimate feel. The Orthodox church building seeks to reflect God's nearness, to reflect the notion that God has come down to humanity through Christ's incarnation and through the gift of the Holy Spirit.

As a rule, the Orthodox rarely use statues and stained glass; but Byzantine-style icons—two-dimensional religious images

26. See Hilarion Alfeyev, *Orthodox Christianity*, vol. 3, *The Architecture, Icons, and Music of the Orthodox Church* (Crestwood, NY: St. Vladimir's Seminary Press, 2014).

—are ubiquitous. Painted on wood, believers have them in their homes, especially in a prayer corner. They adorn the *iconostasis*, the icon screen that separates the nave from the sanctuary, and usually the walls of the church itself are also decorated with frescoes or mosaics. In response to the iconoclastic controversy in the Byzantine Empire in the eighth and ninth centuries, the Orthodox Church developed an explicit theological justification for icons in response to the charge that they violated the commandment not to make "graven images" (Exod 20:4). It accepted the Old Testament prohibition against making images of God the Father as appropriate because God is Spirit and cannot be depicted; in the Orthodox tradition it is not, therefore, customary to make depictions of God the Father. But Christ, by becoming incarnate, became visible and therefore depictable, and doing so is an affirmation of the incarnation. The Seventh Ecumenical Council not only made this argument, but also made clear the distinction between the *veneration* or honor paid to images because of what they represent, and *worship*, which is due to God alone. The Orthodox venerate but do not worship icons, and icons are therefore *not* idols. Icons are intentionally two-dimensional and not realistic, but rather deeply symbolic: they are not meant to represent earthly realities so much as to act as a "window to heaven."

Icons follow certain traditional patterns, so that believers can easily recognize an icon of Christ's birth or of St. Nicholas. At the same time, there is room within those set parameters both for creative expression of the artist and for distinctions of different national (or even regional) traditions within the Orthodox world. The Russian tradition developed a fantastic wealth of icons of different styles and shapes. The most distinctive feature of the Russian church interior is the multi-tiered iconostasis. At the center of the screen stand the Royal Doors that lead to the sanctuary and are used by the priest during the liturgy. On either side of the Doors are always placed two main icons—Christ on the right side and the Theotokos (Mary, literally "the one who bore God") with the Christ child on the left, and above the Door, Christ enthroned. Other icons on other tiers of the iconostasis represent archangels, the four Evangelists, the biblical prophets, and later saints.

Russian iconography followed Byzantine patterns but developed its own particular styles as seen, for example, in the fourteenth- and fifteenth-century frescoes and wooden icons by Andrei Rublev (who was canonized as a saint in 1988) and Dionisius. Overall, iconography followed Byzantine standards until the seventeenth century, when Western artistic influences introduced elements of realism and baroque splendor.

Icons in Russia were not just decorations, illustrations, or reminders; they represent the world beyond, another reality, and they worked as a medium to contact the transcendent. Some special icons acquired through the experience of generations the reputation of being "miracle-working," possessing an extraordinary grace that produces miracles. Miracle-working icons have been known in the Catholic Church as well—some of the Madonna images were said to have such power; however, in Eastern Orthodoxy, including Russia, this kind of veneration seems to be particularly unique. In effect the first miraculous icon, according to tradition, was the Mandylion (or the "image of Edessa"), the image of Christ imprinted on a cloth for King Abgar of Edessa; copies of this image were believed to be the model for the "Savior Not Made with Hands" icon, popular in Russia. The most revered icons in Russia, however, have been those of Mary the Theotokos.

Some of the icons became national symbols, such the

Vladimir and Kazan icons of the Theotokos. The first, the Vladimir icon, a Byzantine icon (according to legend painted by Luke the Evangelist), was sent to the key medieval city of Vladimir; it is said to have miraculously protected the country several times and is now preserved in a chapel built for that purpose in the Tretyakov Gallery in Moscow. A second one, the Kazan Theotokos, designed in a Byzantine style, appeared (or was "found"), according to the legend, in the city of Kazan at the end of the sixteenth century, then moved to Moscow, where it is said to have played a central role in reviving the Russian state during the so-called Time of Troubles, in 1611 and 1612. This miracle of protecting the city and the nation came, significantly, from a copy of the icon, not the original, which attests to a widespread tradition of disseminating miraculous grace among many copies. Although the original of the Kazan icon strangely disappeared, many copies were venerated as miracle-working. The Kazan icon is special indeed, because the day of its celebration (November 4) became a national holiday in 2005, called the Day of People's Unity, to commemorate the end of the Time of Troubles (and to replace the holiday of the Bolshevik Revolution, which fell on November 7).[27]

---

27. On icon veneration in Russian Orthodoxy, see Vera Shevzov, "Iconic Piety in Russia," in *A People's History of Christianity*, vol. 6, *Modern Christianity to 1900*, ed. Amanda Porterfield (Minneapolis: Fortress, 2007), 178–208. On the Kazan icon in the Russian tradition, see Shevzov, "Scripting the Gaze: Liturgy, Homilies and the Kazan Icon of the Mother of God in Late Imperial Russia," in *Sacred Stories: Religion and Spirituality in Modern Russia*, ed. M. Steinberg and H. Coleman (Bloomington: Indiana University Press, 2007), 61–92; and "On the Field of Battle: The Marian Face of Post-Soviet Russia," in *Framing Mary: The Mother of God in Modern, Revolutionary, and Post-Soviet Russian Culture*, edited by Amy Singleton Adams and Vera Shevzov (Dekalb: Northern Illinois University Press, 2018), 270–311.

Distinctive Characteristics
of the Russian Tradition

Most of the elements outlined above are intended to describe the general characteristics of Orthodox Christianity. The structure, beliefs, practices, and worship are shared by all Orthodox Christians. Virtually everything that has been said applies equally to all Orthodox Churches—Greek, Slavic, or otherwise—though emphases in any element can and have varied by tradition and era. Naturally in Orthodoxy, as in most other religious traditions, the formal teachings and rationale for ecclesiastical structures is understood and assimilated by ordinary believers in their own fashion, frequently in ways that would not be acceptable to the theologians or church officials. This is particularly the case in contemporary Russia, where religious education was formally banned for most of the twentieth century.

As we speak further of a particular identity of the Russian Church, distinguishing it from the rest of the Orthodox commonwealth, we should turn to those historical and sociopolitical circumstances that shaped this particular national tradition (as will be done in subsequent chapters). In Russian there are two distinct adjectives that are both translated into English as "Russian"—*russky* and *rossiisky*. The difference may be elusive but sometimes becomes significant. *Russky* is associated with ethnic national culture, while *rossiisky* has political and imperial connotations, referring to *Rossiia*—the official name of the country, from the imperial times of the Romanov dynasty (*Rossiiskaia imperia*—Russian Empire) to the twenty-first century (*Rossiiskaia Federatsiia*—Russian Federation).

Throughout its history, the Russian Orthodox Church used both terms (*russkaia* or *rossiiskaia*) for its name, each providing different connotations. In Imperial Russia, the Church was *Rossiiskaia*, to stress that the Church (like the Empire) consisted of more than ethnic Russians and included many other Slavic or non-Slavic peoples. In the twentieth century, when the Church was decoupled from the state by the communists, and when the term *Russia* became downplayed as a part of the new Soviet empire, the official title for the Church became *Russkaia*. Over time, this usage has taken on new implications for the Church's outreach: it refers not so much to the state borders or to the empire or a multi-ethnic state, but rather to the (ethnic) Russian people in a way that includes those who live outside the Russian Federation, with significant numbers living in the new states succeeding the Soviet Union as well as in the diaspora around the world. In this sense, *Russkaia* refers both to a national ecclesiastical tradition and also to what may be called a new transnational reality—the global spread of ethnic Russians.

In modern times, Eastern Churches have been closely associated with particular ethnicities or nationalities to the degree that religious and national identity were often enmeshed. This is also true of the Russian Orthodox, who have frequently had a special sense of "chosenness." Yet this close identification of faith and nation is in tension with Christianity's universal claims, including the Orthodox Church's own claims to be the one true Church for all humanity (or "catholic" as proclaimed in the creed). This is a tension not unique to the Russian or any other Orthodox Church, however, and many Christians, from Irish Catholics to American evangelicals, have conceived of themselves as somehow special in God's eyes.

The "ethnic" overtone in the very name of the Russian Orthodox Church presumes that all ethnic Russians wherever they live—in Russia proper, in France, or in China—are considered as bearers of this same religious tradition. It then becomes an "endemic" national religion. People born from Russian parents are "supposed" to be Russian Orthodox. However, this conception of a "national religion" creates confusion. What about those who have converted to another religion? Have they somehow lost their "Russianness" if they are no longer Orthodox? Or, conversely, what about someone of a different ethnic background (for example, Tatar or Jewish) who converted to Russian Orthodoxy?

Moreover, because of historical developments and because of the imperial sway of the Russian state, the Russian Orthodox tradition tended to unify or absorb distinct ethnic traditions under one umbrella. First of all, three Eastern Slavic groups: Russians proper, Ukrainians (once called Little Russians, *Malorossy*), and Belorussians (translated as "White Russians"); then Moldovans (in today's Republic of Moldova); and, finally, some other ethnicities in the vast territories of the former empire. After the collapse of the Soviet Union, the Russian Orthodox Church remained dominant among these ethnic populations, although this has recently been challenged dramatically, especially in Ukraine. (This topic will be further treated in chapter 6.)

Structure of the Contemporary Russian Orthodox Church

According to the Charter of the Russian Orthodox Church, the main body that represents "the fullness of the Church" is the Local Council (*Pomestnyi Sobor*). Although the Local Council is supposed to be summoned periodically, it is not obliged to meet at fixed intervals; the Charter says that the Local Council is convoked "if necessary" to address such issues as the election of the Patriarch, granting autonomy or autocephaly to a part of the Church, and solving fundamental issues of relations with the state or other churches. The Local Council brings together bishops, priests, and elected laity. After the end of the Soviet Union in 1991, the Council of 1917–1918 (see chapter 3) garnered attention because the fundamental decisions made there resonated with the democratic mood of the 1990s. The two recent Local Councils of 1990 and 2009 served to elect Patriarchs, Aleksy II and Kirill I respectively, but fundamental reforms that many believed urgent were not discussed. Overall, the newly emerged structure of decision-making is authoritarian, especially since Kirill (Gundiaev)* became Patriarch.

---

*In the Orthodox Church, a person receives a new name when they take monastic vows, signifying that they have renounced their old worldly identity and taken on a new one. Because formally they have renounced their secular name, their last (family) name is indicated (in order to distinguish them from others with the same monastic name) but placed in parentheses. The rite of taking monastic vows is referred to as tonsure; the bishop or abbot performing the rite choses the name, not the one taking the vows, as a sign of the latter's obedience.

An effective instrument of the ecclesiastical administration is the Council of Bishops, which has been convened frequently and which has produced important guiding documents for the Church, canonized saints, and other important actions. Though authority is conciliar in matters of religious belief, it has been strictly hierarchical in the day-to-day operations and administration of the Church.

The Russian Church's highest prelate is the Patriarch of Moscow. The Holy Synod is the highest regular ruling body under the Patriarch; the Synod includes a few permanent members—bishops of the major dioceses and heads of major patriarchal departments. The Patriarchate and the Synod have a number of departments under them dealing with various issues; they routinely manage the regular administration. The bishop, according to the early Christian experience and canons, occupies the central position within the church: he has the real authority within his diocese and is in regular contact with the parish clergy and laity. Bishops, following tradition, are required to be celibate. In 2020, there are just over three hundred dioceses worldwide, with approximately the same number of ruling bishops, plus a number of auxiliary or assistant bishops.

The parish priests must be ordained by bishops and are subject to them. There were about thirty-five thousand priests at the end of the 2010s. In the Russian Church, unlike the Roman Catholic Church, the regular (parish) priests are all supposed to be married; the priests' wives, *matushkas,* have always been important community figures. In Russia, the contrast between the monks and the regular priests has always been crucial; they were called, respectively, the *black* and the *white* clergy; some monks were also priests (*hieromonks*), conducting services in monasteries, and only monks could become bishops.

The cleavage between the white and black clergy, which often, especially in the twentieth century, ignited criticism from the "white" against the "black," is, therefore, a structural tension between the married clerics, who are often closer to laity, and the monastic elite. Though the ruling elites of the Church are all monastics, most ordinary monks are not part of the ecclesiastical structures.

The locus of religious life for ordinary believers is the parish. The parish is the traditional form of Christian congregation. Historically, similar to Roman Catholicism, it was territorially defined and part of the state-church symbiotic system of administration, whose function went far beyond purely religious matters. In the Russian empire a parish, with its priest and its church building, was a local unit of state organization with a number of functions, from census recording to ideological control. As the church system was decoupled from the state, the religious, spiritual functions have been separated from "secular" administration, though the parishes still are territorial units of ecclesiastic administration. The Soviets attempted to reduce parish life merely to the performance of sacraments so that the parish had no meaning as a community of people; such an autonomous, religiously motivated community was anathema for the communist regime.

Parish life was only revived in the 1990s. From the beginning, the traditional territorial structure was contested by some in the church as being too rigid and bureaucratic and too subordinate to the ecclesiastical hierarchy. Critics argued that the times required a more autonomous, democratic, and tight-knit local congregation—a *community* in the full sense, as built upon the sacrament of communion and the inner commitment of members. In this way people would come to the parish community and priest of their choice, and not necessarily because they live in the neighborhood. This model of a tightly knit social and mystical community would evoke the early congregations of the first centuries of the Christian era, and the champions of this revival were referring to that legacy as being truly authentic. This model was realized in some places around popular charismatic priests, but the dominant trend of the early twenty-first century has been the strengthening of a hierarchical ecclesiastic institution with parish priests dependent upon the bishops, and the latter upon the Patriarch.

Economically, the parish is supposed to live by the donations of the flock. Priests do not receive a salary either from the ecclesiastical administration or from secular authorities. The priests' salary is defined by the parish council in coordination with the local bishop. Money for the upkeep of church property comes also from donations. In practice, the state—mostly at the local level—sometimes supports the maintenance and even the building of churches either within a program of restoration of cultural heritage or by direct investments. In the latter case the state's support is often criticized by political activists or scholars as a violation of the principle of church-state separation, but defended on the grounds that it was the (Soviet) state that had destroyed or damaged church properties to begin with, and this damage should be redressed.

In any event, the parish income is the main source of economic life of the parish. A part of this income is given as an assessment from the parish to the diocese and the central church administration, and therefore the Patriarchate as a large bureaucratic institution lives off parish assessments. Everything that is left after this "tax" remains within the parish and goes toward salaries and other expenses. This makes a particular parish, in a way, a private enterprise, dependent upon the churchgoers. There is no tradition in

Russian Orthodoxy of tithing or parish members making regular contributions. Therefore "donations" constitute a wide category that includes many things: most importantly, income from candles—inexpensive but used in huge amounts as they are so central to Orthodox worship; emoluments given for conducting sacramental services such as baptisms, weddings, or funerals; amounts donated for regular prayers (for the dead, sick, or others) offered by the priest during the liturgy and at other special services; income for the books or church paraphernalia at the special kiosks; and direct donations that can be very small, or great ones offered by wealthy believers. The offerings for sacraments and prayers are somewhat controversial, for in many local churches there are fixed rates for everything, and these "price lists" are unofficially but openly displayed at the church kiosks. Although officially the Church rejects this practice as noncanonical and violating the voluntariness of the donation, it was common and widespread until very recently, since there was no practice of regular membership contributions.

As parishes are partly such independent economic enterprises, it is clear that some of them are flourishing and some are poor. Big churches in large cities are packed on holidays and regularly visited on Sundays, and their incomes are substantial enough to be able to keep several priests, a few deacons, and church lay workers such as wardens, treasurers, or janitors. A remote rural church that hardly gathers a few people on a regular basis cannot count on more than a subsistence income, unless a local wealthy patron generously offers help. Much of the economic viability of the parish depends on location, but also on the popularity of the priest or on something that makes the church particularly attractive such as a saint's relic or miracle-working icon.

When it comes to administration, the parish is less independent. Although the senior priest (or rector) is the center of the parish defining its style and congregational culture, he can be easily removed and transferred from one place to another by the bishop or patriarch. The vulnerability of parish priests has been the subject of criticism. In spite of this uncomfortable bureaucratic dependency ensured in the Church Charter, parish administrative independence in many local practical matters is uncontested. In fact, it is a long tradition of Eastern Orthodoxy to endorse much more local variety and require much less rational uniformity than is typical of Roman Catholicism or even some Protestant churches.

The priest is the true center of a parish; he is supported by a parish council elected by the entire congregation. The council allocates the income and decides on expenses; the lay counterpart to the priest is a warden who is usually a quite influential figure. The warden is elected from the core of the regular churchgoers. Though priesthood in Orthodoxy is an incontestably male vocation, the warden can be either male or female, and in Russian practice, with a stronger female demographic profile among active believers, female wardens are common. According to the parish charter, a parish assembly is supposed to be the highest decision-making body of the congregation. In practice, however, its authority is nominal because Russian churches do not maintain parish membership lists. Therefore, the real power within a parish belongs to an unofficial core of a few fervent parishioners, headed by the priest and the warden.

Parish life in Russia can be defined as consisting of two aspects: the sacramental and the social. The former includes regular services according to the church calendar and other religious ceremonies, such as life-cycle rituals and other sacraments. The social activities are mostly educational (Sunday schools and other classes) and charitable (soup kitchens, support for refugees, work in hospitals and prisons). The early twentieth century saw the rise of this social involvement of the Church, yet the Bolshevik revolution stifled this development. According to Soviet religious policy, the Church had to be completely cut off from any social and public sphere, and only a limited sacramental life was tolerated.[28] Since the end of Soviet restrictions, the Church had ample opportunities to develop new social projects but completely lacked experience for such work. In most parishes the support is limited to their own fellow parishioners while only a few active urban congregations developed a wider range of social and charitable services.[29]

Russian Orthodox faithful go to their parish priest for the regular performance of sacraments and regular confession. Many Russian believers will also seek out a "spiritual father" for deeper spiritual guidance, someone (usually a monastic) who is regarded as an "elder" (*starets*), who has gained a reputation for sanctity and wisdom. Sometimes informal networks of an elder's spiritual children develop. The network of such informal spiritual ties covers the entire space of the Russian Church, representing an alternative to formal, institutionalized hierarchical structure extending from the local parish to the Patriarch on the top. Believers are guided through life by these spiritual fathers—*dukhovniki*, or confessors, according to a traditional mechanism of blessing and obedience. Any decision in life should be blessed (approved) by one's spiritual

28. Scott M. Kenworthy, "To Save the World or to Renounce It: Modes of Moral Action in Russian Orthodoxy," in *Religion, Community, and Morality after Communism*, ed. Mark Steinberg and Catherine Wanner (Washington, DC: Woodrow Wilson Center Press; Bloomington: Indiana University Press, 2008), 21–54.
29. See John Burgess, *Holy Rus': The Rebirth of Orthodoxy in the New Russia* (New Haven: Yale University Press, 2017); Detelina Tocheva, *Intimate Divisions: Street-Level Orthodoxy in Post-Soviet Russia* (Berlin: LIT Verlag, 2017).

father, and his direction should be followed faithfully. Such practices may create excessive dependence, but it has also served as a strong system of moral and social control. In today's Russia many regular churchgoers find a time to visit their spiritual father at least a few times a year.[30]

Lived Christianity

When we think of Russian Christianity, we imagine various elements, most often icons, images of the saints, large monasteries, monks in black robes, gold onion-shaped domes, fragrant incense, colorful garments of bearded priests, Old Slavonic script, a capella singing, and a beautifully elaborate, long liturgy. In what follows we will try to put together some of the major elements that shape Russian *lived* religion. Lived religion is an integral category that includes formal doctrinal teaching and norms, although they may be practiced in a mixed, popular way sometimes going beyond the ecclesiastical norms. Lived religion may also include elements that are *not* considered normative by the Church at all but are practiced on an everyday basis.

Let us take as an example the veneration of the saints, which has been incredibly important in Russian Orthodoxy. An array of saints are presented in the *Menologion*, a service calendar book organized by months and containing the commemoration of all the saints; this book is traditionally used by believers to give names to newborn children. It contains a few thousand

---

30. For vivid stories of spiritual fatherhood, see the bestseller by Tikhon Shevkunov, *Everyday Saints and Other Stories*, trans. Julian Lowenfeld (Moscow: Pokrov, 2012). The most detailed description of the formal and informal structure of the post-Soviet Church is Nikolai Mitrokhin, *Russkaia pravoslavnaia tserkov': sovremennoe sostoianie i aktual'nye problemy* [Russian Orthodox Church: Current State and Problems] (Moscow: Novoe literaturnoe obozrenie, 2004).

names, all referring to particular saints. Saints include many individuals canonized in the early centuries of Christianity and therefore venerated in both Western and Eastern Christendom, beginning with Mary, the apostles, and other biblical figures. After the schism of 1054, the canonization process diverged as well. In addition to many post-1054 Eastern Orthodox saints of Byzantine (Greek), Romanian, Serbian, or other origin, there are Russian saints, including monks, clerics, princes, laymen and women, and even holy fools. Most recently, almost 1,800 new saints were canonized who represent the victims of Soviet persecutions of the twentieth century. There are many local saints as well—those venerated as such in particular regions but not included in the calendar of either national or pan-Orthodox saints.

Each particular saint is believed to have his or her own character and is associated with a particular kind of help, similar to the respective icons devoted to him or her. In most cases, the prayer request is for healing, and there are saints responsible for healing particular illnesses. The healing power of Mary the Theotokos and St. Nicholas of Myra (or Nicholas the Wonderworker) are by far the most universal in their effects. Also, St. Penteleimon, a Greek saint (d. 305 CE), is the patron saint of medicine, and his icons are ubiquitous in hospitals. Now in hospitals Panteleimon is often flanked by an image of St. Luke Voino-Yasenetsky (1877–1961), a Russian practicing surgeon and bishop, canonized in 2000. The holy martyr Tatiana is traditionally believed to be a patroness of university students. The holy princes Alexander Nevsky and Dmitry Donskoi, as many others, work as patrons of soldiers. Xenia of St. Petersburg (d. 1803) and Matrona of Moscow (d. 1952) were canonized as saints relatively recently and became important references especially for women, most typically widows and single women of simple origin, who engage in a full gamut of popular devotional practices around these two saints, of which the most central is venerating their tombs in Russia's two largest cities.

A particular aspect of the veneration of the saints is the veneration of their relics (remains). In the Orthodox view, the human person is a psychosomatic whole, and a person who follows God's will becomes holy—a saint. At death, not only is their soul with God in heaven, but their body on earth awaits the final resurrection. Their human remains on earth therefore act as a meeting place between heaven and earth, and Russian popular piety finds expression in the belief that prayers said at such places were particularly powerful; the relics act as conduits of God's grace to heal or work other miracles. These practices, which were commonplace before the Revolution of 1917, have experienced revival in post-Soviet Russia.

Trinity-St. Sergius Lavra. *Photo copyright © 2008 Scott M. Kenworthy. Used by permission.*

Trinity-St. Sergius Lavra. *Photo copyright © 2008 Scott M. Kenworthy. Used by permission.*

The most sacred places in Russia are usually connected to particularly revered saints, typically monasteries where their relics still reside. Perhaps the most famous site is the Trinity-St. Sergius Lavra in Sergiev Posad, some forty-five miles (seventy-five kilometers) from Moscow, founded by St. Sergius of Radonezh in the fourteenth century. St. Sergius has long been one of Russia's most revered saints, and his monastery has been the destination of pilgrimage for all, from common peasants to the tsars and their families. Up until the Revolution of 1917 there were regular reports of miraculous healings, both from the relics of St. Sergius and from miraculous icons at the monastery. Trinity-St. Sergius Lavra was historically a holy place simultaneously promoted by the ecclesiastical hierarchy and state interests, as well as popular with ordinary believers; it is returning to a similar status in contemporary Russia, where there are major plans to develop the monastery and the surrounding town into a major religious and pilgrimage center.[31]

Another particularly popular sacred place is the Diveyevo monastery near the city of Nizhny Novgorod. The monastery was founded by St. Seraphim of Sarov, who lived in the area in the early nineteenth century, was canonized in 1903, and has become one the most venerated saints throughout the Orthodox world. Seraphim's glorification as a saint was a truly national affair led by the last Russian emperor, Nicholas II. Seraphim became, indeed, the saint of both the people and the monarchy, and his relics were widely venerated until they were confiscated by Soviet antireligious activists. The remains were removed from the church in Sarov, and, ironically, Sarov itself became a quintessential atheistic city, home of Soviet nuclear bomb research, and a "closed town" because of its secret industry. After the Soviet Union fell, on the wave of Orthodox revival the relics of St. Seraphim were "miraculously rediscovered" in 1991 in St. Petersburg, and with great solemnity they were transported back to Diveyevo monastery near Sarov. Since that time, Diveyevo became a common marker of a widespread type of devotion for millions of pilgrims, comparable to European sacral places such as Lourdes in France or Compostela in Spain. Diveyevo, according to popular lore, contains an enormous energy of grace through Seraphim's otherworldly prayer for the dead and the living; these prayers are, so to speak, confirmed and this energy is contained in the relics of the saint. Numerous places similar to Diveyevo, although less

---

31. Scott Kenworthy, *The Heart of Russia: Trinity-Sergius, Monasticism, and Society after 1825* (Oxford: Oxford University Press, 2010).

powerful as sacred places, are the destination of popular pilgrimages flourishing in twenty-first-century Russia.[32]

In popular Russian Orthodoxy, holy springs are regarded as another significant vessel of divine blessing. Both Sergiev Posad, the town surrounding the Trinity-St. Sergius Lavra, and Diveyevo, have many of such springs that contain the *living water* because of their proximity to the saints. The springs and the use of them around the sacred site are elaborated and ritualized. Immersing oneself in the springs, drinking from them, and taking water home in bottles are common practices. Sometimes, these practices are criticized by the more rigorous Orthodox as "magic" and "superstition"—especially when natural water springs are spontaneously venerated by locals, with no involvement from the Church. In many cases, however, the Church takes these springs under its own control by building chapels or sending priests who bless the water. As soon as the Church gets involved and performs a ritual of blessing, the water's special quality is no longer considered simply "magic" and is seen as an element of Christian grace. The springs become a part of a complex system of water symbolism deeply engrained in the Christian tradition and manifested in the sacrament of baptism, the feast of Epiphany, and on other occasions, even though the ordinary believers who are drawn to these springs are not referring to higher theologies. This example shows how "lived religion" works as a combination of simple sacred instincts and the institutional order.[33]

---

32. J. Kormina, "Nomadic Orthodoxy: On New Forms of Religious Life in Contemporary Russia," *Ab Imperio* 2 (2012): 195–227.

33. On various forms of folk religion, see Stella Rock, *Popular Religion in Russia* (London: Routledge, 2009); C. Hann and H. Goltz, eds., *Eastern Christianity in Anthropological Perspective* (Berkeley: University of California Press, 2010).

If we tie together a few features—the apophatic (negative) theology, the mystical monastic piety, the otherworldly emphasis of the liturgy, the strong icon veneration, and the popular devotion to saint relics and other sacred spaces/places—we will not be able to draw a unique, noncontradictory formula. The Russian Church may be attributed a special "other-worldliness," as many writers accept, but this does not fit the deep historical involvement with politics and worldly affairs in general. We can dub this tradition utterly spiritual in some of its monastic, kenotic pursuit of deification, but this would not fit at all the extreme sense of materiality of the sacrum, such as in icon and relic veneration, with elements of enchantment infiltrated into the entire ritual order, which led some critics to call the tradition *obriadoverie*—"the faith in rites," rather than in teaching; commitment to *orthopraxy* instead of *orthodoxy*. It is hard to say to what extent all these contradictory characteristics are true or stereotypical. We need to be careful in final assessments.

There are, in short, many features that distinguish Orthodox Christianity and its ethos from its Western counterparts that touch every aspect of the faith, from theological articulation of Christian beliefs to expressions of spirituality, from forms of worship to religious arts, from conceptions of church-state relations to manifestations of popular piety. These distinctions often strike Western Christians as exotic—in either attractive or repellent ways. There are also features of Russian Orthodoxy that differentiate it from other national forms of Orthodoxy. Each national Orthodoxy has its own distinctive expressions in terms of liturgical language and music or iconographic styles. But within the Orthodox commonwealth, the Russians are perceived as the strictest: they still adhere to the old (Julian) calendar and medieval liturgical language, and they have the longest worship services and the most stringent expectations for dress (e.g., women are expected to cover their heads in church). The Russian Orthodox tend to be more closed, more likely to be suspicious of ecumenical dialogue with other Christians. Finally, in contrast to the Ecumenical Patriarchate of Constantinople, which embraces certain "progressive" causes such as environmentalism, the Russian Orthodox Church in recent years has assumed the position of being a staunch defender of "traditional Christian values" over liberalizing and modernizing tendencies in the West.

But this very strictness arguably produces other paradoxes, hinted at in the beginning of the chapter: on the one hand, Russian Orthodoxy has again become a central feature of Russian national identity, which has resulted in a tremendous surge in the number of Russians identifying themselves as Orthodox and has led to a close alliance with the state under President Vladimir Putin. On the other hand, by contrast with other Orthodox countries, which rank among the most religious countries in Europe, levels of regular religious participation remain very low in Russia.[34] This situation may result, at least in part, from the very strictness of Russian Orthodoxy—one must either participate fully or not participate at all, rather than faith being naturally integrated into one's life; this may also partially explain why phenomena such as relics or holy

---

34. According to a 2018 Pew study, the five most religious countries in Europe are all Orthodox majority: Romania, Armenia, Georgia, Greece, and Moldova. Russia ranks twentieth, the lowest of all Orthodox majority countries. Jonathan Evans and Chris Baronavski, "How Do European Countries Differ in Religious Commitment?" (December 5, 2018), https://tinyurl.com/y2e4j2kk.

springs are more popular than regular church-going. It is necessary to understand what Russian Christianity has undergone, especially in the past century, in order to make sense of these paradoxes, which is what we hope to do in the remainder of the book.

2

Geographies of Russian Christianity

Russia's millennial history was one of perpetual territorial expansion, either by conquest, agreement, or simply by acquisition of uninhabited lands, but also, sometimes, by conversion of the local population to Christianity. Rus, the first Eastern Slavic state, emerged in the tenth century as a Christianized principality; it was then reshaped many times through several clashes and mergers, and acquired large territories, initially alien and even hostile. By the eighteenth and nineteenth centuries Russia had forged itself into a predominantly Christian, but multicultural, Eurasian empire that absorbed the lands of many ethnic groups and faiths scattered in surrounding territories. "Russia" has been a flexible concept, and what we have in mind now is both the "real and imaginary geography of Russianness."[1]

1. S. Franklin, E. Widdis, *National Identity in Russian Culture: An Introduction* (Cambridge: Cambridge University Press, 2004), 30–49. In our book we use a relatively loose geographical focus, speaking of this "real and imaginary space" whose ter-

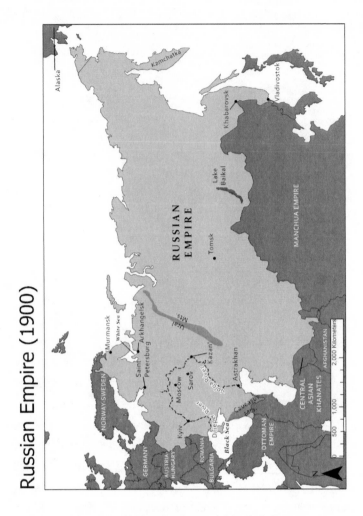

Map by CJ Mescher, Miami University Geospatial Analysis Center.

ritorial borders were fluctuating throughout history, from the Russian Empire, to the Soviet Union and to the post-Soviet space, where the Russian Federation is just one of the independent states.

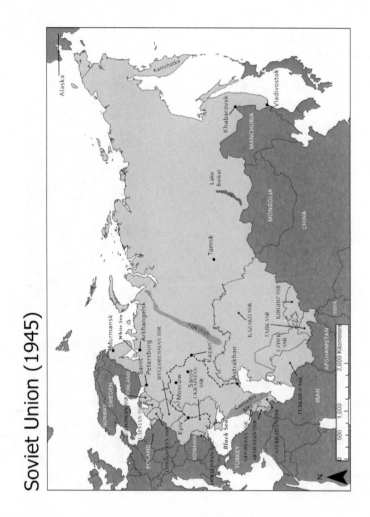

Map by CJ Mescher, Miami University Geospatial Analysis Center.

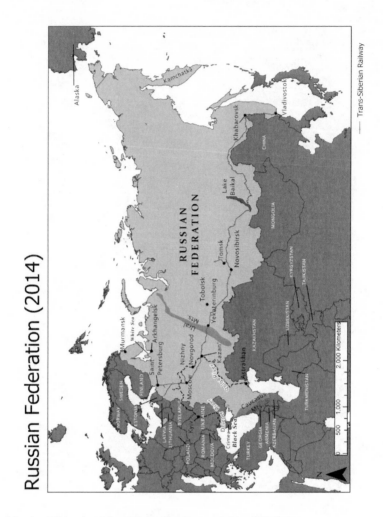

Map by CJ Mescher, Miami University Geospatial Analysis Center.

The Russian Empire reached its greatest geographical expanse by the beginning of the twentieth century, and though it nearly collapsed during the Revolution of 1917, the Soviet Union reconstituted most of the former Empire. The Soviet Union was built upon quite different ideological principles:

clearly anti-Christian, antireligious, and internationalist, though it was still technically an imperial construction that included a variety of geographically and culturally specific peripheries. After the dissolution of the Soviet Union in 1991, Russia emerged as the Russian Federation, along with fourteen other newly independent states that had previously consti-tuted the Soviet state. Although we focus here on the Russian Federation, each of the fourteen other post-Soviet indepen-dent states warrants analysis of its relationship with the for-mer metropole. The whole territory has been sometimes called "Post-Soviet Eurasia," but in the course of time, this associa-tion with the old Soviet Union was challenged and gradually yielded to new configurations of geopolitical and cultural loy-alties.

Nevertheless, there are some common elements deeply woven into the cultural fabric of the entire space in and around contemporary Russia. This is not surprising since many non-Russian peoples were under Russian rule for centuries. The Russian language still serves as a lingua franca, despite recent challenges from globalized English. Russian-speaking peoples continue to live in the former colonies, although their popula-tion has definitely decreased in places like Central Asia and the Caucasus. The political interests of a more self-assertive Rus-sia under Vladimir Putin are expanding toward what the Rus-sians call "the near abroad"—the former Soviet territories. The most controversial example, the annexation of the Crimean peninsula from Ukraine in 2014, was a clear act of reasserting Russian nationalist, territorial, and even religious claims. In public statements legitimizing the "unification," there were references to the semi-legendary account of the baptism of the saint prince Vladimir in the tenth century CE in the city of Chersonesus, an ancient Greek colony in the place of today's

Crimean city of Sebastopol. (In fact, the reason he was baptized in Chersonesus was precisely because it was a Byzantine city from where Vladimir accepted Christianity, not a territory that belonged to the Rus—but this is a detail overlooked by those seeking to assert the "Russianness" of Crimea. On the baptism of Rus by Prince Vladimir, see chapter 3.)

In terms of religion, the entire territory of the former Russian and Soviet empires has been viewed as the "canonical territory" of the Russian Orthodox Church—that is, a geographical sphere of ecclesiastical jurisdiction that was said to have been accorded to the early Russian prelates by the then unified Eastern Orthodox Church. These claims have been challenged by some local church administrations in the newly independent states in the twenty-first century, most dramatically in 2018 to 2019 when a movement in Ukraine sought to form an autocephalous (independent) Ukrainian Church. In any case, the real presence of the Russian Church in the non-Russian areas of the former empire is another trace of Russian imperial memories.

To make more sense of the religious and cultural structure of this vast territory, let us turn to demographic statistics over the past century. The most reliable figures we have before the Soviet period come from the 1897 Census of the Russian Empire, which was the first in Russian history to use the methods of total direct questioning of the entire population. One of the questions was about religious belonging. The Christian population constituted approximately 84 percent of the empire's population. Muslims—mostly in the central Volga region, the Caucasus, and Central Asia—made up 11 percent. Jews were 4 percent, most of whom lived in the western parts of the empire, restricted to the "Pale of Settlement." The Buddhists were just a tiny minority of 0.3 percent and were concentrated in Kalmykia near the Caspian Sea and in the south Siberian region of Buriatia.

Among Christians, Catholics made up 9 percent of the entire population, and the majority of them lived in the Kingdom of Poland, a Russia-governed portion of Poland. Protestants, who made up less than 4 percent, were mostly Baltic ethnic groups (Finns, Latvians, Estonians, and Germans). Armenian Christians, who mostly lived in the South Caucasus, constituted about 1 percent. Finally, the Eastern Orthodox, including a relatively small portion of Old Believers, made up by far the largest group—about 70 percent of the entire population—and they were spread out more or less everywhere, while the greatest concentration was, of course, the Central European plain, where, in half of the administrative regions, their share was as high as 99 percent. Among the Eastern Orthodox, there were not only Russians, who constituted less than half (44 percent) of the population of the empire, but also Ukrainians, Belarusians, Georgians, and Moldovans.

The Soviet Union inherited the territory of the empire as it also tried to erase religion altogether. Since the end of the Soviet Union, imperial unity has been a waning reality morphing into memory, while at the same time religion partly regained its relevance. The Muslim areas of the former empire, especially the recently independent Central Asian states, are now moving toward transnational Islamic networks; the Baltic states are already a part of Europe's (post-)Christian culture; other former peripheries emphasize their particular, independent traditions. The Russian Orthodox world still nominally includes the Orthodox territories of the former empire —Belarus and Ukraine, as well as Moldova, yet Moldova is torn by intensifying ties with ethnically kindred Romania. Ukraine, after the 2014 revolution and ensuing conflict with Russia, has been rapidly moving toward its own independent Church, proclaimed in 2019, and distanced from Russia.

If we take today's Russian Federation only, without former imperial peripheries, its religious composition is, sociologically, a hard question to tackle. Religious belonging is no longer on the list of the census questions. Independent surveys yield contradictory results, with a solid part of the population, between 50 and 80 percent, identifying themselves as Orthodox Christians; between 5 and 10 percent claim to be Muslim, and there are small minorities of Catholics, Protestants, Buddhists, Jews, and others (no more than 1 percent each). We will turn closer to the current life and current society in the last chapter.

Returning to religious history and geography, Russian Christianity has shaped the gigantic Eurasian space where it unfolded through the centuries, and it was shaped *by* this space. The major instruments of spiritual colonization of remote areas, proceeding together with political expansion, were missions, monasteries, and pilgrimages. These three forces knitted the space together. The missions and monasteries created pious outposts, while pilgrims wove these outposts together in a mobile, intense devotional network tied to the old central pivots of Russian faith and culture. Conversely, such unusually vast and open space, in its own turn, deeply affected the character and style of Russian Christianity.

Let us go over the main areas that are defined by history, geography, and demography. If we speak of the Russians, or even Eastern Slavs, who are the main participants in Eastern Christianity in this region, the population and its density is extremely uneven across this vast territory. European Russia is the mostly densely populated part of the country, with Moscow in the center of this human geographical space. We will start with this deep mainland, and will then travel in all directions to see how the geography of the Russian civilization and Christianity unfolded.

European Russia

The core of Russian civilization is the vast central plain to the west of the Ural Mountains (conventionally viewed as the boundary between Europe and Asia). It stretches through the Dnieper and Volga basins, until it reaches the regions of Russia that border on Belarus and Ukraine. In fact, these three nations, now separate and independent, go back to the same root of those people who are usually called Eastern Slavs, as opposed to Western Slavs (Poles, Czechs, etc.) and South Slavs (Serbs, Croats, Bulgarians, etc.). This territory, although not as sizeable as Siberia beyond the Urals, is also quite large and, for nearly a millennium, was a space of conquests, nomadic movements, shifting spheres of influence, and cultural mixing. The movements were facilitated by the landscape—mostly flat plain, with only a few elevation changes in the middle, giving birth to the main rivers. The climate is highly continental, with long, cold winters and hot summers, abundance of woods (more in the center and the north), and moderately fertile soils. The type of society that emerged here reflected the climate and geography, with no direct access to the sea, tending to fortify itself from the precariously open social and natural environment.

The core of this civilization emerged first at the shores of Dnieper, with Kiev (Kyiv in current Ukrainian form) as the capital of the first state of the Eastern Slavs, Kievan Rus. By the fourteenth and fifteenth centuries, the center of gravity had shifted northward to Moscow.[2] In the early eighteenth century St. Petersburg became the capital of the empire, and about the same time Russia started gradually to expand and to acquire what it was lacking at the start, including access to the seas. The center shifted back to Moscow in the twentieth century.

European Russia (2014)

Map by CJ Mescher, Miami University Geospatial Analysis Center.

2. On Muscovy, see Valerie Kivelson, *Cartographies of Tsardom: The Land and Its Meanings in Seventeenth-Century Russia* (Ithaca: Cornell University Press, 2006).

Since the first millennium CE, the Eastern Slavs have been the dominant ethnic element in the Russian Empire, and they constitute the majority population in contemporary Russia, Ukraine, and Belarus: about 80 percent in Russia and more than 90 percent in both Ukraine and Belarus. The density of the population varies, with core areas being denser than in the eastern regions of Russia, but still lower than the European average (about twenty-seven people per square kilometer against about 128 in the European Union).

The Eastern Slavic pre-Christian, tribal, and ethnic religion is now a high-profile theme for scholars and those who are busy with historical reconstructions of festivals, crafts, and arts. The historical records show a rich pantheon of deities and a wide variety of practices and myths, close to other branches of Slavs, cognate to Baltic and Scandinavian pre-Christian religious systems, and going back to ancient Indo-European roots.[3] The political and cultural unification of the Eastern Slavs was greatly enhanced by the conversion to Orthodox Christianity in the tenth century. Since then, the Russian state and culture have been Orthodox Christian by definition, and this became decisive in all outward contacts of early Rus and of all its successors.

Eastern Slavic Christianity has always been anchored in the central plain around the oldest churches and monasteries, the very core of Russian and Ukrainian Orthodoxy. While traveling across this huge plain, one cannot escape the splendid silhouettes with gilded domes that still define the landscape. Such monasteries as Kyiv Caves, Trinity-St. Sergius, or New

---

3. Boris Rybakov, *Iazychestvo drevnei Rusi* [Paganism of Ancient Rus] (Moscow: Nauka, 1987), has long been the main source on the Slavic historical religion. It has been criticized for depicting an overly systematic picture based on the scattered and fragmentary sources, mostly by later Christian polemists.

Jerusalem, and dozens of other big monasteries scattered around the old cities, create a grid of coordinates of both Christianity and East Slavic culture. If one happens to be in cities like Novgorod, Pskov, Suzdal, or Yaroslavl, one surely feels how the entire urban atmosphere breathes with white-gold facades and darkened, icon-filled interiors of the old churches.

Ascending North

The Russian North—a less populated and colder landmass between Scandinavia and Northern spurs of the Ural Mountains—includes today's regions of Karelia, Arkhangelsk, Murmansk, and Vologda. These areas, once populated by Finno-Ugric tribes, were colonized by the Slavs later than the central plain, and from the very beginning this Slavic colonization was characterized by a combination of a harsh struggle with nature and the spiritual feats of Christian pilgrims. The area was remote and, for a long time, beyond the reach of the state. This made the North a suitable place for a relatively free economic life, some degree of liberty, and intense monastic endeavors. It was a harsh environment that served as the Russian equivalent of the desert for early Christian ascetics.

With the rise of the centralized state in Moscow, Russia gradually transformed into a bureaucratic empire with growing control over its population. The peasantry was transformed into serfs—virtually slaves of the aristocratic families and gentry, a condition that lasted until 1861 when serfdom was officially abolished. Yet in the remote North, serfdom was almost nonexistent. Most of the peasants there were officially ascribed to the state, not to the nobility; but as the real control of the state was weak, the local people were relatively free of imperial control. Yet, though the North thus enjoyed more social freedom, it suffered from stronger climatic challenges, weaker infrastructure, and cultural isolation.

This combination affected the Christian enterprises that developed there, including monasteries established amid lakes and dreamlike forests. The North became home to individual hermitages and monasteries, which escaped the control of the growing central bureaucracies. Monasteries began to be established in the North especially in the age after St. Sergius of Radonezh, in the late fourteenth and fifteenth centuries. (See chapter 3.) That is how the famous Valaam Monastery on the islands of Lake Onega, the Kirillo-Belozersky Monastery at Siverskoe Lake, and the Solovetsky Monastery on the shore of the White Sea emerged. The number of monasteries continued to grow, and the region acquired an aura of a severe, but spiritually intense, wonderland, imbued with a mystical quietude and silence that attracted thousands of pilgrims from the Russian core.

Big monasteries, however, were not only places of intensive prayer and meditation. The monasteries, wittingly or not, served as agents of the growing empire, of the political presence of the Russian state in these loosely controlled areas, and focal points of economic activity. Sometimes, the northern monasteries with their impressive stone walls also functioned as fortresses. Eventually, they were used as prisons for criminals or political exiles as the state gradually increased its control over the entire area, which became simultaneously a place of escape or one of exile for religious dissenters.

In the North thus emerged a unique religious culture—more ascetic, less hierarchical, more mystical and meditative—than was found in other parts of the empire. Apart from large monasteries with big, white stone walls, a unique wooden architectural style was developed there. Such churches can still be seen today, for example on Kizhi Island, although they are especially vulnerable because of the materials from which they were constructed.

In the twentieth century, Soviet power largely eradicated the local monastic culture and used the Solovetsky Monastery as one of the first concentration camps for thousands of victims of the Stalin terror.[4] In the late Soviet period, the North, with its forests, lakes, and semi-forgotten churches, was romanticized as a sublime home of a future spiritual revival. After the collapse of the Soviet Union, with many monasteries and churches reopened and restored, the North has come to be viewed as a place of unique religious, social, and ethnographic heritage.

Engaging the West

Europe, to the west of the East European plain, was once labeled as the realm of Latin Christianity, an object of competition, and the source of both inspiration and resistance. Its inhabitants, including fellow Slavs such as the Poles and the Czechs, regarded their Russian neighbors—and were regarded by them in turn—as heretics. Curiously, however, according to historical records, the first rulers of Rus were a tribe of Vikings who settled (or, in some versions, were "invited") in major cities such as Pskov, Novgorod, Vladimir, and Kiev. The first East Slavic political rulers, therefore, were actually Scandinavians who mixed with the local Slavic population. Nevertheless, this new elite eventually converted to Eastern Orthodoxy instead of Roman Catholicism, and this choice determined the future history of Russia. (See the whole story in chapter 3).

4. Roy Robson, *Solovki: The Story of Russia Told Through Its Most Remarkable Islands* (New Haven: Yale University Press, 2004).

This fundamentally religious decision worked to demarcate an imagined border that separated Russia from "the West." This line was drawn from north to south, approximately from the Baltic Sea area to the shores of the Black Sea. Along this flexible cultural border, Russia waged wars and developed trade with many European powers struggling for expansion of the lands across this imaginary line. There were wars with Teutonic knights, Sweden, and Poland; a few times with Germany, including the two World Wars; with France during the Napoleonic wars; and other smaller conflicts. Twice, in the early seventeenth and the early nineteenth century, Moscow was briefly taken by Western troops: the Poles-Lithuanians in the first case and Napoleon's army, in the second.

Over the course of several centuries Russia absorbed vast territories populated by Ukrainians and Belarusians; annexed the lands of Baltic peoples—Lithuanians, Latvians, Estonians, and Finns; and took over a major part of Poland and a part of Romania (the east of Moldova [Bessarabia]). Poland and Finland became independent after World War I and remained so. Part of western Ukraine was briefly independent and then part of Poland, while Bessarabia became part of Romania, and the Baltic states became independent. But all of these were forcibly re-annexed by the Soviet Union in 1939; the Baltics and Moldova were folded into the Soviet Union, becoming independent only in 1991.

The cultural and religious boundary separating Russia from the West was never stable, and it shifted along with the Russian state's political and military fortunes. In all of the western regions that once belonged to the Russian Empire, there was always intense cultural interaction as the Russian language, culture, bureaucracy, and religion spread everywhere the Russian state held sway. In many cases, they spread under forced orders and through working settlers, officials, or soldiers. Forced Russification always engendered fierce resistance by local populations. Yet among the settlers from the imperial core, there were always people from the educated class, intellectuals, and other dissenters who sympathized with the conquered peoples.

At the same time, the impact of the West upon Russia was also extremely important, and the oscillation between Russophilia and Westernization has often been identified as one of the major leitmotifs in Russian history. The western borderlands, of course, were the space through which European culture, technologies, and ideas penetrated Russia. Whether these influences were adopted or rejected, they were in any case always a matter of enriching debate. Peter the Great, who conquered the Baltic coast for Russia and founded St. Petersburg, sought to "hack a window into Europe," from which he took inspiration for his radical reforms. Indeed, the Petrine reforms are frequently seen as Russia's entrance into European politics and European culture.

Russia's western borderlands were an arena of intense competition between Eastern and Western Christianities. One of the results of such competition was the so-called Greek Catholic church (the Uniates, or those in union with Rome)—quite small in today's Russia but very active in Ukraine and the countries of the imagined, movable East/West cultural border. The Greek Catholics follow modified Byzantine Eastern liturgical rites but administratively belong to Roman Catholicism and recognize the primacy of the pope. The difficult relationship between the Russian Orthodox Church and the Greek Catholics endured for few centuries: the Uniates were suppressed in the Russian Empire but survived outside of it, then again suppressed in the Soviet Union and finally revived after the collapse of the USSR, especially in Western Ukraine.

The Roman Catholic Church itself was also present and influential in the western Russian borderlands. It was firmly established as a "national" faith in both Poland and Lithuania, which once composed a united commonwealth. Catholic influence in Ukraine and Russia, as well as the Orthodox "anti-Catholic" ("anti-Latin") resistance, has been a factor in culture wars since at least the seventeenth century. Policies toward Catholics have been mostly polemical and restrictive, although many Catholics were prominent in the sciences and arts, and many Russian intellectuals—especially the so-called Westernizers—were Philo-Catholics or even converts. Ambivalent policies toward Roman Catholics continued under the Soviet regime. After the collapse of the Soviet Union, many Catholics emigrated, but those who stayed in Russia still made up approximately half a million people by the end of 2010s, most of them living either in Siberia or in central areas in and around Moscow.

Protestants of many stripes entered the Russian imperial and cultural orbit, first with the reforms of Peter the Great, who invited many of them to live and work in Russia, and again with the annexation of what are now Latvia, Estonia and Finland, where Lutherans dominated. Many Baltic German Lutherans, who were Russified and converted to Orthodoxy, became prominent not only in industries and academies but in the ruling class.[5]

Most of Protestants, such as Lutherans, were tolerated in

5. Some Russian rulers were partly (or entirely) of German origin, starting with Peter III and Catherine II (the Great) in the mid-eighteenth century; Alexandra, the wife of the last Russian tsar, Nikolas II, was also a German who converted to Orthodoxy. Important twentieth-century theologians such as John Meyendorff and Alexander Schmemann were descendants of Baltic Germans.

imperial Russia, while other groups such as Baptists and evangelicals were considered as alien "sects" and persecuted, and this policy continued through the Soviet period.[6] After the collapse of the Soviet Union, a totally new history started. Since the early 1990s, Protestant activism had a global origin: hundreds of evangelical missionaries founded communities of various sizes in major Russian cities; with time, however, they started to be viewed suspiciously by the Russian Church and the authorities.[7]

Besides the religious communities and nationalities already mentioned, Russia was also home to a large Ashkenazi Jewish population that lived in what is now Poland, Ukraine, and Belarus. In spite of the huge emigration in the early twentieth century, mostly to the United States, a great many Jews remained throughout the Soviet period. Many of those who lived in the western Soviet borderlands, which suffered under Nazi occupation during World War II, did not survive the Holocaust; according to detailed estimates, about 2.7 million Soviet Jews, or about 55 percent of the pre-war Jewish population, had perished by the end of the war.[8]

Religious policies toward the Jews in the Russian Empire were based on restrictions and the assumption of their eventual conversion to Christianity. The Jews were largely restricted to living in the so-called Pale of Settlement, which essentially constituted the western and southern regions out-

---

6. See Heather Coleman, *Russian Baptists and the Spiritual Revolution, 1905–1929* (Bloomington: Indiana University Press, 2005); Abraham Friesen, *In Defense of Privilege: Russian Mennonites and the State before and during World War I* (Winnipeg: Kindred, 2006).

7. Geraldine Fagan, *Believing in Russia: Religious Policies after Communism* (London: Routledge, 2014).

8. *The Electronic Jewish Encyclopedia*, https://eleven.co.il/jews-of-russia/history-in-ussr/15417/ (in Russian); Viacheslav Konstantinov, *Evreiskoe naselenie byvshego SSSR v XX veke* [The Jewish Population of the Soviet Union in the Twentieth Century] (Jerusalem: LIRA, 2007), 16–17.

side of Russia proper, and they were not allowed, with some exceptions, to settle in big cities. Jewish converts to Orthodox Christianity, the so-called *vykresty,* acquired full legal rights in the Russian Empire. Anti-Judaism was rather strong in conservative Orthodox Christian circles, and it later evolved, alongside incipient nationalism, into Russian "everyday" anti-Semitism.[9] In the Soviet Union, under a consistent antireligious policy, Judaism was crushed in the same way as other religions, but those Jews who left religion and "converted" to communism acquired better positions, moved to larger cities, and played an important role in Soviet history, being both among the communists but also among their victims, including the dissidents of the later Soviet period. The end of the Soviet Union brought about another wave of Jewish emigration and some revival of Christian anti-Judaism. Finally, there remains a quite important urban subculture of Orthodox Christians of ethnic Jewish origin.[10]

Overall, at the western borderland of the "Russian world," Orthodox Christianity has been in constant negotiations with Western Christianities and Judaism. The record of these negotiations is ambivalent. The medieval doctrinal suspicion toward the "heretics," the "people of alien faiths" (*inovertsy*), turned at times into visceral everyday hostility that led to persecutions and pogroms against the Catholics, Protestants, and Jews. At the same time, they worked for Russian Christians as significant cultural "others," in contrast with whom they defined their own identity. Catholic education and theology, imported through the western Russian imperial borders,

9. V. Shnirelman, *Koleno Danovo: Eskhatologiia i antisemitizm v sovremennoi Rossii* [The Tribe of Dan: Eschatology and Anti-Semitism in Modern Russia] (Moscow: BBI, 2017).

10. J. Kornblatt, *Doubly Chosen: Jewish Identity, the Soviet Intelligentsia, and the Russian Orthodox Church* (Madison: University of Wisconsin Press, 2004).

namely through Ukraine, deeply impacted the Russian Church's institutional structure and ways of thinking—even though this impact was exercised, paradoxically, through resistance to "Latin heresies." The Protestants brought to Russia their incomparable biblical expertise, strong faith, and rigorous ethics, as well as the efficient industries based upon them. Many Russified Jews, attracted by Orthodox spirituality, contributed to Russian Christianity a deep liturgical sensibility based on a sense of sacramental continuity between the Old and New Testaments.

Descending South

The most significant expansion of the Russian state and culture was directed southward and eastward, and these stories are rather different from the interactions in the western borderlands.

Russian expansion to the south, initially scarcely populated steppes, started as an attempt to secure the frontier against nomadic incursions. In the early centuries, the Eastern Slavs ran across a few Turkic speaking seminomadic tribes—Bulgars, Pechenegs, Khazars, and others. Behind the steppes, Crimea and the Caucasus loomed as old, strong centers caught up in a competition for influence between the two major Muslim empires, Persia and the Ottomans. By the eighteenth century, the Russians had begun to seriously consider conquering these territories and joined the geopolitical fight for influence.[11]

The Black Sea coast has always been home to various ethnicities. Here the Russian state came into contact with, among others, Pontic Greeks, who were Orthodox and had lived on

11. See M. Khodarkovsky, *Russia's Steppe Frontier: The Making of a Colonial Empire, 1500-1800* (Bloomington: Indiana University Press, 2004).

the shores of the Black Sea for centuries. Gradually these lands were incorporated into the Russian Empire, and the Greeks were active in local commerce and culture until they were deported to Kazakhstan by Stalin in the twentieth century; subsequently, many emigrated to Greece. The Crimean peninsula was populated by the Islamized Crimean Tatars—relatives of the Volga Tatars and largely dependent on the Ottoman Sultan, despite the Crimean Khan's illustrious status as a direct descendant of Genghis Khan. Other ethnicities settled on the shores of the Black Sea, including a small and unique Turkic-speaking group called Karaites, who adopted a specific version of Judaism. Crimea was annexed by Russia in 1783 and then populated by Russians and Ukrainians, pushing the Muslim Tatars out. The major deportation of the Tatars, however, took place in 1944 during Stalin's wartime deportations. At the end of the twentieth century, the Tatars came back en masse, and the peninsula continues to be multiethnic and multireligious until now.[12]

The Caucasus was another complex and, to Russian eyes, hostile region to the south of the Russian core territory that was supposed to be Russified and Christianized. The Caucasian mountain range and the highlands to the north and south of it are home of a number of ethnicities—some Turkic, some autochthonous Caucasian, some Indo-European. The Caucasus continues to be one of the world's most multicultural areas. Most of the indigenous Northern Caucasians and the Azerbaijanis are Muslim, while Georgians and Armenians are Christians. The Russian conquest of the area, which occurred in the eighteenth and nineteenth centuries, brought Russians into

---

12. After the end of the Soviet Union, Crimea was a part of Ukraine until it was annexed by the Russian Federation in 2014 in an act not recognized by most countries.

competition with the Ottoman and Persian Empires for influence in the region. These conflicts, which totaled more than fifteen wars, dragged on for nearly two centuries. The entire region eventually fell under Tsarist, and later Soviet, control. In the twentieth century, Western European powers became involved in the Caucasus, particularly during the World Wars. After the collapse of the Soviet Union in 1991, the North Caucasus, including Dagestan, Chechnya, North Ossetia, and a few other regions, became part of the Russian Federation, while the South Caucasus split into three independent states: Armenia, Azerbaijan, and Georgia.

The clash with the Muslim empires in the south was the peak of Russian colonial ambitions. This was especially true in the case of the Ottoman Empire, whose capital was the former Byzantine capital of Constantinople, the wellspring of the Russian Orthodox faith. Russia believed itself to be the spiritual successor of the Byzantine Empire, and in the nineteenth century, a wave of Russian imperial chauvinism framed the wars with the Ottomans as a kind of "reconquista" aimed at wresting control over the Bosporus and Dardanelles, the straits between the Black Sea and the Mediterranean Sea, and over Constantinople (Istanbul) itself, away from the Ottomans. For Russians, this would represent a profound material and symbolic victory for Christian Orthodoxy, to say nothing of its political and economic significance. This goal, however, was never reached.

The Caucasus, after many wars, was wrested away from the Ottomans and the Persians. Most of the peoples of the northern Caucasus remain Muslim. The few exceptions are mostly Christian Alans, or Ossetians, an ethnicity of Indo-European origin, and the Buddhist Kalmyks, or Oirats. The former reside in what is now the Republic North Ossetia-Alania within Russia, and the latter in Kalmykia, in the steppe area next to the Caspian

Sea. To the south of the Caucasus mountain range, as said before, the Azerbaijani are mostly Shiite Muslims, while Georgians and Armenians are old Christian nations.

For Russia, as well as the Caucasian peoples, the acquisition of the Caucasus led to enormous human and economic losses. Not only the Turkish and Persian armies, but many local peoples, including the Circassians, Chechens, Ingush, and Avars, furiously resisted Russian conquest. These peoples waged a decades-long war in the nineteenth century under Shamil, the local leader who proclaimed the *Imamat*, an Islamic state, and so the conquest of the Caucasus by the Russian Empire was often seen by both sides in terms a religious war, a clash between a Christian empire and the indigenous Muslim population.

The religious peace has been rather fragile or simply nonexistent in these mountainous areas and the Russian Christians have felt not quite comfortable there. And yet, at the same time, the Caucasus' wild, rocky beauty had a deeply romantic impact on the Russian cultural imagination. This was true for both secular and religious intellectuals.

The idea of a Christian mission, of converting the local people, sometimes motivated colonial efforts in the southern steppes, Crimea, and the Caucasus, though frequently imperial administrators were more concerned with maintaining peace.[13] While the city name Vladikavkaz in Russian means "rule over the Caucasus," Stavropol, the name of another major Russian city at the foothills of the Caucasus, is a Greek word for the "city of the cross." The presence of the post-Byzantine

13. Nicholas Breyfogle, *Heretics and Colonizers: Forging Russia's Empire in the South Caucasus* (Ithaca: Cornell University Press, 2005); Mara Kozelsky, *Christianizing Crimea: Shaping Sacred Space in the Russian Empire and Beyond* (DeKalb: Northern Illinois University Press, 2010).

Greeks in Crimea and on the Black Sea shores, as well as some older Christian traces among other local groups, made it easier for Russian Christians to move here, build churches, and establish monasteries. The mountainous or maritime ambience and landscape did not allow for huge monastery-fortresses dominating the infinite plains, as in the North. Yet pockets of Christian Orthodoxy quickly appeared around the area becoming important new centers of Russian Christianity. One major monastic center was created in the nineteenth century in *Novyi Afon,* or New Athos, in what is now Abkhazia. Ignaty Brianchaninov, a famous bishop of the Caucasus in the mid-nineteenth century, is considered one of Russia's great spiritual and mystical theologians.

In the Soviet period, all religions in the area were repressed as in other parts of the country, including both local Islam and Russian Orthodoxy. In the post-Soviet Caucasus, religious identities revived. To keep the region under control, the Russian state is relying partly upon reviving Orthodox Christian presence, through believers, dioceses and churches, Russian Orthodox settlers, and the Cossacks. Islam has recovered considerably as well, and this revival took both peaceful forms (as in the system of education, and the growth of Islamic legal norms and of the market of Islamic goods) and more militant expression, reacting against the Russian military efforts to keep control over the lands. The two Chechen wars in the 1990s were catastrophic: the first had the character of a more nationalist insurgency, and the second had more religious undertones, including foreign fighters who came to wage jihad against Russia. Chechen insurgents of the late twentieth century proclaimed an Islamic state in the same way as their ancestors in the mid-nineteenth century, but they were opposed not only by the government but also by a part of the local Muslim population.

Russian state and culture were also deeply involved in the history of the peoples on the southern slopes of the Caucasus range, in what the Russians called Transcaucasia. The Georgian Church was once absorbed by the Russian Orthodox Church; now the Georgian Church is an independent institution. The Armenian Apostolic Church belongs to the so-called Old Oriental Orthodox and continues its own tradition of Christianity. Russia's contacts with the Armenians has had a long history, as the Armenian diaspora communities have long lived in Russia's southern borderlands and Eastern Europe. What is now the Republic of Armenia was annexed by Russia in the nineteenth century after a war with the Ottoman Empire. Azerbaijan was once populated by the Turkic nomads who settled in the eastern part of the Caucasus, then fell under the power of Persia, and then emerged as a nation first under the Russian and Soviet empire and then, since 1991, as an independent state. Azerbaijani culture is a mixture of Turkish and Persian influences, and Azeris, like Iranians, are mostly Shiite Muslims, although Azerbaijan claims to be the most "secular Muslim" country in the world.

The Caspian Sea and the huge lands to its east became part of Russian Central Asia in the nineteenth century, when the resistance of local Muslim emirs and khans was crushed by the Russian military. These lands were then under Soviet control until they transformed into five independent states of Kazakhstan, Uzbekistan, Kyrgyzstan, Turkmenistan, and Tajikistan, in 1991. Similar to the Caucasus, the influence of Islam increased immensely in Central Asia, fueling nationalism and the process called decolonization. In the twenty-first century, the Russian diasporas in Central Asia dwindled but are still important, at least in Kazakhstan. All these new states are more or less politically authoritarian, and all are secular, thus ensuring a degree of religious freedom, at least for the churches of the Russian Orthodox diocese covering the entire area. Some regions of Kazakhstan were locations for labor camps, internal exile, and deportation, and as a result became religiously diverse. Kazakhstan celebrates its religious diversity and tolerance by, for example, hosting the Congress of Leaders of World and Traditional Religions every three years since 2003.

All of the countries of Southern Caucasus and Central Asia have long been influenced by Russian culture and, therefore, by European culture as well. This is true of Christian Georgia and Armenia, as well as of the Muslim cultures to the southeast. Tbilisi, Baku, Tashkent, and other capital cities have been multicultural spaces and strongholds of Russian cultural influence. In political terms, all these countries have many conflicting interests, and Russia continues to assert its own geopolitical presence. Regardless of cultural and religious affinities, however, Russia's image is ambiguous in all these lands—it is an imperial power whose legacy brought both cultural fruits and oppression. The Orthodox Church and Christian tradition are among the main pillars of the Russian cultural presence in these regions.

Moving East to the Urals

Moscow is between seven hundred and eight hundred kilometers from Minsk and Kyiv, and it is more than nine thousand kilometers from Moscow to the Pacific shore in the Far East. The spaces and distances are hardly comparable. Demographic density, and developed culture along with it, wane dramatically beyond the Ural mountain range into Siberia, where we still find the world's largest unpopulated landmass. Yet, cultural encounters in the East were as intense and rich as in the West, and even more varied. You take a fast train in Moscow directly eastward, and in a few hours you find yourself amid an unusual religious and cultural mixtures of the Volga area. You go further east to get to the Urals area where big imperial cities such as Orenburg, Ekaterinburg, Tomsk and Tobolsk contain the traces of strong Orthodoxy, enclaves of Western Christian and Muslim settlements, and gloomy, rationalistic Soviet atheism. You take the famous Trans-Siberian Railroad and spend a week going directly eastward up to the Chinese border and Pacific cities of Khabarovsk and Vladivostok, noting on your way a changing cultural landscape with old and new churches, as well as Buddhist and Shamanic shrines in the middle of standard Soviet apartment blocks and post-Soviet, postmodern constructions.

In the east, Russian Orthodoxy came to dominate the vast areas from Moscow to the Urals: from Nizhny Novgorod and Saratov on the Volga to Astrakhan on the shores of the Caspian Sea and Chelyabinsk and Ekaterinburg in the Urals. And unlike the western regions, which were populated to a great extent by other Slavic peoples, in the east Turkic and Finno-Ugric peoples made up a substantial, and historically older, population.

From very early times, Rus faced the nomadic Turkic and Mongol incursions emanating from the south steppes, which are now part of Russia and Ukraine, and from Central Asia and southern Siberia. The most dramatic and fateful historical encounter was with the Tatars, whose origins are among the Turkic peoples coming from the depth of Asia who settled around the Volga basin. The Tatars were allies of the Mongol armies that overthrew Kievan Rus and subdued its lands for more than two centuries. Like most other Turkic peoples, the Tatars at some point converted to Islam.

The area of the middle Volga continued to be the stronghold of the Tatar ethnicity even after the Russian conquest of the sixteenth century. Today, the Republics of Tatarstan and Bashkortostan are the biggest Muslim-populated regions of the Russian Federation, and about two million Tatars make up more than 50 percent of the population in Tatarstan alone. Roughly twice as many live in other parts of Russia as well. Since the medieval period, the Turkic Volga people have been deeply intermixed with the Slavs, through mixed marriages and numerous settlements of Tatars across European Russia, and through similar interactions in Siberia and the Far East. The Tatar elite in particular were incorporated into the Russian aristocracy and bureaucracy, and there was a deep ethnic, linguistic, and cultural intermixture in the modern urban settings of the last two centuries. This has been true of Moscow, where the Tatars make up the biggest minority group, and Kazan, the old Tatar capital and present-day capital of Tatarstan, a republic within the Russian Federation, where the population is equally divided between Russians and Tatars.

In spite of such encounters, the major Turkic minorities of Russia continue to adhere to Sunni Islam. Religion, along with language and territory itself, continues to be one of the main markers of identity. At the time of the Russian conquest, the annexation of the middle Volga Tatar territories was seen in religious terms as Christianization of the "heathen" (as Muslims were seen). Indeed, the Russian conquest, first initiated by Ivan IV ("the Terrible") in the sixteenth century, is now seen by some Tatar nationalists as being analogous to a Crusade, one that left mosques destroyed and replaced by the Christian churches. However, in the last few centuries, in spite of occasional interethnic and interreligious tensions, Orthodox Slavs and Muslim Tatars usually coexisted peacefully. Mass Christianization did not occur. It is true that many Tatars and Bashkirs, especially those who settled in Russian cities, converted to Christianity, but in Tatarstan itself only a relatively small subethnic group of the so called *kriashen*, Christian Tatars, were baptized into the Christian faith.[14] Overall, radical, militant Islamism is relatively weak in this area, and in spite of a rather strong new Tatar nationalism, the Tatarstan government promotes the agenda of multiculturalism. Kazan positions itself as an important cultural center of both Tatars and Russians, of both Islam and Christianity.

Volga Tatars and Bashkirs are not the only non-Slavic ethnicities who were integrated into the orbit of the Eastern Slavic Christian culture and state. We also find in the Middle Volga region descendants of the Finno-Ugrian Mordva, Udmurt, and Mari peoples, who were imbued with nominal autonomy during the Soviet period. These administrative units persist as Mordovia, Udmurtia, and Mari El within the present-day Russian Federation. These regions have large Slavic Russian populations as well. There is here a long story of Christianization, often forced, of local people, who were classified as "pagan" in the same way as the native tribes of Siberia and of the far North.[15] Now, with the post-Soviet religious revival, many people here would identify themselves with Orthodox Christianity and others with churches of Protestant origin (as in many places across Russia, though the overall figures of Protestants are modest). However, there has also been an ongoing revival

14. Agnes Kefeli, *Becoming Muslim in Imperial Russia: Conversion, Apostasy, and Literacy* (Ithaca: Cornell University Press, 2014).
15. P. Werth, *The Tsar's Foreign Faiths: Toleration and Fate of Religious Freedom in Imperial Russia* (Oxford: Oxford University Press, 2014).

of the "native faith"—a set of traditional beliefs and practices that were once labeled as "pagan" by Christian missionaries and that acquire now a new form of a "reconstructed" ethnic and spiritual identity.[16]

Finally, as in other peripheries of the Russian core regions, we find the descendants of the Old Believers around the Urals—those who emigrated or were expelled during the long conflict with the Orthodox Church dating back to the seventeenth century. The Old Believers, with their special strict work ethic, made up the basis of flourishing local industries of the Urals.[17] Many left Soviet Russia, but some, who did not join back the mainstream Orthodoxy, are still trying to conserve old rites and customs (on Old Believers, see more in chapter 3).

What happens to the further east, beyond the Ural range? There a different story starts, to which we now turn.

Beyond the Ural Mountains: Siberia and the Far East

By far the largest part of Russia's territory is the *taiga* (wild forests), tundra (treeless permafrost), and mountains covering the broad northern and eastern part of the country, Siberia, and the Far East. These areas, which border China and Mongolia to the south, were home to scattered northern nomadic tribes for thousands of years. The entire landmass beyond the Ural mountain range was nominally annexed by the Russian

---

16. Sonja Luehrmann, *Secularism, Soviet Style: Teaching Atheism and Religion in a Volga Republic* (Bloomington: Indiana University Press, 2011); Z. Kormina, A. Panchenko, S. Shtyrkov, *Izobretenie religii: Desekuliarizatsiia na postsovetskom prostranstve* [The Invention of Religion: Desecularization in the Post-Soviet Space] (St. Petersburg: European University, 2015).

17. Douglas Rogers, *The Old Faith and the Russian Land: A Historical Ethnography of Ethics in the Urals* (Ithaca: Cornell University Press, 2009).

Empire during the seventeenth and eighteenth centuries, either through formal agreements, conquest, or simply by the arbitrary decrees of the Russian tsars. Colonization was slow, and it largely followed the thousands of kilometers of the southern Trans-Siberian track (later the famous Trans-Siberian Railroad). The Russians finally reached the Far Eastern shore of the Pacific and continued to Alaska, which was under the Russian authority until 1867, when the US Congress begrudgingly approved the purchase of this "icebox" for about $7 million.

Today, after four hundred years of colonization, the Russian Far East is home to large cities such as Nakhodka (translated as "discovery"), Blagoveshchensk ("city of announcement"), and Vladivostok ("ruler of the East"), as well as smaller cities on the Kamchatka Peninsula and Sakhalin Island. In Siberia, there are major urban centers such as Novosibirsk, Krasnoyarsk, Tomsk, and Tobolsk—all of them along the Trans-Siberian Railroad—and other smaller cities. A few urban centers are scattered in the Siberian North, where some heavy and mining industries have been developed. But for the most part, the majority of the region is almost completely unpopulated due to the extreme cold and lack of accessibility.

The colonization of Siberia by the Russian Empire produced unique cultural outcomes. Throughout four hundred years, soldiers, state officials, and traders moved east along with Russian Orthodox missionaries. As in other parts of the world, the colonizers' explicit goal was conversion of the local population and the land itself, and the entire history of the Siberian conquest was a long saga of Christian missionary work.

The native peoples professed animistic belief systems and practices that were usually designated as varieties of shamanism; the very word *shaman* is of Siberian (Tungus/Evenk) origin. Christianization was a goal of the Siberian conquest, and it came along with elements of technological progress that brought about, as usual, both positive and negative effects for the natives.[18] The city of Tobolsk was founded by the Cossacks in 1590 and became the anchor of both administrative and religious authority for the entirety of Siberia. The Tobolsk Kremlin (fortress) and the churches inside it were among the oldest in the city. Now there are cathedrals and churches in all big Siberian cities, and the vast majority of the population, including the native Siberians, would count themselves as belonging to Russian Orthodoxy, though the first decades of the twenty-first century saw not only the revival of the Christian church but also of the old, "native" tribal beliefs and practices.[19]

The involvement of the native peoples in the Russian Christian culture and the spread of the government-sponsored Russian trade and industries were not, however, the only cultural effects on Siberia and the Far East. The Russian and Soviet governments also forcibly resettled millions of people from other parts of the country to the east. The composition of Siberian immigration was thus complex: there were adventurers and traders, similar to the American Wild West; criminals and misfits of all kinds; and finally the endless row of political and religious dissidents, as well as entire ethnic groups who felt uncomfortable in Europe or Central Russia and moved east, where they established new villages and small towns. As for the dissidents, many were aristocrats, intellectuals, and revolutionaries exiled from the Russian capitals and main cities, and some of them founded universities and cultural centers in

18. Andrei Znamenski, *Shamanism and Christianity: Native Encounters with Russian Orthodox Missions in Siberia and Alaska, 1820-1917* (New York: Praeger, 1999).
19. Aileen Friesen, *Colonizing Russia's Promised Land: Orthodoxy and Community on the Siberian Steppe* (Toronto: University of Toronto Press, 2019).

Siberia and the Far East. These people included such widely known and diverse a group as the early-nineteenth-century members of the Decembrist movement; Fyodor Dostoevsky and other intellectuals and early socialists; and Vladimir Lenin, Joseph Stalin, and other Bolshevik revolutionaries, some of whom would later come to power after the 1917 Revolution and exiled dissidents to Siberia and the Far East.

The tsarist government also exiled to the east individuals and groups that somehow threatened the unity of the state Church: the Old Believers and all sorts of disturbing "spiritual movements" (or "sects"), both of native Russian and foreign (mostly Protestant) origin. There were also some groups of Protestant and Catholic voluntary colonizers (mostly German, Polish, and Dutch), who later were joined by those exiled. In addition, some Siberian cities acquired groups of Muslims, mostly Tatars, who moved from the Volga region of European Russia. The territory close to Lake Baikal and Mongolia was populated by the peoples converted to Tibetan Buddhism. From the very beginning of the colonization, Orthodox missionaries targeted the Buddhists in the same way as they were trying to convert others, though with less success.

Forced migration to Siberia reached its peak in the twentieth century in the Soviet Union. A major part of Stalin's terror was the Gulag—famously documented by Alexander Solzhenitsyn in his "Gulag Archipelago"—an unprecedented system of concentration and labor camps.[20] Here criminals, political dissidents, political rivals of the regime, religious people, and millions of innocent men and women considered "class ene-

---

20. A. Solzhenitsyn, *The Gulag Archipelago: An Experiment in Literary Investigation*, trans. Thomas Whitney and Harry Willets, 3 vols. (New York: Harper & Row, 1974-1978). See also A. Applebaum, *Gulag: A History* (New York: Anchor, 2004). Gulag is the Russian acronym for the main administration of the camps.

mies" of the communist regime were mobilized for unpaid work. Many lost their lives, and others simply settled in Siberia after their release. Particularly during World War II, Stalin's regime would continue to deport groups marked by religious or ethnic origin, such as Germans, Chechens, Crimean Tatars, and others.

Overall, the landscape of the relatively scattered, scarcely populated lands in Siberia and the Far East has a quite complex genealogy in terms of social, ethnic, linguistic, and religious origins. Nevertheless, the secularization of the twentieth century strongly affected the religious landscape. In recent times, thousands (especially German or Polish Catholics and Protestants) have left the area, but it is still unique in terms of religious developments. Although some groups are closely tied to religious identities, the bulk of the population—descendants of colonists, prisoners, exiled people, and especially large numbers of those young communist volunteers who were encouraged by the Soviet governments to industrialize the area—are of very weak or no religious background, with no strong religious roots or religious knowledge. If they try to recapture their spiritual life now (which has been a trend since the collapse of the Soviet Union), these masses of former "nones," or "hereditary" non-believers, often choose evangelical Protestant denominations, whose missionaries have been very active, or "new religious movements" of various origins. Indeed, the share of Protestants, according to surveys, is higher here than in the European mainland of the Russian Federation.[21] To be sure, most people tend to declare themselves Russian Orthodox, but church life here is somewhat different—its roots are less deep and pervasive.

21. S. Filatov and R. Lunkin, "Statistics on Religion in Russia: Reality behind the Figures," *Religion, State and Society* 34, no. 1 (2006): 33–49.

Transnational Religioscapes

As Russia transformed into an imperial power involved in international geopolitical games, the groups and communities of Russian travelers, traders, military, and working people settled in many places of the unstable, shifting borderlands, as well as in neighboring countries. The aristocracy and other wealthy people established their secondary residences in France, England, Italy, Switzerland, or other European lands. Starting in the mid-nineteenth century, this led to the emergence of Russian Orthodox parishes in Western Europe to serve immigrants who chose not to convert to Catholicism or Protestantism.

The two most important landmarks of the Russian Christian presence abroad were Mount Athos and the mission in the Holy Land. In Jerusalem, the entire Russian Compound is just a few hundred meters from the Old City. The famous Orthodox Palestine Society was created in 1882 under imperial patronage and was widely supported by the state and private capital. The Society worked as a research facility but also functioned as a shelter and mission for the hundreds of thousands of pilgrims who visited holy places in Jerusalem. In the late nineteenth century, the Russian Orthodox Church became a major patron of the St. Panteleimon Monastery, which grew into one of the largest monasteries on Mount Athos, the "monastic republic" in Greece.[22] Both the Palestine mission and St. Panteleimon Monastery were agents of Russian influence and, at the same time, the channels of religious connections with Middle Eastern Christians.

Gradually, some Russian Christian presence took root in

---

22. Nevertheless, all twenty monasteries of the Holy Mountain, including St. Panteleimon, are subject to the Patriarchate of Constantinople, not Moscow.

Iran, India, China, Japan, and other Asian countries, as well as North America. The most remote point was Japan, where Nikolai Kasatkin (1836–1912) worked. He was a priest, missionary, and the founder of the local church and was later canonized as St. Nikolai of Japan. When Alaska was colonized, many native Alaskans converted to Christian Orthodoxy, and at least 5 percent of the state population are heirs of those converts, and they deeply revere St. Herman of Alaska (d. 1836), a mystic and hermit, and bishop St. Innocent Veniaminov (d. 1879), known as the Apostle of Siberia and America.[23] Missions were created on the west and east coasts of the United States, and in Latin America, Australia, and Africa.

Russia's internal political turmoil, combined with growing cosmopolitan connections abroad, resulted in several waves of Russian emigration, starting in the nineteenth century, mostly to Europe and the United States. First, there were political dissidents who fled the Tsarist government, most of whom were democrats, liberals, and revolutionaries. These groups had little to do with the Church, which was seen as a pillar of the monarchy. There was, however, also a substantial emigration of various religious and ethnic minorities. Some of these were non-Christians, such as Jews, while others were dissident and "heretical" Christians, such as Old Believers, Dukhobors, Molokans, and other groups.

Another massive wave of emigration began after the 1917 Revolution, with millions of people of quite a different type. These were mostly mainstream Orthodox believers, driven out by the Bolsheviks, including many bishops and priests. At this time, the Church itself split over differing attitudes toward the Revolution, with the Russian Orthodox Church Abroad emerg-

---

23. Michael Oleksa, *Orthodox Alaska: A Theology of Mission* (Crestwood, NY: St. Vladimir's Seminary Press, 1992).

ing to represent those who rejected the Bolshevik regime. Some parishes that were loyal to the Moscow Patriarchate and to the Soviet authorities developed a parallel structure alongside the parishes of the Church Abroad, until they reunited in 2007.

Large Russian diasporas in the West have developed distinct church traditions. The biggest one, in the United States, was granted autocephaly by the Moscow Patriarchate in 1970 to create what is now known as the Orthodox Church in America (OCA). In Europe, the legacy of Russian Christianity, in terms of administration, is divided between the two patriarchates: dioceses and parishes are loyal to either Moscow or Constantinople. In Western cities, the onion-shaped domes are an easily recognizable sign of Russian presence—be it St. Nicholas Cathedral in Manhattan or the newly built Holy Trinity Cathedral on the banks of the Seine River in downtown Paris.

The largest Russian diasporas emerged, however, at the very end of the twentieth century, thanks to two major factors. The first was a new wave of emigration, and the second was the breakdown of the Soviet Union itself, when millions of Russians found themselves as minorities in the newly independent nations that emerged in 1991. Emigration abroad thrived because the doors were open after the decades of isolation ensured by the Iron Curtain. But there were also millions who were the first-, second- or third-generation settlers of various occupations, who had no intention of migrating and who now constituted new diasporas in the Baltic states, Ukraine, Belarus, Moldova, South Caucasus, and Central Asia. Russians became citizens of new states, or turned into foreigners, and many moved to Russia proper. Those who remained kept their churches either linked to Moscow—which sometimes created tensions with local governments—or chose to integrate into the new independent churches, although of similar tradition. The Ukrainian case is, of course, the most striking and challenging: a part of the older Russian Orthodox Church there, since the 1990s, wanted to be an autonomous Ukrainian Church and thus completely independent from Moscow. (See chapter 6.)

Geographic Spaces and Signs of Russian Religion

The vast Eurasian territory we are speaking about is, in spite of its unique size, relatively homogenous in terms of forms of Orthodox Christianity. The Russian main religious tradition tended to reproduce itself in a similar shape across the imperial scope. However, the cultural areas within this huge territory are very diverse by themselves both initially, with their various indigenous cultures, and as a result of historical developments and political-economic arrangements. In the above overview we have identified a few geographical zones; now we will try to give a more systematic typology.

After the initial period of Kievan Rus, the city of Moscow and its hinterlands have been the definitive center of Russia's religious life. Moscow is home to the "alliance of altar and throne," of spiritual and temporal powers, which lasted for centuries. Up to now, Moscow and the central region contain the largest number of cathedrals, churches, and monasteries in Russia. The city was and continues to be the seat of the Patriarch. Meanwhile, St. Petersburg, the second largest city in Russia, which was the imperial capital for two centuries until 1918, is also the second stronghold of Russian Orthodoxy. Both capitals are, at the same time, the most multicultural places in Russia, with various ethnicities and religions living next to each other: old communities and representatives of the Catholics,

Protestants, Jews, Muslims, Apostolic Armenians, Buddhists, Old Believers, and, more recently, new religious movements coming from around the world. The two megapolises are also strongholds of secularism, anticlericalism, atheism, and religious indifference. They are the places where antireligious communist ideas emerged and where current anticlerical and liberal movements are actively developing.

Central and northern Russia—the provinces around the Moscow region, Vladimir, Novgorod, Pskov, Yaroslavl, and a few others—make up the core of Russian Christianity, which moved there from ancient Kiev. In these parts of Russia you can now find traces of old churches and majestic monasteries, but also traces of the Soviet antireligious campaigns. The network of famous cathedrals and monasteries make up the "sacral map" of Christianity in this space.

To the west and southwest, we find three important regions where the East Slavic Christian tradition has deep roots and a vibrant church life: Belarus, Moldova, and Ukraine. These regions are significant because they are now independent states that claim their own religious identity—and rightly so, because each of the three ethnicities developed their own special religious culture. The Church of Belarus, which belongs to the Moscow Patriarchate, shares a religious space with Catholic and Protestant Christians, who have always been present in this borderland. The Church of Moldova, which is also under the Moscow Patriarchate, tends to be close to Romanian Orthodox Christianity because the people share language and culture; in the 1990s this led to tensions resulting in a claim by some Moldovan clerics to shift from Moscow to the Patriarchate of Bucharest.

Ukraine represents a very special case: it was the center of Eastern Slavic Christianity (then Kievan Rus), the two key monasteries, the famous Kyiv Cave Lavra and the Pochaev Lavra, and ancient Kyiv cathedrals, which marked the importance of this land for Christianity. Ukrainian religious life has strongly affected Russian Christianity as a whole. Even today, as was the case before, the overall religiosity in Ukraine is more vibrant than in Russia: the number of Orthodox parishes per population of Ukraine is much higher. Ukraine is also more diverse and religiously plural: several Christian churches are separated from each other, including a few Orthodox, Catholic, Greek-Catholic (Uniates), and a variety of Protestant communities, some historical and some quite new. The movement toward independence from Moscow that started since the 1990s and culminated in 2018–2019 dramatically changed the relationship of the Ukrainian and Russian Orthodox churches, even though they remain very similar in terms of practices and doctrines.

Further south and east, Russian Christianity enters other spaces of ethnic and religious diversity—in the Caucasus and the Volga-Ural areas. Here Orthodoxy had contacts with other ethnicities and faiths, first with Islam and the numerous ethnic groups it embraces, but also with Buddhist Kalmyks, Orthodox Greeks, Apostolic Armenians, Finno-Ugrian "pagans," and others. These close contacts with religious and ethnic others made Russian Christians here more identity conscious, sometimes more pragmatic and flexible, and sometimes more closed and nationalistic. Places like Circassia, Chechnya, or Tatarstan have seen both religious conflicts and negotiations. Russian Orthodoxy here is ethnically pluralistic because of a long history of conversions of indigenous populations.

Finally, the enormous space beyond the Urals and up to the edges of the Sea of Japan created yet another type of Russian Christianity—the sparse, diffused churches, parishes, and remote missions scattered across the area, with sometimes hundreds of kilometers between churches. This space was open to settlers of different kinds—voluntary and forced; enthusiastic and deported; Christians of many stocks; Muslim Tatar communities and Buddhists around the Baikal; and various local faiths of Siberian natives. Overall, religiosity has been thin—Orthodox Christianity had weaker roots, and the spread of Protestant or new religious groups in the post-Soviet times was more impressive than in the "old" Orthodox areas.

Sacred Places and Networks of Russian Christianity

The main landmarks of an East Slavic Christian presence—the spiritual hubs that create the map of the tradition—are monasteries, church structures, reliquaries, miracle-working icons, and holy springs. They all are connected, not so much by administrative ties, which are sometimes limited or interrupted for political reasons, but rather by pilgrimages that have always been frequent and now are prevalent across the entire region.

The monasteries have been places of both spirituality and political power; they served as missions and fortresses, similar to Christian monasteries elsewhere. Now they have lost most of their political significance but still retain their spiritual authority. Almost all men's monasteries and women's convents were closed under the Soviet government. But the late twentieth century has witnessed a revival. Altogether, there are more than nine hundred monasteries belonging to the Moscow Patriarchate,[24] from the biggest complexes to small shelters

24. Official figures from the official site of the Moscow Patriarchate, www.patriarchia.ru.

for just two to three people. The most important and biggest monasteries mark the regions of the deepest Christian presence. The most famous monastic complex, the Trinity-St. Sergius Lavra, which played a primary role in the history of Russian Christianity, is located outside Moscow.[25] A few other *lavras*—the biggest monasteries—include the oldest Kyiv Cave Monastery in Ukraine and the Alexander Nevsky Monastery in St. Petersburg; other key monasteries include the New Jerusalem Monastery, an imitation of the Holy Land, designed by Patriarch Nikon in the seventeenth century, also outside Moscow; the monastery of Optina Pustyn around the city of Kaluga, south from Moscow, which was a place of inspiration for many Russian intellectuals; in the very North, the remote monasteries such as Solovki, Valaam, Ferapont, and others, each with its particular history and special function.

The famous old cathedrals in the city centers are important aesthetic and tourist landmarks. Such is the eleventh-century St. Sophia Cathedral in Kyiv, the center of East Slavic Christianity. The same is true of the Dormition Cathedral in Vladimir, the second biggest of the ancient urban centers, and dozens of surviving cathedrals of Novgorod. More recent cathedrals were built in the newly acquired lands along with the Russian colonization. Massive churches were also built in the key cities: Kazan Cathedral in St. Petersburg, Christ the Savior in Moscow, and St. Vladimir's in Kyiv. The smaller churches are scattered across "deep Russia"—the central plains and woods, and across all other regions, most of them reproducing the recognizable architectural design with onion-shaped, often gilded, cupolas. In rural areas, the villages and crossroads are marked with wayside crosses and small chapels.

25. Kenworthy, *The Heart of Russia*.

Thousands of church buildings were destroyed during the Soviet period, and thousands more turned into government offices or industrial warehouses. A large number were rebuilt after 1991. Since then, hundreds of brand new churches, still in the same traditional design, have been built, profoundly altering the landscape. In many ethnically plural places—the big cities and culturally diverse areas—they appear next to new mosques, synagogues, or other religious places.

Since the veneration of the saints is a key practice in Russian Christianity, the relics of the saints are placed across the entire space and connect itineraries of pilgrimages. They are most concentrated in the core regions of Russia, such as in the Trinity-St. Sergius Monastery, with the remains of St. Sergius of Radonezh; the Alexander Nevsky Monastery in St. Petersburg, with the remains of the famous thirteenth-century prince; and the Diveyevo complex with the relics of Seraphim of Sarov, around Nizhny Novgorod on the Volga River. Pilgrimages to these places are thriving, such that today they constitute one of the largest forms of population movement in Russia. After the canonization of the last tsar's family in the year 2000, the place of their murder in 1918 and the place where their corpses were dumped near the city of Ekaterinburg saw a growth in the number of churches, as well as practices devoted to commemoration of the royal victims. Besides the relics of nationally canonized saints, there is a large number of locally venerated saints whose relics are objects of devotion, local pilgrimages and processions. The church calendar, in the entire Church and locally, is a sort of "dynamic grid" that covers the entire space of Russian Christianity.

This spiritual network of the saints' relics and loci overlaps with another one: many churches and monasteries possess what believers call miracle-working icons that have always played an exceptional role in Eastern Christianity and especially in Russia (see more in chapter 1). Many such icons refer to particular key geographical names related to the icons' stories: Vladimir, once the capital of a powerful ancient principality where the Byzantine icon was brought and kept; or Kazan, conquered in the "holy war" with the Muslims, where the icon was miraculously found. These "national" icons are associated with widely recognized church narratives of their salvific role at various critical points in national history, including the Napoleonic wars and World War II.[26] But there are plenty of less famous icons of regional or local acclaim, which are of huge importance for the flock who expect from them health and protection. Countless people make pilgrimages on various days to particular places to express their faith in the miraculous power of the icons.

Thus, Russian Christian geography is a dense network of monasteries and churches, symbols and relics, icons, and people's movements and performances; and behind all this, the spiritual authority of monks and priests who are in constant interaction with the believers through ritual or pastoral conversation; and finally, still behind the ecclesiastic-parish structure, the movement of the senses, emotions, and imagination. The immense Russian spiritual space—with its dense centers; its mixed, quiet peripheries; its little drops spilled around the world up to the far corners of other continents—all are tied together by the memory of the millennial tradition.

---

26. See Shevzov, "Scripting the Gaze," 61–92.

3

The History of Christianity in Russia

The moment the first East Slavic state—the precursor of today's Russia, Ukraine, and Belarus—began to coalesce was the same moment of its Christianization a thousand years ago. Therefore, Christianity has been central to Russian culture throughout its history.[1] Russian Christianity, however, is frequently misunderstood and mischaracterized in the West. The

1. Although we do not presume the reader is familiar with Russian history, a basic knowledge is certainly very helpful. The best place to start is Geoffrey Hosking, *Russian History: A Very Short Introduction* (New York: Oxford University Press, 2012). For an overview of Russian church history that takes a thematic approach, see Thomas Bremer, *Cross and Kremlin: A Brief History of the Orthodox Church in Russia*, trans. Eric Gritsch (Grand Rapids: Eerdmans, 2013). There is no adequate narrative history of Russian Orthodoxy in English; older attempts include Nicholas Zernov, *The Russians and Their Church* (Crestwood, NY: St. Vladimir's Seminary Press, 1978); and Dimitry Pospielovsky, *The Orthodox Church in the History of Russia* (Crestwood, NY: St. Vladimir's Seminary Press, 1998). The classic monumental histories in Russian were written by Makarii (Bulgakov) in the nineteenth century, Evgenii Golubinskii in the early twentieth, and Anton Kartashev in the mid-twentieth, and all have been reprinted in post-Soviet Russia. The scholarship in Russian since the collapse of the Soviet Union is voluminous.

religion of the Russian people has been caricatured as semi-pagan superstition, its clergy as ignorant or obscurantist, and its church as being little more than a "handmaiden of the state." The characterization of the Russian Church as especially subservient to the state—as if churchmen were more concerned to serve the state's interests than the Gospel—is particularly prevalent in interpreting both Russia's past and its present. This type of exoticization of Russian Orthodoxy has served to reinforce the notion of Russia as "other" from the West. An upsurge of specialist research into the history of Russian Orthodoxy in recent decades has dismantled these stereotypes, though they still persist in popular depictions and are still perpetuated in general histories of both Russia and Christianity. From the perspective of world Christianity, Russia is its own distinct case of the broader phenomenon of inculturation, the way in which Christianity takes root and adapts to particular cultures and, in turn, shapes the development of those cultures. It is important to understand the development of Russian Orthodoxy on its own terms, from the nature of popular religiosity to church-state relations.

The Christianization of Kievan Rus (988–1240)

The official date for the conversion of the Eastern Slavs to Christianity is 988. In that year, Grand Prince Vladimir of Kiev (Kyiv) adopted Christianity not only for himself, but for his realm, in an event known as the "Baptism of Rus." Kievan Rus was a federation of Slavic and Finnic tribes and city-states ruled over (according to the ancient chronicles) by Viking Norsemen who adopted the Slavic language and culture. At the height of its power, Rus stretched from the Baltic Sea in the north to the Black Sea in the south from the late ninth to the mid-thirteenth century. The modern peoples of Russia, Ukraine, and Belarus all trace their history back to Kievan Rus; it would therefore be anachronistic to speak of the "Christianization of Russia" in the tenth century.[2]

There is a legend in the *Chronicles* that Christianity was first introduced into the region in the first century by the Apostle Andrew, who, on his missionary journeys around the Black Sea, traveled up the Dnieper River and planted a cross on the hills of the future city of Kiev. This account is clearly legendary, as no continuous presence of Christianity persisted in the region in the intervening centuries, but it gave the new Christians in Kiev the sense of having some apostolic roots, so the legend became embedded in Russian and Ukrainian memory.

Relatively little is known about pre-Christian paganism of the Eastern Slavs, which left no written records and few archeological remains; temples and idols were made of wood. Most of what is known about it is indirect, coming either from Christian sources or from nineteenth-century folklore. Slavic paganism shared basic similarities with other Indo-European (especially Scandinavian) paganism, including a prominent thunder god (Perun), but it also included an important mother-goddess figure ("moist mother earth" or *Mokosh*). Grand Prince Vladimir was not the first to embrace Christianity: since the Rus were on trading routes between the Baltic and Black seas, Christian traders and merchants were living in Rus, and there were also local converts. The most prominent convert was Princess Olga, Vladimir's grandmother, although her choice was a personal one with no expectation that others would

2. For the early period of church history, see Maureen Perrie, ed., *The Cambridge History of Russia*, vol. 1, *From Early Rus' to 1689* (Cambridge: Cambridge University Press, 2006), chaps. 3–4; John Fennell, *A History of the Russian Church to 1488* (London: Routledge, 2014); Sophia Senyk, *A History of the Church in Ukraine*, 2 vols. (Rome: Pontifical Oriental Institute, 1993, 2011).

necessarily follow. Her son Sviatoslav regarded Christianity as weak and considered the old paganism as more appropriate for warriors.

Since Kievan Rus was a loose confederation of tribes and city-states, Grand Prince Vladimir of Kiev (r. 980–1015) sought to strengthen and consolidate the realm. The process of state formation required a more unified, monolithic, and institutionally strong form of religion than the more fragmented and localized polytheism. The main source for the story of the Baptism of Rus is the *Primary Chronicle*, written about a century after the events, which relates Vladimir's "testing the faiths." According to this account, Vladimir was visited by missionaries from the surrounding monotheistic faiths: from the Bulgar Muslims on the Volga River to the east, Jews from the state of the Khazars on the Black Sea, Western Christians from Germany, and Greek Christians from Constantinople. Vladimir listened to and questioned them. He rejected Judaism after the Jewish missionary told him that the Jews had been expelled from their homeland as punishment by God for their sins—not an appealing message for a ruler trying to consolidate his realm. Vladimir was attracted to Islam when he was promised seventy maidens in heaven (for, according to the *Chronicle*, Vladimir "was fond of women"). His attitude changed when he found out he would have to be circumcised and would be prohibited from eating pork and especially drinking alcohol because—according to what has become an oft-repeated phrase from the *Primary Chronicle*—"drinking is the joy of the Rus." The Greek missionary, finally, gave a compelling account of salvation history.

Vladimir wisely stated that everyone claims their religion is the best, but the only way to really know was to see it for oneself, so he sent emissaries to each of the realms to come back and report to him. Vladimir's emissaries were not impressed with the worship of any but that of Constantinople, which, they reported, was so remarkable that "we knew not whether we were in heaven or on earth. For on earth there is no such splendor or such beauty, and we are at a loss how to describe it. We only know that God dwells there among men, and their service is fairer than the ceremonies of other nations. For we cannot forget that beauty."[3] Although the account contains legendary elements and was certainly embellished, it is very significant that, for the Eastern Slavs, the intellectual arguments in favor of Christianity were less decisive than the beauty expressed in the splendor of its worship—calling to mind the Slavic term for Orthodoxy (*pravoslavie*) as the "right glory" of God. It is also noteworthy that, in the medieval period, the Russians developed spiritual life and the religious arts to a far greater extent than they did the intellectual pursuits of theology.

Legendary elements aside, the choice to adopt the faith from Constantinople was practical as well as strategic. Constantinople supported a century-old tradition of Slavic Christianity, which began in the ninth century with the Greek brothers Cyril and Methodius. As missionaries to Bohemia and Moravia (the modern-day Czech Republic), Cyril invented an alphabet (known as Glagolitic) for the previously illiterate Slavs and began translating the worship services and Scriptures into their language. Their efforts were continued by their successors in Macedonia, Bulgaria, and Serbia, who also created the Cyrillic alphabet by modifying Cyril's alphabet to be closer to the Greek. The choice between Western and Eastern Christianity was, therefore, also a choice between receiving Christian-

---

3. From the *Primary Chronicle* in Serge Zenkovsky, ed., *Medieval Russia's Epics, Chronicles, and Tales* (New York: Penguin, 1974), 67.

ity in Latin (which would have been totally incomprehensible to everyone, elites and commoners alike) or in Slavic, with texts already translated and an alphabet specifically designed to reflect the peculiarities of Slavic languages.

Finally, there was the political dimension: in the late tenth century, the Byzantine Empire was far more powerful, wealthy, and sophisticated than any of Rus's other neighbors, and especially given their geographical location, it was in a sense inevitable that the Rus would have come into the Byzantine orbit.[4] The specific circumstances of Vladimir's conversion involved a military alliance with the Byzantine Emperor in exchange for marrying the Emperor's sister—a rare instance of an imperial princess marrying a barbarian prince—which necessarily entailed his conversion to Christianity. According to the *Chronicles*, Vladimir changed after his baptism, giving up his harem with hundreds of concubines as well as his bloodthirsty ways. But for Vladimir this was not only an individual choice: he ordered the pagan statues cast down and destroyed, and the people of Kiev were instructed to come to the river for a mass baptism.

The Christianization of Rus did not happen overnight, of course. Nevertheless, the change was a significant one: promoting Christianity became a feature of princely rule, and none of Vladimir's successors attempted to restore paganism. Formal pagan practice tied to temples, idols, and communal rituals disappeared. But the churches and clergy would have been established in the cities and towns first, and only gradually extended out to the villages. Thus the Christianization

---

4. On Byzantium's influence on the world around it, see Colin Wells, *Sailing from Byzantium: How a Lost Empire Shaped the World* (New York: Delacorte, 2007). On Byzantine Christianity, see Averil Cameron, *Byzantine Christianity: A Very Brief History* (London: SPCK, 2017).

of the common people took time—decades or even centuries. Nineteenth-century Russian intelligentsia created a caricature of the Russian peasantry that characterized their faith as *dvoeverie* or "dual faith," meaning that they remained basically pagan with only a veneer of Christianity. This notion was uncritically taken over by Western observers and scholars. However, there was nothing particularly unique about the Eastern Slavs (or later the Russians) in the process of their Christianization that would have distinguished them from other northern Europeans in the Middle Ages (or in more modern times in Latin America), where there was a process of inculturation by which elements of prior beliefs and practices were Christianized. Only the Protestant Reformation declared such elements "superstition" and vigorously tried to root them out in Western Europe.[5] Despite whatever "pagan" elements may have survived in Russian popular religion, the people considered themselves Christian, and paganism as a belief system disappeared.[6]

In the century after Vladimir, Kievan Rus developed a rich Christian culture that included church architecture and iconography as well as literature. The age produced the first East Slavic saints: Boris and Gleb, two of Vladimir's sons who were killed by their brother in his attempt to seize power. They were canonized as "passion bearers" because of the Christ-like way in which they accepted their deaths (by contrast with martyrs, who are killed for the faith). The church of the Rus remained subordinate to the Patriarchate of Constantinople, and the metropolitan bishops were mostly Greek. Other bish-

---

5. John Bossy, *Christianity in the West, 1400-1700* (Oxford: Oxford University Press, 1985); Keith Thomas, *Religion and the Decline of Magic: Studies in Popular Beliefs in Sixteenth and Seventeenth Century England* (Oxford: Oxford University Press, 1997).
6. Rock, *Popular Religion in Russia*.

ops were probably Greek or Bulgarian in the beginning, but gradually locals were elevated to all ranks of the clergy. The one East Slav metropolitan[7] of Kiev in the mid-eleventh century, Hilarion (1051–1054), was the author of the first known piece of East Slavic literature, the "Sermon on Law and Grace," a rhetorical masterpiece in which he spoke of the spread of the gospel across the world that had "finally reached" the land of the Rus.[8] Although this text is sometimes misinterpreted as implying that the Rus were a "chosen" people, the intent is rather a "last but not least" motif: though late to joining the Christian family, they were nevertheless now equal members. Hilarion was metropolitan during the reign of Iarloslav the Wise (1019–1054), who was known for promoting Christianity by supporting the building of churches, the preparation of clergy, and the copying of books.

The development of Kievan Christianity included monasticism, which proved crucial to the spread of Christian culture. The first important monastery, that of the Kiev Caves, was established in the early eleventh century by Anthony, who became a monk on Mount Athos before returning to Kiev. Anthony began his monastic career as a hermit, digging a cave for himself on the banks of the Dnieper River to live in complete isolation from the world. Theodosius joined Anthony, but eventually he founded a cenobitic communal monastery (above ground) that would flourish into the most important monastery in Rus. The monastery mediated conflicts between rival princes, fashioned many religious leaders, and produced most of the important early monuments of literature, including the life of Theodosius and the *Primary Chronicle*, both attrib-

---

7. *Metropolitan* is a title that refers to the bishop of a major city (*metropolis*), who ranks above bishop and archbishop.
8. Zenkovsky, *Medieval Russia's Epics*, 85–90.

uted to the monk Nestor. It also served as a model for later monasteries. In short, Christianity in Kievan Rus flourished for two and a half centuries, developing rich expressions in architecture and religious literature as well as models of Christian living, from saintly princes to ascetic monks.[9]

The Mongol Invasion and the Rise of Muscovy (1240–1550)

Despite its rich Christian culture, Kievan Rus was politically unstable and collapsed in the face of the Mongol invasion that culminated in the fall of Kiev in 1240. Widespread physical destruction resulted from the Mongol conquest—their policy was to level cities that resisted. But the Mongols, who were still adherents of traditional shamanistic religion, were religiously tolerant everywhere they conquered, and protections for the clergy and church property were enshrined in Mongol law. (This branch of the Mongols, the Golden Horde, accepted Islam later, in the fourteenth century.) The Mongols ruled indirectly, leaving the Kievan princes in place, who, in turn, owed taxes and military recruits to the Mongols. The century and a half after the Mongol conquest was a dark age for Rus, which produced little in terms of written or constructed religious culture.[10] After the collapse of Kievan Rus with the Mongol conquest, the southwestern part of Rus was then conquered by Poland, while the northwest region was conquered by the Lithuanians. This geographical division and the differing his-

9. See Muriel Heppell, ed., *The Paterik of the Kievan Caves Monastery* (Cambridge, MA: Harvard University Press, 2011).
10. On the Mongol and early Muscovite periods, see Perrie, ed., *Cambridge History*, vol. 1, chaps. 7, 15; Michael Angold, ed., *The Cambridge History of Christianity*, vol. 5, *Eastern Christianity* (Cambridge: Cambridge University Press, 2014), chaps. 11, 12.

torical trajectories of these regions of Rus over the next several centuries contributed to the emergence of three distinct peoples: the Russians in the territories ruled by the Mongols, and the Ukrainians and the Belarusians in the regions ruled by Poland and Lithuania. The Lithuanians adopted elements of Slavic culture in the early centuries and were tolerant of the Orthodox Church.[11]

At the same time as the Mongols invaded, the Roman Catholic Swedes and the Teutonic Knights invaded the northern part of Rus. The latter, in particular, came with a crusading spirit to convert the "heretic" Eastern Christians as well as to conquer them. Prince Alexander Nevsky (1221–1263) made the strategic decision to submit to the Mongols but to fight against these northern invaders, whom the Rus saw as a greater threat to Orthodoxy than the Mongols. Prince Alexander, who received the epithet Nevsky after his defeat of the Swedes on the Neva river in 1240, was later canonized a saint in the Russian Church. The exemplars of the Christian faith canonized as saints in Rus were mostly either princes (such as Vladimir, Boris, Gleb, and Alexander Nevsky), or monks (such as Anthony and Theodosius).

Rus was challenged simultaneously from the East and from the West, and in both cases its identity was under question. To contrast themselves with the Mongols, they emphasized their Christian identity, but at the same time the West and Western Christians appeared as an even greater threat to their Orthodox identity. In effect this "in-betweenness,"—between Europe and Asia, Christian yet different,—would become a fundamental building block of Russian identity.

The political revival of the part of Rus that became Russia

---

11. Serhii Plokhy, *The Origins of Slavic Nations: Premodern Identities in Russia, Ukraine, and Belarus* (Cambridge: Cambridge University Press, 2010).

centered further to the northeast in the region around Moscow, which also became the locus of a spiritual and cultural revival. The key figure in the religious revival was St. Sergius of Radonezh (d. 1392). Following the example of early Christian monks who went into the desert, Sergius went into the Russian equivalent—the uninhabited forest—and lived alone as a hermit for years, devoting himself to prayer. Hagiographical accounts of his life depict him as a man of deep humility, exemplifying a characteristic expression of Russian Christianity, namely its *kenotic* nature, with a reference to the condescension and humility of the Son of God in becoming human and willingly undergoing his self-sacrificial suffering.[12] Eventually word of his holiness spread, and disciples gathered around him until a monastery was established with Sergius as abbot. Sergius combined the contemplative impulse of Orthodox hesychasm with a communal monastic setting. Sergius was so renowned in his lifetime that princes came to him for guidance; according to the hagiographical account of his life, he blessed Grand Prince Dmitry Donskoy (1350–1389) before the Muscovites' first victory over the Mongols at the Battle of Kulikovo in 1380. In time, the spiritual authority of his monastery added legitimacy to Moscow's claim as the new political center. In the wake of this spiritual revival came the greatest flowering of religious art, architecture, and liturgy, expressed above all by the famous iconographer Andrei Rublev (d. 1428). Rublev would be rediscovered in the modern period and regarded as medieval Russia's greatest artist.

Muscovy emerged as the new center for the East Slavs rather

---

12. The Life (Vita) of St. Sergius and other saints, as well as other religious texts, can be found in G. P. Fedotov, ed., *The Way of a Pilgrim and Other Classics of Russian Spirituality* (New York: Dover, 2003). The emphasis on the kenotic nature of Russian Orthodoxy was put forward by Fedotov, *The Russian Religious Mind*, 2 vols. (Cambridge, MA: Harvard University Press, 1966).

rapidly in the fifteenth century, finally putting an end to Mongol dominance in 1480. The growing strength of Muscovy and its church coincided with the decline of Byzantium. In the mid-fifteenth century, the remains of the Byzantine Empire, facing an imminent threat of Ottoman conquest, appealed to the West for help and became willing to negotiate a reunion of the Eastern and Western churches on terms dictated by Rome. This reunion was signed at the Council of Florence in 1445. One of the supporters of the union was the Greek Isiodore (d. 1463), who had been appointed metropolitan of Rus. When he arrived in Moscow and declared the union with Rome, the Russians rejected the union and arrested Isiodore (who later fled West). The bishops in Muscovy proceeded to elect their own metropolitan in 1448, thus signaling their ecclesiastical autocephaly from Constantinople. This independence of the Russian Church, although not immediately accepted by Constantinople (which itself repudiated the union with Rome after the fall of Constantinople in 1453), was permanent. Although the lands of Kievan Rus were divided between Polish, Lithuanian, and Mongol rule, until this point the Church had remained united (for the most part) under the bishop, who retained the title "Metropolitan of Kiev and all Rus" even though he ceased to reside in Kiev. After the autocephaly of the Russian Church in 1448, its head bore the title of the Metropolitan of Moscow, and became separate jurisdictionally from the Church in Poland and Lithuania.

So long as the Russian Church was subordinate to Constantinople, there was a consciousness that it was part of something larger. The autocephaly, however, meant a complete identity of the church with the nation. Formally, the model of church-state relations remained the Byzantine one of symphony (see chapter 1). In Muscovy, however, the ruler had the upper hand in the relationship. He was believed to be God's anointed ruler, and he had the right to call church councils, influence the selection of metropolitans and patriarchs, and enforce the Church's rules.

The fifteenth and sixteenth centuries was a period of political, territorial, and spiritual consolidation that resulted in the creation of an independent national Russian Church with its own pantheon of saints and traditions that paralleled in glory the growing power of the nation and state. This culminated in a special sense of Russia as the last true Christian kingdom and therefore a notion of "Holy Russia." The Muscovites interpreted the fall of Constantinople as divine punishment for the union with Rome, leaving the Russian Church as the sole bearer of true Orthodoxy. The Rus had not only been subordinate to Constantinople in ecclesiastical terms; being a part of the "Byzantine Commonwealth" meant that the emperor (Caesar) ruled in Constantinople, and those who ruled in his orbit—even if politically independent—could at most be "Grand Princes."[13] It was not until after the fall of Constantinople and the independence of the Russians from the Mongols in 1480 that Russian rulers began to take the title "tsar," the Slavicization of "Caesar"; Ivan IV the Terrible (1533–1584) was the first crowned with the title *tsar* in 1547.

In their perception, Muscovy grew strong politically and gained its political independence, and its Church had preserved Orthodoxy untarnished, at the same time as the Byzantines compromised their Church to a union with Rome and lost their political independence. From these coincidences Muscovites concluded that Russia had succeeded Byzantium as the ecclesiastical and political center of Orthodox Christianity.

---

13. Dimitry Obolensky, *Byzantine Commonwealth* (Crestwood, NY: St. Vladimir's Seminary Press, 1971).

This was articulated in a letter by the monk Filofei (Philotheus) to the Grand Prince Vasily III in 1510 as the idea that "two Romes had fallen"—that is, Rome fell away to heresy, and Constantinople, the "new Rome," had fallen to the Turks. Moscow was the "third Rome," that is, the third (and final) center of true Christian civilization and empire.

St. Sergius of Radonezh inspired a remarkable monastic resurgence that lasted more than a century as his disciples and their successors planted monasteries throughout the Russian north. Many, including St. Sergius's own Trinity Monastery, became major landowners as wealthy aristocrats bequeathed property to them in exchange for perpetual prayers for their souls. By the early sixteenth century, two great monastic leaders and authors emerged, one of whom, Iosif Volotsky (d. 1515), codified communal monastic life along strict disciplinary and hierarchical lines focused on liturgical worship combined with study. The other, Nil Sorsky (d. 1508), emphasized inner contemplative prayer in a simple setting in which the monastic brotherhood did not own property. Though once thought to be opponents, recent scholarship has demonstrated that they were in fact collaborators, and the conflict between the defenders of monastic property ("Possessors") and its detractors ("Non-Possessors") occurred only in the next generation.[14]

The divide between the Possessors and Non-Possessors also found expression in a range of other issues, such as how to deal with heresy. As in the West, though to a lesser extent, the religious ferment of the age produced some movements rejected by the established church as heretical, particularly the so-called Judaizers, in the late fifteenth century, who appar-

---

14. David Goldfrank, trans. and ed., *Nil Sorsky: The Authentic Writings* (Kalamazoo, MI: Cistercian Publications, 2008); Goldfrank, trans. and ed., *The Monastic Rule of Iosif Volotsky*, 2nd ed. (Kalamazoo, MI: Cistercian Publications, 2000).

ently rejected some traditional Christian teachings as well as the growing power and wealth of the Church. The chief figure condemning the Judaizers was Iosif Volotsky, who justified taking harsh measures against them; Nil Sorsky, by contrast, believed that heretics should be dealt with through persuasion. As a rule, the execution of heretics in medieval Russia was very rare. Perhaps most importantly, Iosif Volotsky also developed a political theology defending Muscovite autocracy.

Both Nil Sorsky and Iosif Volotsky were eventually canonized by the Russian Church, yet the differences between their approaches embody the paradox of Russian Orthodoxy concerning the Church's relationship to the world. How should the Church relate to political power—by being involved through blessing or alliance, or by being distanced and autonomous? What role should the clergy play—active involvement or withdrawal and contemplative prayer? The Possessors (or Josephites) promoted strict monastic communal discipline, active involvement in worldly affairs, intolerance to religious deviance, and militant alliance with secular power. The Non-Possessors emphasized mystical individual piety, noninvolvement, ascetic restraint, tolerance of dissidents, and priority of inner contemplation over liturgical performance. Although the two parties argued about details of monastic practices, the significance of the debate was much broader: they represented the two images of Holy Rus. Although these tensions have always been present in the history of Christianity, in Russia the Possessors became the dominant trend, and the material wealth of the monasteries, the Church's institutional discipline, and involvement in worldly affairs continued to grow. However, the tradition represented by the Non-Possessors was never entirely rejected by the Russian Church and always remained an ideal and an undercurrent that periodically came to the fore again.

The Russian Empire was born in the sixteenth century, when Ivan the Terrible expanded the realm beyond gathering the lands of Kievan Rus (i.e., Orthodox Slavs) under Moscow to conquering territories of the former Mongol Khanates that consisted of ethnic and religious others. This process of expansion would continue until the fall of the Russian Empire in 1917. With imperial expansion, Russia was faced with a new question of identity: Was it an Orthodox Christian Empire, Byzantium's successor and the "third Rome," or was it a multi-ethnic and multi-confessional empire like the Mongols? Although the Orthodox Church preferred the former, not all Russian rulers or imperial administrators agreed; the tension would persist until the end of the empire.[15]

Early Modern Russia and Ukraine

After the autocephaly of the Russian Church in 1448, the Orthodox Church in Ukrainian and Belarusian territories of Kievan Rus remained headed by the Metropolitan of Kiev under the jurisdiction of Constantinople; these territories fell under the rule of Poland and Lithuania, and later the combined Polish-Lithuanian Commonwealth (a massive state in east-central Europe in the sixteenth and seventeenth centuries). At this point the Muscovite and Ukrainian traditions diverged. In the sixteenth century the Commonwealth was the most confessionally diverse nation in Europe, home to Roman Catholics, Orthodox, Protestants, and Europe's largest Jewish population. After the Reformation, the Orthodox came under greater pres-

15. Geoffrey Hosking, *Russia: People and Empire* (Cambridge, MA: Harvard University Press, 1997), 6–7.

sure and competition from both Catholics and Protestants. Both Orthodox hierarchs and laity sought to defend and revitalize their church in the face of this competition. The laity formed brotherhoods that promoted education and publishing activities, including the creation of the Ostrog Bible in 1581, the first printed Old and New Testaments in Church Slavonic.

Toleration disappeared under King Sigismund III (1587–1632), a militant Roman Catholic who aggressively sought to bring both Protestant and Orthodox Christians into the Roman fold. Aspects of Counter-Reformation Catholicism appealed to the Orthodox hierarchy in Ukraine, and most joined the Union of Brest in 1596. This Union created the Uniate, or Greek Catholic Church, and allowed the Orthodox converts to retain Eastern Christian practices, including Slavonic liturgy and married priesthood, but brought them under the jurisdiction of Rome instead of Constantinople. Many of the parish clergy, laity, and brotherhoods chose to remain with Constantinople, however, despite the fact that the Orthodox were deprived of bishops. Only with the death of Sigismund in 1632 were the Orthodox of the Commonwealth allowed to restore a legally recognized hierarchy.[16]

The energetic Peter Mogila became Metropolitan of Kiev from 1632 to 1647; he reshaped and revitalized Orthodoxy in Ukraine.[17] Education and publication were at the center of his program: the school he established in Kiev introduced the highest standards of learning, epitomized by Polish Jesuit schools. The service books he published also became standard,

16. For the early modern period, see Perrie, ed., *Cambridge History*, vol. 1, chap. 27; Angold, ed., *Cambridge History of Christianity*, vol. 5, chap. 13; Boris Gudziak, *Crisis and Reform: The Kyivan Metropolitanate, the Patriarchate of Constantinople, and the Union of Brest* (Cambridge, MA: Harvard Ukrainian Research Institute, 2001).

17. Mogila, though metropolitan of Kiev, was Moldavian; his name is therefore spelled variously (Movila by the Romanians, Mohyla by the Ukrainians).

even in Russia. Kiev thus became the cultural center for much of the Orthodox world by the mid-seventeenth century.

The Cossacks, who were self-governing, semi-military communities on the borderland between Muscovy, the Polish-Lithuanian Commonwealth, and the Ottoman Empire, rebelled against the Polish lords for greater independence in 1648. The Cossacks turned to Moscow for support in 1654, with the end result that by 1667 Moscow gained control of all of Ukraine east of the Dnieper River as well as of Kiev. In 1686, the newly elected Metropolitan of Kiev, Gedeon, transferred his allegiance from Constantinople to Moscow, thus subordinating the Ukrainian Orthodox Church to the Russian.

This subordination began a process of Russifying the Ukrainian Church traditions, although it also opened the door for the transfer of significant influence from Ukraine to Russia (on this, see chapter 5). At the same time, the Uniate Church, which was subordinate to Rome, extended its control over all the Orthodox dioceses in the Ukrainian and Belarusian territories west of the Dnieper that remained in the Polish-Lithuanian Commonwealth. As a consequence, the distinctive Ukrainian Orthodox tradition, which had existed in parallel with the Russian tradition for centuries, gradually disappeared after the mid-seventeenth century.

During this period, Orthodoxy in Moscow was acquiring new strength. This process culminated in its church being elevated to the status of a patriarchate, with the election of the first Patriarch, Job, in 1589. This status was conferred by the Patriarch of Constantinople, and Moscow was given the last place in the traditional scheme of the pentarchy (see chapter 1). The Patriarch of Constantinople and the other Greek patriarchs viewed the Greek Church as the "mother Church" that was still the final arbiter of Orthodoxy. The Russians, by contrast, emphasized their position as the only powerful Orthodox state, which they felt accorded them the leading role in the Orthodox world. This tension between Moscow and Constantinople for leadership in the Orthodox world continues today.

The Russian patriarchs would soon be called on to provide leadership for the country as a whole during the interregnum known as the Time of Troubles (1598–1613), when the Rurik dynasty that had ruled Rus and Muscovy since the beginning came to an end. Patriarch Germogen of Moscow called on forces in Russia to cast out the invading Polish army and defend Orthodoxy against Catholicism. This era of state collapse and foreign incursion—and the potential of the church and its patriarch to lead the nation out of crisis—was recalled during the crises of the twentieth century.

The Time of Troubles ended with the establishment of the Romanov dynasty as the ruling family in Russia when the Assembly of the Land elected the young Mikhail Romanov as tsar in 1613. Mikhail's father Filaret (1553–1633) was unable to become tsar because he had been forced to take monastic vows years earlier precisely to prevent that possibility. Filaret instead became the patriarch of the church, and he had a powerful influence over affairs of state. He also increased the power and prestige of the patriarchate. Filaret and his successors felt the need to reform church life, in particular to enforce uniformity of liturgical practice and rigorously uphold morality among the parish clergy and laity in efforts similar to the Western Christian "confessionalization" campaigns that aimed to regularize and unify religious practices and eradicate elements considered superstitious.

Attempts at reform continued through the seventeenth century. When Nikon (1605–1681), one of an elite group of reformers known as the Zealots of Piety, became patriarch in 1652, the reform took a catastrophic turn. At first Nikon was close to and had full support of Tsar Aleksei (r. 1645–1676). In printing liturgical books for the first time, Nikon had to choose among the diverse practices that had evolved in Russia itself and particularly between Russian and Greek practice. Because Nikon wanted to position Moscow as a leader in the Orthodox world as a whole, he was willing to adapt Russian practice to the Greek in order to make it acceptable to the Greeks. In the mid-1650s he published reformed liturgical books, symbolized by changing the way worshippers made the sign of the cross from two to three fingers. Moreover, he made these changes in an imperious and autocratic fashion rather than with the backing of a church council as would have been normal in the Orthodox tradition; he also insisted that those who continued to practice the old rituals were heretics. Nikon's reforms split the reform movement, with many of the leading figures in the Zealots of Piety rejecting Nikon's reforms, asserting that the Russians had maintained the pure Orthodox tradition when the Greeks had compromised during the Council of Florence. Much more was therefore at stake than a few simple liturgical changes, but even the significance of those should not be underestimated, since they impacted every believer in the most commonly repeated gestures and words. Nikon's reforms were backed by the state, however, and opponents were exiled.[18]

Nikon emphasized patriarchal authority both within the Church but also vis-à-vis the state, claiming a superiority of the spiritual over the temporal in ways more similar to the

---

18. For an overview, see Nadieszda Kizenko, "The Church Schism and Old Belief," in *A Companion to Russian History,* ed. Abbott Gleason (Hoboken, NJ: John Wiley & Sons, 2009), 145–62; Robert Crummey, *Old Believers in a Changing World* (DeKalb: Northern Illinois University Press, 2011).

medieval papacy than the traditional Orthodox formulation of symphony. The patriarch and the tsar had a falling out, and Tsar Aleksei convened a Council that was presided over by representatives of the Eastern patriarchates. The Council deposed Nikon but reaffirmed the liturgical reforms as well as the harsh line condemning as heretics those who did not adopt the reformed liturgical practices. Because the state sided with church reform, opposition to the reforms also entailed rejection of the authority of the state. The second half of the seventeenth century also witnessed the development of serfdom and worsening conditions for the peasantry so that social unrest, political opposition, and religious dissent frequently coalesced in explosive ways.

Those who opposed the reforms became known as the Old Believers (in English; in Russian known as *staroobriadtsy,* "old ritualists," or simply as *raskolniki,* "schismatics"), who accepted an apocalyptic view that the betrayal of true Orthodoxy by the state and official church signaled the end of times. In a few extreme instances, groups of Old Believers locked themselves in churches that they set on fire when government troops approached. The opposition leaders, including Archpriest Avvakum (author of the first Russian autobiography), were burned at the stake in 1681 in a relatively rare instance of Orthodox execution of heretics. Greater numbers of Old Believers retreated to Siberia or other remote areas on the fringes of the empire out of the authorities' reach, where they established a dissenting Orthodox tradition.

The number of Old Believers only grew in subsequent centuries. Forced to band together as an oppressed minority, they created a particular subculture of resistance and survival, which combined self-isolation and concern for purity with an efficient work ethic. In the nineteenth and early twentieth century many provincial businesses and industries in Russia were run, paradoxically, by the officially under-privileged Old Believers. They survived imperial and Soviet persecutions over three hundred years, and in the twenty-first century many communities can be found scattered across Eurasia and overseas.[19] Paradoxically, at the very moment when the Russian Church reached a pinnacle of its power and authority, it was weakened, especially vis-à-vis the state, by internal division. Unlike the split in Western Christianity stemming from the Protestant Reformation, no substantive theological issues were at stake in Russia, and the protesters in the Russian tradition were those who opposed reform.

Imperial Russia (1700–1917)

The reign of Peter the Great (1682/1696–1725) brought massive changes to the Russian Orthodox Church, as it did to Russian society and culture generally. Peter regarded Russia as isolated and backwards, and sought to modernize and integrate it into European great power politics. This modernization entailed reforms not only of government administration and the military, but also of the Orthodox Church. Foremost among these were the abolition of the patriarchate, for Peter considered that a single head of the Church could undercut the singular power of the tsar. The patriarchate was replaced by a collegial body of senior clergy known as the Most Holy Governing Synod. The patriarchate would not be restored until after the fall of the monarchy in 1917. The period between 1700 (the death of the last patriarch) and 1917 is often referred to as the Synodal period of Russian Orthodoxy, which corresponds to

19. See Douglas Rogers, *The Old Faith in the Russian Land: A Historical Ethnography of Ethics in the Urals* (Ithaca, NY: Cornell University Press, 2009).

what historians refer to as the Imperial period of Russian history centered in Peter's new capital city, St. Petersburg.[20]

Peter the Great's reforms are usually characterized as having decapitated the Church (or even placing himself as its head), subordinating it to the state, and making the Holy Synod little more than a department of state headed by a lay bureaucrat, the chief procurator; all this is viewed to have effectively secularized the Russian Church. Such a depiction is not accurate, however. Peter's reforms, embodied in the *Spiritual Regulation* (1721), were certainly motivated by a desire to reduce the Church's political influence. At the same time, Peter wanted to strengthen the Church because he regarded it as a necessary part of a well-ordered state. The reforms led to the development of the church administration so that religious practice could be standardized and norms enforced. He also saw an educated clergy as essential for a modern Church and mandated the establishment of a network of seminaries to train them. Although church and state structures and interests were certainly intertwined and both ultimately subordinate to the Tsar, neither the church nor the Holy Synod was a "department of

20. On the Synodal period, see Gregory Freeze, "Russian Orthodoxy: Church, People and Politics in Imperial Russia," in *The Cambridge History of Russia*, vol. 2, *Imperial Russia, 1689-1917*, ed. Dominic Lieven (Cambridge: Cambridge University Press, 2015), 284–305; Angold, ed., *The Cambridge History of Christianity*, vol. 5, chaps. 14–15; Paul Werth, "Religion," in *The Oxford Handbook of Modern Russian History*, ed. Simon Dixon (Oxford: Oxford University Press, 2015); and the introduction to Randall Poole and Paul Werth, eds., *Religious Freedom in Modern Russia* (Pittsburgh: University of Pittsburgh Press, 2018), 1–43. There has been a flowering of scholarship on Orthodoxy in Imperial Russia in the past several decades, pioneered by Freeze and developed by others. For an overview of Freeze's contribution, see Scott Kenworthy, "Gregory L. Freeze: Historian of the Orthodox Church in Modern Russia," in *Church and Society in Modern Russia: Essays in Honor of Gregory L. Freeze*, ed. Manfred Hildermeier and Elise Kimerling Wirtschafter (Wiesbaden: Harrassowitz Verlag, 2015), 211–29. For an overview of the new scholarship, see the introduction to Heather Coleman, ed., *Orthodox Christianity in Imperial Russia: A Source Book on Lived Religion* (Bloomington: Indiana University Press, 2014), 1–20.

state." At the most basic level, the clergy never received state salaries (except in special cases). The lay chief procurator was established to be a liaison between the Holy Synod and the tsar. Despite ubiquitous repetition by historians, the chief procurator was never the "head" of the Synod (which was usually chaired by the Metropolitan of St. Petersburg), and the procurators grew in power—to the point at which they controlled the affairs of the Synod—only toward the end of the imperial period.[21]

By the nineteenth century the Church had constructed an entire educational system to educate future priests, and a seminary degree became a prerequisite for ordination. The majority of bishops studied not only in the seminary but also one of the four elite theological academies (Moscow, St. Petersburg, Kiev, and Kazan), the Church's parallel to the university. This educational system was reserved primarily for sons of the parish clergy, which meant that the clergy virtually became a hereditary caste. Despite stereotypes about the ignorance of the Russian clergy, they were in fact one of the most educated segments of Russian society. At the same time, the clergy in Russia were not particularly privileged; their income depended on their parishioners, who were most often impoverished peasants, and the clergy's levels of income typically matched their parishioners. To survive, the clergy frequently had to work the land alongside the peasants, which contributed to their benighted image.

Although monasticism had been a central expression of Orthodoxy since late antiquity, Peter the Great and his successors regarded monks as idle and monasticism as socially

21. A seminal article on this topic is Gregory L. Freeze, "Handmaiden of the State? The Church in Imperial Russia Reconsidered," *Journal of Ecclesiastical History* 36 (1985): 82–102.

useless. In 1764, Empress Catherine the Great (1729–1796) confiscated monastic estates altogether, closed more than half the monastic institutions, and restricted the number of monks and nuns. Monasticism suffered a severe decline for the next half century, and in 1825 there were less than half the number of monks and nuns than a century earlier (from twenty-five thousand to eleven thousand). Yet monasticism experienced a dramatic revival: in the course of the nineteenth century the number of monasteries doubled to around one thousand, and the number of monks, nuns, and novices exceeded one hundred thousand by 1917. By the time of the 1917 Revolution, three-quarters of the monastics were women, many of whom were engaged in charitable activities such as education, health care, and care for the poor and elderly. The resurgence of monasticism was connected with a broader resurgence of popular religiosity, which found expression in an explosion of pilgrimages to famous holy places and monasteries.[22]

The revival was in part driven by a revival of contemplative spirituality. A key figure in this process was Paisy Velichkovsky (1722–1794), who went to Mount Athos, the international Orthodox center of monasticism, where he discovered and translated early texts of contemplative spirituality; this culminated in the publication of the Slavonic *Philokalia* (literally the "Love of the Good") in 1793. Paisy's disciples brought these traditions of Orthodox spirituality and hesychasm back into Russia in the early nineteenth century. A key component of this tradition was the figure of the *starets*, or spiritual elder, a person of exceptional holiness who also had special gifts for guiding others. These elders were a traditional feature of

---

22. See Scott M. Kenworthy, "Monasticism in Modern Russia," in *Monasticism in Eastern Europe and the Former Soviet Republics*, ed. Ines Angeli Murzaku (London: Routledge), 265–84; Kenworthy, *Heart of Russia*.

monastic life, with experienced monks guiding novices. But in nineteenth-century Russia, some elders grew famous for their abilities of spiritual direction and attracted thousands of ordinary faithful to visit them. The most famous of these included Serafim of Sarov (1754–1833) and the elders of the Optina Hermitage. The age also produced several very important spiritual writers who articulated older traditions for a modern age, most notably Ignatius Brianchaninov (1807–1867) and Theophan the Recluse (1815–1894). Optina Hermitage, about 185 miles (three hundred kilometers) south of Moscow, attracted not only many ordinary pilgrims but also the leading lights of Russian culture, including thinkers such as Ivan Kireevsky and Vladimir Solovyov as well as the writers Nikolai Gogol, Fyodor Dostoevsky, and Leo Tolstoy. The phenomenon was important enough to play a central role in Dostoevsky's major novel *The Brothers Karamazov.*[23]

The popularity of Optina Hermitage among intellectual and literary giants points to a broader phenomenon, namely the flowering of Russian culture in the nineteenth century. This flowering, especially in literature and music, reached a pinnacle that is universally recognized. Although some Russian culture, like its Western European counterparts, was predominantly secular in orientation, religious themes were very important to a number of Russian authors (see chapter 5). In the realm of music, Russia's greatest composers, such as Petr Tchaikovsky (1840–1893) and Sergei Rachmaninoff (1873–1943), composed liturgical music, and others incorporated liturgical themes into their compositions. Russian artists such as Mikhail Nesterov (1862–1942) and avant-garde painters

23. Irina Paert, *Spiritual Elders: Charisma and Tradition in Russian Orthodoxy* (DeKalb: Northern Illinois University Press, 2010). Some texts of Russian spirituality can be found in Fedotov, *Way of a Pilgrim.*

such as Natalia Goncharova (1881–1962) and Wassily Kandinsky (1866–1944) also engaged spiritual motifs in their work.

The Synodal period also witnessed a flowering of missionary activity in the Russian Orthodox Church. The greatest of the Russian missionaries were sensitive to distinguish between the gospel and Russian or European culture and sought to preach the gospel in the vernacular, to Christianize but not to Russify. This was true of some missionaries within the Russian Empire, such as Nikolai Ilminsky (1822–1891) among the Tatars and Makary (Glukharev, 1792–1847) in the Altai region, and was particularly the case among the missionaries on the fringes of the Empire or beyond it altogether. One of the greatest, Innocent (Veniaminov, 1797–1879), was a missionary among the natives in Alaska, where he learned the local languages and translated the gospel into them. Because the Russian missionaries in Alaska respected native cultures, native Alaskans became even more devoted to Orthodoxy after the sale of Alaska to the United States, which was accompanied by aggressive efforts to Protestantize and Americanize them.[24] Nikolai (Kasatkin, 1836–1912) was a missionary in Japan who spent many years learning Japanese culture and language before beginning his missionary work, and he endeavored to create an indigenous church that was led by Japanese converts rather than being dependent upon Russian missionaries.

During the second half of the nineteenth century, Russia experienced forces of modernization and rapid social change, including urbanization, industrialization, and the spread of lit-

---

24. On Alaska, see Sergei Kan, "Russian Orthodox Missionaries at Home and Abroad: The Case of Siberian and Alaskan Indigenous Peoples," in *Of Religion and Empire: Missions, Conversion, and Tolerance in Imperial Russia,* ed. Robert Geraci and Michael Khodarkovsky (Ithaca, NY: Cornell University Press, 2001), 173–200; Michael Oleksa, *Orthodox Alaska: A Theology of Mission* (Crestwood, NY: St. Vladimir's Seminary Press, 1993).

eracy. The impact that these changes had on religion was complex. Greater social and physical mobility combined with literacy resulted in the proliferation of popular religious literature and an upsurge in pilgrimage. Although the institutional Church and the overburdened parish clergy certainly had their challenges in meeting the spiritual needs of the faithful, expressions of popular Orthodoxy flourished. At the same time, modernity also brought new alternatives in the form of new religious groups such as Baptists, which also experienced increased numbers of converts, as well as those who rejected religion altogether for radical political movements. The phenomenon of secularization—the decline of religious belief and participation that affected Western Europe—seems to have had only a marginal impact on Russia, however. Even up to the 1917 Revolution itself, rates of religious participation—at least as measured by annual participation in confession and communion—remained extraordinarily high in Russia (nearly 90 percent) by comparison with the West.[25]

Some Orthodox clergy responded to the modern challenges by increasing their social involvement. Renewed ideas of pastoral theology sought increased engagement with the world, especially with new social elements such as industrial workers and educated urbanites. Some even advocated something akin to the Social Gospel in the West at the same time.[26] One of the most extraordinary figures of the turn of the twentieth century was Father John of Kronstadt, who, as a married priest, drew people in a way similar to renowned elders; his spirituality combined the personal and contemplative approach with

25. Freeze, "Russian Orthodoxy," 299.
26. Scott Kenworthy, "An Orthodox Social Gospel in Late-Imperial Russia," *Religion and Society in Central and Eastern Europe* 1 (2005): 1–29, https://tinyurl.com/qrbob8j.

the liturgical and sacramental, all of which was complemented by an active social program for the poor.[27]

The Orthodox Church, as the state church of the Russian Empire, for the most part supported the political status quo. Although early nineteenth-century elites embraced a kind of ecumenical vision of Christianity, Tsar Nicholas I (1825–1855) adopted an official ideology of "Orthodoxy, Autocracy, and Nationality" that gave a central role to Orthodoxy both in the political order and in conceptions of Russian national identity. Political opposition and revolutionary movements therefore generally opposed the Orthodox Church because of the its links to the state; the hostility of the revolutionary intelligentsia to the Church would have enormous consequences after the 1917 Revolution.

As Russian society became more polarized in the early twentieth century, the Church was beset by its own internal tensions. Particularly damaging was the scandalous relationship between the royal family and Grigory Rasputin (1869–1916), the Siberian peasant who gained a reputation as a charismatic spiritual healer. The royal family believed in his healing effect on their hemophiliac son and successor to the throne, Alexei. Since they regarded him as a holy man, Rasputin exercised great influence in affairs of state such as government appointments and church posts. Rasputin was not a monk and had no formal role in the Church, which mostly resented his meddling interference.[28]

In 1905, Russia experienced its first mass revolutionary upheaval, which proved as much a watershed moment for the

---

27. Nadieszda Kizenko, *The Prodigal Saint: Father John of Kronstadt and the Russian People* (University Park: Pennsylvania State University Press, 2000).
28. Douglas Smith, *Rasputin: Faith, Power, and the Twilight of the Romanovs* (New York: Picador, 2017).

Church as it was for society. The revolutionary movement was ultimately defeated, but it forced the monarchy to make concessions, creating the Duma (parliament) and greater legal extension of religious tolerance. The introduction of party politics into Russia brought to the fore political polarities, and some clergy—though by no means all—embraced the cause of right-wing monarchist and nationalist movements that deployed anti-Semitic rhetoric. The extension of religious tolerance awakened a kind of liberation movement within the Church as well—that is, a call for liberation from state tutelage. After the tsar granted greater religious liberty, some felt that the Orthodox Church was disadvantaged and fettered by its ties to the state. Virtually all of the clergy advocated a Church Council that would address systemic problems hampering the Church's responsiveness to believers' spiritual needs. Proposed reforms included the restoration of the patriarchate, which would give the Church an independent voice vis-à-vis the state, though for precisely that reason the state blocked the Council.[29]

World War I exacerbated pre-existing political and social turmoil in Russia, and the monarchy's failed leadership led to its collapse in February 1917, when Nicholas II abdicated the throne. Euphoria of freedom swept the country, and Russia had a brief moment of democracy. The provisional government, which was supposed to rule until a new constitution was written, also failed to stabilize the country. Once the monarchy fell, there was a break in the union of throne and altar that was experienced as a kind of emancipation by many within the Orthodox Church. The Church took the opportunity to call a major Council, which began in August 1917. The Church had

---

29. James Cunningham, *A Vanquished Hope: The Movement for Church Renewal in Russia, 1905-1906* (Crestwood, NY: St. Vladimir's Seminary Press, 1997).

its own democratic moment, and local congresses of clergy and laity sometimes ousted their bishops and held elections for their replacements. The All-Russian Church Council, the first since the seventeenth century, was a monumental event. Virtually every aspect of church life was on the agenda: the administration of the Church, education, liturgical practice, monasticism, the reform of the parish, and the role of the laity and particularly women in the church. More than half of the delegates were laymen. The Council had great potential.[30]

All-Russian Church Council of 1917–1918. *Photo courtesy of Wikimedia Commons.*

By the fall of 1917, however, the political situation was growing increasingly unstable, and the most radical left-wing group—the Bolshevik faction of the Social Democratic (Marxist) Party—seized power at the end of October. The Bolsheviks proceeded to establish a single-party state with a radical social-

30. Hyacinthe Destivelle, *The Moscow Council (1917-1918): The Creation of the Conciliar Institutions of the Russian Orthodox Church*, trans. Jerry Ryan (Notre Dame: University of Notre Dame Press, 2015).

ist program designed to bring about the realization of a communist utopia. The Church Council was still in the early stages of its work when the Bolsheviks seized power, and conditions rapidly changed. The Council voted to restore the patriarchate immediately after the Bolshevik seizure of power, and then elected Tikhon (Bellavin) to the office (see chapter 4), although the Council was unable to accomplish much else before it was closed down a year later.

Taken as a whole, the Synodal period (1700–1917) was characterized by the development of the Church as an institution (the proliferation of diocesan structures, seminaries, etc.) that eventually became too bureaucratized and subordinated to state tutelage to be completely responsive to changing social conditions. At the same time, the Orthodox faith remained vibrant both among many of the intellectual elites and among the common people, who expressed their faith through such phenomena as monasticism and pilgrimage.

Religious Diversity in the Russian Empire

Peter the Great envisioned his new city of St. Petersburg as a multi-confessional one, and it became one of the few European cities in which one could encounter churches of so many different denominations in such close proximity to one another. Peter's secular orientation continued with his successors in the eighteenth century. Not all of the intervening empresses advocated religious tolerance (as evidenced by forced conversions of Muslims in the 1730s and 1740s), though Catherine the Great (r. 1762–1796), who styled herself an enlightened monarch, promoted it. Although Russia is not usually thought of as religiously tolerant, in fact the record during the Imperial period was quite complex, varying widely according to religion, region, and time period.

The general rule was that the Orthodox Church was enshrined in law as the "predominant and preeminent" faith, and the non-Orthodox were prohibited from proselytizing or converting Orthodox Christians away from Orthodoxy. At the same time, the Russian Empire was multi-ethnic and multi-confessional. Religion in the Russian Empire was associated with ethnicity, so it was considered "natural" for Russians, Ukrainians, Georgians, and others to be Orthodox; Poles and Lithuanians to be Roman Catholic; Germans to be Lutheran; Armenians to belong to the nationally specific, ancient Armenian Apostolic Church; Tatars and Bashkirs to be Muslims; Buriats and Kalmyks to be Buddhists; and Jews to profess Judaism. The state recognized certain administrative structures through which it sought to integrate these religious communities into the empire. As a rule, Russian administrators were more interested in keeping the peace than they were in achieving religious homogeneity, at least before the late nineteenth century when there were greater pressures to "Russify" and create more unity in the Empire.[31]

Among the non-Christians, Jews were a unique case in the Russian Empire: they were essentially missing from Russia before the dismemberment of the Polish-Lithuanian Commonwealth by Russia, Prussia, and Austria at the end of the eighteenth century. After the partitions of Poland, Russia received Europe's largest population of Jews virtually overnight. The solution was to restrict them, with some exceptions, to residing in the regions of the Russian Empire in which they already

---

31. Paul Werth, *The Tsar's Foreign Faiths: Toleration and the Fate of Religious Freedom in Imperial Russia* (Oxford: Oxford University Press, 2014); Poole and Werth, eds., *Religious Freedom in Modern Russia*.

resided (known as the Pale of Settlement). Although often associated with anti-Semitism, Russia's history of anti-Jewish violence was much briefer than that of Europe, and only exploded
with particular vehemence after 1881, although it became a
recurrent phenomenon thereafter.[32]

Another large non-Christian population, the Muslims, in
contrast with the Jews, have been interacting with the Russians
for centuries as neighbors, subordinates, and objects of "civ-
ilizing" Russification. Since the Golden Horde and the expansion of the Muscovite state in the Volga region in the sixteenth
century, this was a complex process of cultural interaction,
conversions, and partial coopting of the Muslim elites. Along
with imperial expansion, Russia included first Volga Muslims,
then multi-ethnic Caucasian Muslims, and finally the entirety
of Central Asia.[33]

Since the seventeenth century, the empire incorporated the
Buddhist populations of the Kalmyks and Buriats, ethnicities
of Mongolian origin who lived on the Caspian Sea and around
Lake Baikal, respectively; in the early twentieth century the
Buddhist population also included the Tuvins, a Turkic-speaking people on the border with China. All these peoples practiced a mixture of Tibetan Buddhism and shamanism. The
empire recognized the lamas and sponsored, in the 1910s, the
construction of a large Buddhist temple in St. Petersburg, the
first in Europe.

The Roman Catholic Church was regarded by the Russians as
a serious rival to the Orthodox Church, especially at moments

32. John Klier, *Russia Gathers Her Jews: The Origins of the "Jewish Question" in Russia,
1772-1825* (DeKalb: Northern Illinois University Press, 1986); Klier, *Imperial Russia's Jewish Question, 1855-1881* (Cambridge: Cambridge University Press, 1995);
Eugene Avrutin, *Jews and the Imperial State: Identification Politics in Tsarist Russia*
(Ithaca, NY: Cornell University Press, 2010).
33. Robert Crews, *For Prophet and Tsar: Islam and Empire in Russia and Central Asia*
(Cambridge, MA: Harvard University Press, 2009).

of crisis such as the crusading efforts against the Russian north in the thirteenth century, the attempted Union at the Council of Florence in the fifteenth century, and the creation of the Greek Catholic Church in the sixteenth century. However, like the Jews, large numbers of Roman and Greek Catholics did not live in the Russian Empire until the partitions of Poland at the end of the eighteenth century. The Russian Orthodox Church regarded the Greek Catholic Church as particularly problematic since, in the eyes of the Russian Church and state, its flock had been "poached" from the Orthodox in the sixteenth century. Therefore the Greek Catholic Church in regions that today are Ukraine and Belarus was effectively liquidated and "re-united" to the Orthodox Church in the nineteenth century.[34] It was, however, accepted that Poles and Lithuanians should remain Roman Catholic. After the two Polish uprisings against Russian rule in 1830 and 1863, however, the Catholic Church was seen as a particular threat because Catholic clergy in Russian-controlled territory provided some of the intellectual backing for the anti-Russian resistance.[35]

The most significant Protestant presence came from Germans. The Baltic Germans, who were traditionally Lutheran, were the first to be incorporated into the empire with the territorial expansion in the early eighteenth century. Catherine the Great, herself German, recruited Germans to settle in Russia on very favorable terms. In particular, they were offered religious tolerance and freedom from military constriction, both of which were especially attractive to the Mennonites, who were discriminated against in their native Prussia both because

34. Barbara Skinner, *The Western Front of the Eastern Church: Uniate and Orthodox Conflict in Eighteenth-Century Poland, Ukraine, Belarus, and Russia* (DeKalb: Northern Illinois University Press, 2009).
35. Dennis Dunn, *The Catholic Church and Russia: Popes, Patriarchs, Tsars and Commissars* (Burlington, VT: Ashgate, 2004).

of their rejection of the Lutheran church and because of their pacifism. Other dissenting religious groups like Baptists settled for similar reasons. These Germans settled primarily in the Volga region. Catholic and Lutheran Germans settled in other regions as well, and by the late Imperial period, there were some two million Germans in the Russian Empire. At the end of imperial and in early Soviet Russia, many Russian German Mennonites emigrated to North America.

The greatest restrictions were placed on Christian groups that attracted ethnic Russians away from, and therefore in competition with, the Russian Orthodox Church. These groups included evangelical Protestants such as the Baptists.[36] One local group of Protestants were the so-called Stundists; they appeared in the mid-nineteenth century in southern Ukraine under the influence of German settlers. The name *Stundist* comes from German for "hour," meaning the obligatory hour for Bible study, a key practice of all Protestant evangelicals. Strongly criticized by the Orthodox for their foreignness, the Stundist movement nevertheless spread across some Russian and Ukrainian provinces and became the formative group for ethnically Russian Baptists.

The groups that were most discriminated against were indigenous Russian dissenting religious movements. Such groups included the Old Believers, whose numbers continued to grow in the nineteenth century. It also included an array of so-called spiritual sects; popular forms of emotional, charismatic Christianity sprung among the lower strata of the Russian population, mostly peasants. These sects were the expression of spontaneous Russian spirituality and included the communities of *Dukhobors, Molokans, Subbotniks, Khlysty,*

36. Heather Coleman, *Russian Baptists and Spiritual Revolution, 1905-1929* (Bloomington: Indiana University Press, 2005).

Skoptsy. They all emerged in the eighteenth century in the peasant milieu and varied in particular style and dispositions, but all represented a spiritual alternative based on a hyper-rigorous reading of the Scriptures. They formed peculiar sub-cultures, sometimes around charismatic leaders, practicing trance-like rituals, being frequently iconoclastic, sometimes professing apocalyptic faith, and rejecting the authority of the official Church hierarchy. All these sects were severely per-secuted and forced out to the remote corners of the empire or abroad, notably to North America, where they can be still found in the twenty-first century.[37] The Russian Empire was, in short, very religiously diverse, where various Christians and adherents to other major religious groups coexisted.

The Soviet Period

The Bolsheviks, who later renamed themselves the Communist Party, established the Soviet Union out of the former Russian Empire. As Marxists, the Bolsheviks adhered to an atheist, materialist philosophical worldview. Karl Marx (1818–1883) famously referred to religion as the "opium of the people," an element of the "superstructure" that helped those who held political and economic power exploit the laboring classes by promising them heavenly rewards in exchange for accepting their lot in this life with submission. Marx believed that reli-gion would wither away after the socialist revolution once the social basis for its existence disappeared. The Bolsheviks, and especially their leader Vladimir Lenin (1870–1924), understood Marxism as a totalizing ideology meant to dictate not only

---

37. Sergei Zhuk, *Russia's Lost Reformation: Peasants, Millennialism, and Radical Sects in Southern Russia and Ukraine, 1830-1917* (Baltimore: Johns Hopkins University Press, 2004).

the economy but also the political structure, values, and goals of the entire society. It was, in effect, a secular religion—and therefore traditional religious belief systems represented incompatible competing ideologies that needed to be eradicated.[38]

When they seized power, the Bolsheviks believed that the Orthodox Church, as the majority faith of Russians that was tied to the old regime, represented both a political and an ideological threat. In January 1918, the Bolsheviks passed the Decree of Separation of the church from the State and the school from the church. Although the decree shared some similarities with Western nations that had separation of church and state (particularly France), it went much further than these in that it prohibited any religious education in school, deprived the Church as an institution of the ability to own property, and denied the Church the status of juridical personhood—in short, the Church as an institution ceased to exist in the eyes of the law. Church buildings and other property were declared state property but could be let out to groups of twenty parishioners who signed a contract with the government. In the process of implementing the Decree of Separation, many of the Church's institutions, such as printing presses and candle factories, were closed or confiscated.[39]

At the end of 1918, the Bolsheviks focused their antireligious campaign on elements of popular Orthodoxy by exhuming

38. On Bolshevism as a secular religion, see Yuri Slezkine, *The House of Government: A Saga of the Russian Revolution* (Princeton: Princeton University Press, 2017); see also William Husband, *"Godless Communists": Atheism and Society in Soviet Russia, 1917-1932* (DeKalb: Northern Illinois University Press, 2002).

39. There is no adequate history of Russian Christianity in the twentieth century in English. On the Revolution, see Scott Kenworthy, "Rethinking the Orthodox Church and the Bolshevik Revolution," *Revolutionary Russia* 31, no. 1 (2018): 1–23. See also Catherine Wanner, ed., *State Secularism and Lived Religion in Soviet Russia and Ukraine* (New York: Oxford University Press, 2012).

saints' relics in an effort to convince believers that their faith was just superstition. A second campaign targeted monasteries, closing more than half between 1918 and 1921. Though some were transformed into museums, others befell worse fates: the Solovetsky Monastery became the first prison camp for political prisoners and the prototype for the Gulag.[40] A minority of monasteries survived until collectivization by becoming agricultural collectives.[41] Finally, during the Civil War (1918–1921) and the implementation of the Red Terror—summary justice carried out on those suspected of "counter-revolution"—an estimated twenty thousand clergy (including monks and nuns) were repressed, with fifteen thousand of them simply executed—especially in those regions retaken by the Red Army after a period of occupation by the White (anti-Bolshevik) Army. A large number of clergy who opposed the Bolsheviks and were in White-controlled territories fled with the retreating White Army and subsequently established church structures for Russian émigrés abroad.

By the end of the Civil War, the Bolsheviks were firmly in control. Having defeated the White Army, the Church remained as the last ideological enemy to be vanquished. Leon Trotsky (1879–1940), one of the Bolshevik leaders, taking advantage of a horrific famine that resulted from the Civil War, devised an ingenious plan to undermine the Church. The regime decreed the forcible confiscation of Church valuables. This served as a pretext to (1) arrest clergy who resisted the confiscations, (2) use the money from the confiscated valuables

---

40. *Gulag* means "Main Administration of Camps" and refers to the system of prisons and labor camps in the USSR.
41. Scott Kenworthy, "Monasticism in War and Revolution," in *Russia's Home Front,* book 2, *The Experience of War and Revolution,* ed. Adele Lindenmeyr, Christopher Read, and Peter Waldron (Bloomington, IN: Slavica Publishers, 2016), 221–49; Robert Greene, *Bodies like Bright Stars: Saints and Relics in Orthodox Russia* (DeKalb: Northern Illinois University Press, 2010).

to fund the state, (3) embark on a propaganda campaign to make the Church appear callous to suffering famine victims, and (4) divide the Church from within by allowing clergy who were sympathetic to the regime to take control of the administration after arresting the current leadership. Trotsky's plan worked with devastating effectiveness, and leading clergy, including Patriarch Tikhon, were arrested (see chapter 4).

The Bolsheviks were aware of a group of reformist clergy, known as Renovationists, who resented the monastic control of the church hierarchy, advocated modernizing reforms, and also supported socialism. The Bolsheviks allowed them to seize control of the church administration after Tikhon's arrest, and they succeeded in taking over the majority of parishes. They enacted sweeping reforms such as the consecration of married men to the episcopate and the use of modern Russian (in place of Church Slavonic) in the liturgy. After the patriarch's release from prison in 1923, there were great defections from the Renovationist side, and the movement dissipated.[42] In 1927, the Bolsheviks pressured Tikhon's successor, Metropolitan Sergius, to issue a declaration of loyalty to the Soviet Union that created further divisions within the Church, resulting in an underground "catacomb" Church that existed in parallel with the official church.

At the same time as attacking the Church hierarchy, the Bolsheviks eased the assault on ordinary believers in the 1920s. The antireligious campaign came primarily in the form of antireligious propaganda, carried out by the so-called League of Militant Godless, which was formed in 1925. It appears, however, to have been largely ineffective. In fact, by placing the control of the church in the hands of parishioners, religiosity

---

42. Edward Roslof, *Red Priests: Renovationism, Russian Orthodoxy, and Revolution, 1905-1946* (Bloomington: Indiana University Press, 2002).

strengthened rather than declined in the 1920s. In many ways ordinary believers were gaining control over local church affairs, something they had aspired to for the last decades of the old regime.

The antireligious campaigns of the 1920s were directed primarily against the Orthodox Church, which the Bolsheviks regarded as the greater threat because the majority of the population adhered to it and because of its prior connection to the state. The Catholic Church, as subordinate to a head outside the Soviet Union (and a very anti-communist one at that), was regarded as a threat and also subjected to the confiscation of valuables, arrest, and execution of clergy. Dissenting Christian groups such as Baptists and other evangelicals as well as Russian "sectarians" were left unmolested by the regime for most of the 1920s. The Bolsheviks regarded them as potential allies since they too had been repressed by the tsarist government, and some of them regarded this as a kind of "golden decade." Similarly, Muslims were also left more or less alone in the 1920s because the Bolsheviks, fearing a backlash, had only a tenuous hold on Muslim regions such as Central Asia.

By the end of the 1920s, however, Joseph Stalin (1878–1953) consolidated his power, and he and his supporters sought to implement the communist program in a more radical way, especially through the collectivization of agriculture, rapid industrialization, and intensification of the antireligious campaign. In April 1929, a new decree on religious associations prohibited virtually all forms of religious activity outside of specifically designated religious buildings, outlawed any form of religious education to anyone under the age of eighteen, and banned any charitable activities performed by religious organizations. The constitution was also changed from guaranteeing the "freedom of religious and antireligious propaganda" to "the freedom of religious confession and antireligious propaganda"—making any teaching of religion, including to one's own children, against the law.

A massive closure of rural churches accompanied the campaign to collectivize agriculture. Village parish priests were repressed and exiled to Siberia as "kulaks," a term that technically referred to rich peasants but became a label applied to anyone who resisted collectivization. An estimated sixty thousand clergy and believers were repressed during this time (1929–1931)—the majority being sent to the Gulag or into exile for three to five years. From 1929, repression applied to all religions equally, and to lay believers as well as to clergy. The years 1932 to 1936 were labeled the "atheist five-year plan" (in parallel with the five-year plan in industrialization), in which the closure of churches and antireligious propaganda accelerated with a new intensity.

After two decades of repression and antireligious propaganda, Stalin was confident that most people considered themselves atheists, and therefore he personally added a question on the 1937 census about religious belief. To his dismay, well over half the population (56.7 percent) dared to state that they were religious believers.[43] The results came as a complete shock to the regime, which then suppressed the results.

Clergy and religious activists were targeted during the most extreme phase of repression in Soviet history, the Great Terror of 1937–1938, in part because of the discovery of the persistent strength of religious belief as revealed by the census. In less than two years, an estimated 1.5 million people from all walks of life were repressed in the Soviet Union; half were executed and half sent to the Gulag. The NKVD (People's Commissariat

---

43. Secret report to the Politburo by the head of the Central Statistical Directorate V. Starovskii (December 20, 1955) (in Russian), https://tinyurl.com/s62zbsy.

for Internal Affairs, as the secret police was then known) issued the Secret Order No. 447 of July 30, 1937, which began the most extreme phase of targeting "enemies of the people," that lasted through November 1938. Specific groups were targeted as anti-Soviet and subjected to summary justice, with quotas set for the numbers targeted for arrest and execution. "Church people" (*tserkovniki*) and "sectarian activists" were specifically listed in the NKVD order as among the "anti-Soviet elements" to be included in the operation. In various regions, killing fields were set aside for mass executions. At Butovo outside Moscow, over twenty thousand people were executed; 739 Orthodox clergy have been identified among them, together with 219 activist lay believers (255 had been canonized as new martyrs by 2003), in addition to more than sixty people who were identified as Baptists and "sectarians." In other words, more than one in twenty victims of the Terror were repressed specifically on religious grounds.

In November 1937, Stalin directed N. Ezhov (1895–1940), the head of the NKVD, to clamp down particularly on the "church people." In reply, Ezhov informed Stalin that in the course of the operation thus far, from August through November 1937 (i.e., just the first four months), 31,359 "church people and sectarians" had been arrested, including 166 bishops, 9,116 priests, 2,173 monks, and 19,904 "activist believers and sectarians" (whom they viewed as a united group, whether Orthodox or not). Of those, half of the clergy and one-third of the believers had already been executed. As a result, according to Ezhov, the NKVD operation had "almost completely liquidated the episcopate of the Orthodox Church, which to a significant degree has weakened and disorganized the Church." They had also repressed half of the priests and "sectarian preachers." But Ezhov admitted to Stalin that more work remained to be done: there were still nearly seven thousand churches and ten thousand Orthodox priests and over two thousand sectarian preachers at large in the Soviet Union—most of whom, no doubt, were arrested in the course of the subsequent twelve months.[44] Out of sixty thousand Orthodox churches in Russia in 1917, fewer than four hundred remained open by the beginning of 1939. Only four bishops remained alive and free. The Orthodox Church had been virtually eradicated. This was certainly one of the fiercest persecutions in the history of Christianity, yet, despite having happened within the past century, is one about which most Western Christians are unaware.

Although the Soviet Union had virtually eliminated the Orthodox Church by 1939, the situation was about to change dramatically. In August 1939, the Soviets and the Nazis signed a nonaggression pact that divided Eastern Europe between them. The Soviets annexed Western Ukraine and Belorussia, Moldova (Bessarabia), and the Baltic states, where there were a great number of churches. Overnight the Orthodox Church added thousands of churches and clergy.[45]

An even more dramatic change accompanied the Nazi invasion of the Soviet Union on June 22, 1941. The Nazis used religion as a propaganda tool by allowing churches to reopen on the Soviet territories they occupied, arguing that the people were better off under them than under the Soviets. In response, the Soviets themselves turned a blind eye as believers reopened churches in the unoccupied territories. The Russian Church called on the faithful to defend the motherland from the fascist aggressors. Repression against the Church

44. I. A. Kurliandskii, *Stalin, vlast', religiia* [Stalin, State, and Religion] (Moscow: Kuchkovo Pole, 2011), 516–18.
45. Daniela Kalkandjieva, *The Russian Orthodox Church, 1917-1948* (London: Routledge, 2017).

stopped once the war broke out, and state policy toward the Orthodox Church officially changed in 1943, when the Russian Church was allowed to hold a council to elect a new patriarch. That same year the Soviets created the Council for Russian Orthodox Church Affairs as the government interface with the Orthodox Church, and the following year the Council for the Affairs of Religious Cults was created to manage other religious groups. (The two merged in 1965 to become the Council for Religious Affairs.) By the end of the war, there were one hundred monasteries and nearly fifteen thousand open churches in the Soviet Union, 2,800 of which were in the territory of the Russian Federation. The greatest number were in Ukraine. Stalin's reversal of policy toward the Church had many causes: to gain the wartime support of the entire population, to counter Nazi propaganda, to respond to pressure from the allies, but also as a means to integrate those predominantly Orthodox Eastern European countries that fell behind the Iron Curtain after the war.

After the war, the regime established a kind of modus vivendi with the Orthodox Church and therefore was more tolerant of it than of other Christian confessions, by contrast with the pre-war period. The Uniate (Greek Catholic) Church had a large presence in Galicia, the region of southwestern Ukraine that became part of the Soviet Union only in 1939. Stalin was especially hostile to the Vatican, which he regarded as a threatening international force, and therefore he viewed Greek Catholics as a particularly undesirable element. Since the Greek Catholics represented Eastern Slavs who had been Orthodox before the seventeenth century, Russian Orthodox leaders justified the forced "reunion" of the Greek Catholics with the Orthodox Church at the Lviv Council of 1946; the hierarchy and clergy who were unwilling to join the Orthodox Church were sent to the Gulag.

Stalin's post-war policy of relative toleration of the Orthodox Church remained more or less in force until his death in 1953. Stalin's successor, Nikita Khrushchev (1891–1971, Chairman of the Council of Ministers, 1958–1964), condemned the excesses and abuses of Stalin's rule and initiated a program of "de-Stalinization." In the cultural sphere, this allowed for a greater openness known as the Thaw. Paradoxically, "de-Stalinization" in the religious sphere meant the reversal of the tolerant post-war policy and a reinvigoration of the antireligious campaign (1958–1964). Khrushchev's policies entailed the return of antireligious propaganda and an assault on the institution of the Russian Orthodox Church: five of eight seminaries were closed, sixteen monasteries remained in 1965 compared to sixty-three a decade earlier, and half the parish churches were closed. Many of the churches that were closed were subsequently destroyed in an effort to secularize urban landscapes.[46]

The two decades that followed Khrushchev's fall from power in 1964 were subsequently known as the "era of stagnation." During this time, there was no aggressive antireligious campaign. Rather, the regime exercised strict control over the Church and carefully monitored all its activities. Certain religious institutions remained open for the purpose of demonstrating to the world that there was supposedly freedom of religion in the Soviet Union.

The state's control over religious bodies gave birth to a reli-

---

46. On post-war history, see Nathaniel Davis, *A Long Walk to Church: A Contemporary History of Russian Orthodoxy*, 2nd ed. (Cambridge, MA: Westview, 2003). On churches, see Catriona Kelly, *Socialist Churches: Radical Secularization and the Preservation of the Past in Petrograd and Leningrad, 1918-1988* (DeKalb: Northern Illinois University Press, 2016).

gious dissident movement. In 1965, the priests Nikolai Eshliman (1929–1985) and Gleb Iakunin (1936–2014) wrote two open letters, one to the head of the state and one to the patriarch, criticizing the lack of religious freedom in the Soviet Union and the Church's leadership for its passivity. Both priests were punished, but throughout the 1970s there were active dissidents (see Ogorodnikov in chapter 4). After the Soviet Union signed the Helsinki Declaration on human rights in 1975, these dissidents were particularly active. Religious dissidents were ecumenical in approach—that is, they would gather reports of violations of religious freedom against believers of all confessions and smuggle such reports abroad, where they were published. These dissidents were punished by the regime by arrest and long sentences in prison camps for their boldness.

The government had much subtler ways of deterring religious participation for ordinary believers, however, such as preventing them from getting promotions in their jobs, denying university entry for their children, and so on. As a consequence, churches were mostly filled with old *babushki* ("grannies")—precisely because they were the ones who could no longer suffer such consequences. Religious practice became disconnected from the Church (children would be baptized at home in secret, for example), which has had significant long-term consequences even in post-Soviet Russia.

Western analysts tend to view the late Soviet period in binary terms, contrasting heroic dissidents with compromised, collaborating church officials, as if every bishop or priest was a KGB agent in a cassock. But neither of these poles describes the majority of clergy or believers. A report by the Council for Religious Affairs in the 1970s stated that the Council exercised control over the Holy Synod, its selection of members, and its decisions. The report characterized the episcopate by dividing it into three categories: one group was loyal to the Soviet state and religiously passive; a second was politically loyal but religiously active, endeavoring to raise the influence of faith in people's lives; and the third group of bishops sought to get around Soviet restrictions in their religious activism. In short, the highest levels of the Church certainly collaborated with the regime, but only a minority, even of the bishops, were completely compromised. Some cooperated to a degree as necessary to carry out their religious work, and others were not cooperative. On the ground, especially among lower-level clergy, the situation was even more complex. Very little research has yet been done on this topic, but stories of ordinary clergy make it clear that the Soviet regime or the KGB was not in complete control of the clergy and that some priests found ways to carry out their mission at least in limited ways while neither cooperating with nor openly resisting the Soviet authorities. Decisions to cooperate with the regime were seldom black and white, but rather entailed compromises in one area to be able to do the Church's work in another.

In the late (post-war) Stalin period, non-Orthodox Christians were subject to much harsher repression than the Orthodox Church, and religious communities that were in territories that became Soviet only in 1939–1940, such as Baptists and Jehovah's Witnesses, were particularly hard hit.[47] In the last decades of the Soviet Union, administrative control replaced repression for the non-Orthodox as it did for the Orthodox, except for active dissidents. Until the 1980s, Roman Catholic church life was limited; the number of churches and priests—both in the West and in the East, the old Siberian communities—was very small and insufficient; and all were tightly

47. Emily Baran, *Dissent on the Margins: How Soviet Jehovah's Witnesses Defied Communism and Lived to Preach about It* (New York: Oxford University Press, 2014).

controlled, with only secret ties to the Vatican. Meanwhile, an intense underground life continued "in the catacomb," similar to Russian Orthodoxy, if the activists could escape arrest and exile. At the same time, Catholic theology, education, discipline, and growing engagement with the world—especially after the Vatican II Council in the 1960s—became a stimulus in the late Soviet times for some Russian clerics and educated public who somewhat ambivalently combined rejection and imitation.

During World War II, Stalin ordered the deportation of Russian Germans to Siberia and Kazakhstan, effectively devastating communities such as the Volga Germans, and resulting in some one million Germans of various Christian confessions living in Kazakhstan at the end of the Soviet period, most of whom have since emigrated to Germany.

Finally, in the late-Soviet period, there was an important new development outside the institutional structures of the Church. With the totalitarian press relatively weakened, by comparison with the Stalinist era, there was a slow, semi-underground, censored rediscovery of the country's religious legacy. The 1960s to 1980s saw what could be called an "urban religious renaissance" among intellectuals, especially in the two capitals, Moscow and Leningrad (St. Petersburg). The groups gathered around various forbidden ideas—starting with occult and mystical explorations and ending with traditional Orthodoxy. The latter was interpreted in different ways: either as a universal spiritual heritage, or a national Russian tradition, or as an existential alternative to the murky materialism of an ossified Marxist ideology. Young seekers wandered around the country in search of old churches, monasteries (or their ruins), icons, and, eventually, spiritual leaders among those few monks who were left. At home, they gathered privately to discuss scraps of otherwise censored old texts disseminated through *samizdat* (self-publishing)—hand-printed brochures, reproductions of pre-revolutionary or émigré authors like Vladimir Solovyov or Sergius Bulgakov (see chapter 5), liturgical and prayer books, or, finally, the Holy Scripture, which was scarcely available. These groups of self-educated seekers were not necessarily looking for priests, regular church-going, or liturgical life, which were hardly accessible anyway because of the limited number of churches and the danger of being registered as a "believer." Rather, these urban groups existed as hidden pockets of spiritual subculture, where people created their own, self-styled religiosity.

It is remarkable that the ruling communist elite itself, after the antireligious rage of the 1960s was over, slightly and gradually changed its approach. Although the atheistic propaganda formally continued, the religious cultural legacy—church architecture, icons, and even some texts—were reinterpreted as "national heritage" that made manifest the nation's genius. The state invested much in restoring some church buildings and allowed new fiction literature—the so-called village prose—which celebrated the long tradition of the old and lost Russian national culture, local, rural, and spiritual. Of course, in no way could the regime directly emphasize the religious nature of this tradition; rather, the propaganda promoted the "Soviet way of life" as a truly spiritual project. Yet the discourse of "spirituality" might have resonated differently among people who became increasingly sensitive to the pre-Soviet cultural heritage.[48]

The late-Soviet period witnessed similar trends in other

---

48. On this dialectic of Soviet and religious spirituality of the late Soviet time, see Victoria Smolkin, *A Sacred Space Is Never Empty: A History of Soviet Atheism* (Princeton: Princeton University Press, 2019), 196–205.

Soviet lands as well. Communist elites in the Baltics and Central Asia, Georgia, Armenia, and other places saw the renaissance of their own national heritage that was heavily charged with religious meanings and styles, yet kept an official distance from directly recognizing it as religious. Thus, gradually, religion became everywhere linked to a sense of ethnic and national particularity, while overall this trend toward independence became a major factor in the final implosion of the Soviet Union.

The situation of the Russian Orthodox Church in the Soviet Union changed dramatically in 1988. In 1985, Mikhail Gorbachev (b. 1931) became leader of the Soviet Union and admitted that the economy was stagnating and that reforms (*Perestroika*) were needed; as a result, he allowed for greater openness (*Glasnost'*). The Council for Religious Affairs admitted that 25 to 30 percent of the population were still religious believers—a significant proportion, whose support could be mobilized. The turning point was the one-thousand-year anniversary of the Baptism of Rus in 988. Gorbachev met with Patriarch Pimen (1910–1990, patriarch 1970–1990) in April 1988 and spoke of the Baptism of Rus as a historical turning point in positive terms, allowing the Church to celebrate the Baptism on a national scale. Changes came very rapidly, as churches were allowed to reopen and religion could be positively discussed in the press. The response was immediate and overwhelming; communist ideology was disintegrating as a viable worldview, and massive numbers of people came for baptism.[49] By the time the Soviet Union collapsed at the end of 1991, the Russian Orthodox Church was experiencing a full-scale revival.

---

49. James Billington, "Orthodox Christianity and the Russian Transformation," in *Proselytism and Orthodoxy in Russia: The New War for Souls,* ed. John Witte Jr. and Michael Bourdeaux (Maryknoll, NY: Orbis, 1999), 56.

4

———

Biographies of Modern Russian Christians

The tremendous upheavals for Russian Christianity in the twentieth century were traumatic for the individuals who lived through it. This chapter will explore the experience of the past century for Russian Orthodox Christians and how they navigated the Revolution, rule by an atheist regime, and the collapse of that regime and revival of Christianity in Russia. We will look at the life stories of church leaders, rank-and-file monks, nuns, and priests, as well as laypeople. The previous chapter outlined the systemic transformations, challenges, and conflicts to Russian Orthodoxy caused by the Revolution and seventy years of Soviet atheist rule. This chapter brings that story to life by viewing it through the lens of representative individuals who lived through it.

The 1917 Revolution caused deep fissures in Russian Orthodoxy. One such fissure was between those Russian Orthodox

Christians who remained in the Soviet Union and those who fled and endeavored to ensure Russian Orthodoxy's survival in less hostile circumstances. Finding themselves uprooted from their homeland as a minority in an environment dominated by Western Christians undergoing their own challenges in the face of modernity and secularism, Russian Christian refugees and émigrés interpreted their tradition in very different ways. Some took the position that the only way to preserve Russian Orthodoxy at its purest was to reject any change to their tradition and any dialogue with Western Christians or modernity. Others believed that the trauma of the Revolution was providential in forcing Orthodox Christianity out of its historical and national confines in a way that could creatively communicate its message in new circumstances and to new audiences. As for those who remained in the Soviet Union, Western observers tended to laud dissidents and condemn those who made compromises, but making such value judgments from the outside was easier than being faced with the actual difficult or impossible dilemmas that believers inside the Soviet Union confronted.

Four Leaders of the Orthodox Church in Revolutionary Russia

Four figures guided the Russian Orthodox Church during the first half of the twentieth century, both within and outside the Soviet Union. Tikhon (Bellavin, 1865–1925) became the first patriarch of the Russian Orthodox Church when the patriarchate was restored in 1917, and he led the Church through the Revolution itself until his death in 1925. Antony (Khrapovitsky, 1863–1938) and Evlogy (Georgievsky, 1868–1946) both fled during the Civil War and became leaders of divergent branches of the Russian Orthodox Church Abroad in the interwar period. Sergy (Stragorodsky, 1867–1944) became Tikhon's de facto successor in the Soviet Union, though he only became patriarch during World War II, shortly before his death. The four were born within five years of one another, and it is only possible to tell their lives in parallel, rather than separately, because their lives were so intertwined, and they were often acting in response to one another. Collectively, their lives reveal the challenges of leading the Church both in the face of a hostile totalitarian regime and in exile under totally new circumstances. Both in the Soviet Union and abroad, each of the figures represents a different alternative of how to face the challenges presented to them.

The oldest of the four was Antony (Khrapovitsky), who was to exercise an early influence on the other three. Unlike the other three, who were all sons of parish priests, Antony was born to an aristocratic family. He was devoted to the Church from a young age, and as a youth was particularly influenced by the Slavophiles, Dostoevsky, and later Solovyov (see chapter 5). After completing the gymnasium, he entered the St. Petersburg Theological Academy, the pinnacle of the Church's educational system, instead of going to university. This was highly unusual because the overwhelming majority of students in the Church's educational system were sons of parish clergy. At the academy he was inspired to take monastic vows. In the Russian Church at the time, future bishops were drawn primarily from academy students who took monastic vows. They were known as "learned monks" because they were highly educated but were also not traditional monks since they began their careers as church servitors straight from the academy without ever living in a monastery. However, no students had taken monastic vows at the St. Petersburg Academy in the liberal atmosphere that prevailed since reforms in the 1860s; Antony's embrace of monasticism shifted the trend.

After graduating from the academy in 1885, Antony spent a year teaching seminary in Kholm (Chełm, now in eastern Poland) before returning to the academy as an instructor while continuing his graduate theological education. Khrapovitsky developed a particular vision of creating a brotherhood of educated monks who would not retreat to a monastery to pursue the contemplative life, but rather devote themselves to finding a way for the Church to speak to the educated public, which was growing increasingly estranged from the Church. This vision would have a profound impact on Antony's students, including Bellavin, Stragorodsky, and Georgievsky, both at the St. Petersburg and later the Moscow Academies.

At the age of twenty-eight, Antony became the youngest dean ever appointed to the Moscow Academy in 1891, and four years later, he transferred to the Kazan Academy. He emerged as one of the Church's leading young theologians, and he tried to break with the dominant scholastic model to find ways of articulating the main Christian dogmas that were relevant to contemporary society. In 1900 he became diocesan bishop first in Ufa, then in 1902 in Volhynia (in today's Ukraine). After the 1905 Revolution, Antony became very politicized and supported conservative and monarchist parties in the newly created Duma (parliament) as well as nationalist organizations such as the Union of Russian People. Though conservative politically, he advocated measures to revitalize Church life, including the restoration of the patriarchate and the Church's independence from the state.[1]

---

1. Vladimir Tsurikov, ed., *Metropolitan Antonii (Khrapovitskii): Archpastor of the Russian Diaspora*, vol. 5, *Readings in Russian Religious Culture* (Jordanville, NY: Foundations of Russian History, 2014).

One of Antony's students at the St. Petersburg Theological Academy was Vasily Ivanovich Bellavin, the future Patriarch Tikhon. Bellavin, the son of a parish priest, was born in a poor village in 1865. He followed the typical path of clergy sons and studied in the ecclesiastical school system set up primarily for them; he, like Stragorodsky and Georgievsky, completed his education in the Theological Academy, reserved for the best seminary graduates. After taking monastic vows and getting ordained, he became dean of the seminary in Kholm in 1892. In 1898 he was appointed the sole Orthodox bishop of North America, where he would serve until 1907. Tikhon accomplished extremely important things in his time in North America: he founded the first monastery and seminary, supported the publication of the first English-language service book, and moved the bishop's see from San Francisco to New York. The American diocese was very diverse ethnically (Russians, Ruthenians, Serbs, Greeks, Syrians, and native Alaskans), and Tikhon sought to create a diocesan structure that would respect this ethnic diversity within a unified structure. Tikhon returned to Russia as archbishop of the ancient and central city of Yaroslavl, then became Archbishop of Vilnius (today's capital of Lithuania) in 1914. Unlike Antony, Tikhon avoided politics.[2]

Sergy (Stragorodsky) was born in 1867, and after finishing his studies at St. Petersburg Theological Academy, he spent much time as a missionary in Japan before returning to the academy as dean and being consecrated bishop in 1901. Between 1901 and 1903 he participated in the Religious-Philosophical Meetings, which brought together intellectuals of the

2. Jane Swan, *Chosen for His People: A Biography of Patriarch Tikhon* (Jordanville, NY: Holy Trinity Seminary Press, 2015); Edward Roslof, "Russian Orthodoxy and the Tragic Fate of Patriarch Tikhon (Bellavin)," in *The Human Tradition in Modern Russia*, ed. William B. Husband (Wilmington, DE: SR Books, 2000), 77–91.

Russian religious renaissance (see chapter 5) and clergy who were open to such meetings, a very important initiative and the first of its kind in Russia. In 1905 he was appointed bishop of Finland, where he would remain until the Revolution.

Evlogy (Georgievsky) followed the same path as Stragorodsky and Bellavin, entering the Moscow Theological Academy, and he was a student there when Antony (Khrapovitsky) became dean. Evlogy left a remarkable memoir in which he described in detail his student years and in particular the influence Antony had on him and other students.[3] In 1897 he replaced Tikhon as dean of the Kholm seminary, and in 1903 he was consecrated bishop of Lublin in the same region. Following the creation of the Duma during the 1905 Revolution, Evlogy was elected to represent his region as a deputy of a Russian nationalist party. Later he opposed a proposal to form and lead a separate party for Orthodox clergy on the grounds that consolidating clerical political interests would only give rise to anti-clericalism. In 1914 Evlogy was appointed Archbishop of Volhynia (replacing Antony).

It is worth noting that all four of these future leaders of the Russian Church had some experience in what was considered missionary territory: three of them had served in the region of Kholm, which was the last region of the Russian Empire where the Greek Catholic Church was forcibly united to the Orthodox Church in 1875 (decades later than elsewhere). Antony had taught at the missionary-focused academy in Kazan and served for two years in the Muslim-dominated region of Ufa. Both of the future patriarchs of the Church had served in missions abroad: Tikhon in America, Sergy in Japan. When the Febru-

---

3. Evlogy Georgievsky and Tatiana Manukhina, *My Life's Journey: The Memoirs of Metropolitan Evlogy*, trans. Alexander Lisenko (Yonkers, NY: St. Vladimir's Seminary Press, 2014).

ary Revolution occurred, none were in central Russian dioceses: Tikhon was Archbishop of Vilnius and Lithuania, Sergy was Archbishop of Finland, and Antony and Evlogy were both in Ukraine (Kharkov and Volhynia). Although they had similar educations and comparable experiences, their political leanings and ecclesiastical politics were quite different from one another. Antony was an ultra-conservative monarchist, Evlogy supported the nationalist cause in the Western parts of the Russian Empire, Tikhon was generally apolitical and centrist, and Sergy was considered a liberal in the Church.

After the 1917 February Revolution and the fall of the monarchy, there was a revolution within the Church as well. Some dioceses ousted their bishops in diocesan assemblies of clergy and laity, which then elected their replacements. Antony was one of those initially forced to resign his post, but later in the year a diocesan assembly in Kharkov chose him again as their bishop. Tikhon, effectively a bishop in exile while his diocese was under German occupation during World War I, became the first popularly elected bishop of Moscow in June 1917.

The All-Russian Church Council that began meeting in August 1917 resolved, after months of discussion, to restore the patriarchate immediately after the Bolshevik seizure of power on October 25. The Council decided to follow the procedure of some of the ancient patriarchates, by which the patriarch's name was chosen by lot (to allow for the "hand of God") from among the three candidates who received the most votes by the Council. Antony (Khrapovitsky) received the highest number of votes; Arseny (Stadnitsky), archbishop of Novgorod, the second; and Tikhon (Bellavin), the third. On November 5, after Liturgy in the Christ the Savior cathedral, a holy elder chose the name of Tikhon—who then became the first patriarch of the Russian Orthodox Church since the patriarchate was abolished by Peter the Great two centuries earlier. Tikhon already anticipated that his patriarchate would not be an honor, but a cross. He was enthroned in the Kremlin on November 21, the last time the Orthodox Church was permitted to hold services in the Kremlin churches until the end of the Soviet Union.

In response to early Bolshevik measures against the Church (see chapter 3), Patriarch Tikhon made a series of strongly worded statements criticizing the actions of the new regime, beginning with his Epistle of January 19, 1918, which anathematized those engaged in anti-Church actions. Although this was interpreted by the Bolsheviks, and by most historians since, as an anathema directed against the Bolsheviks, Tikhon was cautious to condemn specific actions, not actors or political platforms. In the summer of the same year he condemned the execution of the former Tsar Nicholas II. He also issued an appeal to the Bolsheviks on the first anniversary of the Revolution, pointing out that they had not given people the freedom and peace they had promised, and called on them to end the persecution of political opponents. He was one of the few voices in Russia in a position to criticize the new regime, and his voice was listened to by a great proportion of the population—and for precisely this reason the Bolsheviks regarded him as a serious threat.

Patriarch Tikhon. *Photo courtesy of Wikimedia Commons.*

During the Civil War, Tikhon declared that the Church should not take sides, but rather called on all sides to end fratricidal strife. Tikhon was cautious to avoid aligning the Church with "counter-revolution." The patriarch was

157

routinely interrogated and periodically arrested during these years. When famine erupted at the end of the Civil War, Tikhon mobilized believers in Russia and Christian leaders around the world to provide famine relief. His positive contribution, however, was not in the interests of the Bolsheviks, so they devised an ingenious strategy to discredit the patriarch and the Church that entailed confiscating the Church's valuables by force rather than with the participation believers. Tikhon called for passive resistance to the decree, especially regarding consecrated objects such as chalices. In response, the authorities arrested him on May 5, 1922.

The Soviets kept Tikhon under house arrest in the Donskoi monastery in Moscow for over a year while they prepared a show trial against him that was to culminate in his execution. The church administration was taken over by the group of liberal and leftist clergy known as Renovationists, who declared loyalty to the Soviet regime. The Renovationists held their own council in 1923 in which they deposed and defrocked Tikhon as well as tried to legitimize their reforms. Rather suddenly, in the summer of 1923, the Soviets released the patriarch. This reversal was motivated in part by international pressures, especially from the British (urged by the Archbishop of Canterbury), who declared that they would end trade negotiations if the patriarch was executed. At the same time, Tikhon himself became willing to make a public statement "repenting" of his earlier anti-Soviet statements together with declaring his political neutrality and that he was not an enemy of the Soviet of the Soviet state. He also distanced himself from the pro-monarchist and anti-Soviet position of the émigré Church (led by Antony Khrapovitsky).

Tikhon's position had shifted because, by 1923, it was clear that the Soviet regime was firmly in power and some kind of modus vivendi had to be found. By that point, the patriarch had come to believe that the Renovationists posed a greater threat of destroying the Church from within. Tikhon in effect decided to make his peace with the regime in order to rescue the Church from the Renovationists. The Soviets, for their part, decided that rather than make him a martyr, they would discredit him through this compromise, though in fact the majority of the faithful stayed loyal to him, and a massive defection from the Renovationists followed as clergy returned to the patriarch. Sergy was one of those who accepted the Renovationist Church administration after Tikhon's arrest, although he opposed their more radical reforms, and returned to the patriarch immediately after his release.

Patriarch Tikhon spent his remaining years trying to restore order to the Church administration and heal the schism with the Renovationists. He died on April 7, 1925, apparently of natural causes, though there has always been speculation that he was poisoned, which cannot be ruled out. At his funeral, over fifty bishops, five hundred priests, and thousands of laypeople attended. A week after his death, the Soviet newspapers published what purported to be his "last testament," which was more conciliatory toward the Soviets than any of his earlier statements. Many doubted the authenticity of this document, especially the émigrés. Recent research into various drafts of this document indicates that Tikhon was working on a statement, but that the final version that was published was not one he signed or agreed upon.

In the meantime, Antony was elected Metropolitan of Kiev in 1918, and both he and Evlogy (Georgievsky) participated in a Ukrainian church council in 1918. With the collapse of the Russian Empire, Ukraine became briefly an independent nation, and some within the Ukrainian Church sought ecclesiastical independence as well. Both Antony and Evlogy opposed Ukrainian autocephaly, and both were arrested in the short-lived independent Ukraine. After being released, they ended up in southern Russia under the control of the White Army. There they formed the Temporary Higher Church Administration of South-Eastern Russia, headed by Antony. With the defeat of the White Army, both fled abroad.

By 1921, Antony settled in Serbia, where he reconstituted the Temporary Higher Church Administration to minister to Russian refugees. Evlogy was designated by both this the émigré Church administration and Patriarch Tikhon to administer the Russian émigrés in Western Europe. At the end of 1921, a meeting of the leaders of the Church Abroad issued declarations—with Antony's insistence, against Evlogy's wishes—in favor of restoring the monarchy and the Romanov dynasty in Russia, and calling on European powers not to recognize the Bolshevik government but instead assist the White forces in overthrowing them. Such support for monarchism and counter-revolution appeared to confirm the Bolsheviks' fears regarding the Church as a political threat in the period leading up to Tikhon's arrest. Just before his arrest, the patriarch issued a statement declaring that this monarchist declaration did not express the voice of the Russian Church, and he ordered the émigré Church administration disbanded and appointed Evlogy administrator of all Russian churches abroad.

The Church Abroad responded by reorganizing the Church administration, which established a Temporary Holy Synod, still with Antony at the head. The Synod administered the parishes of Russian émigrés in the Balkans and in Asia directly, while those in Western Europe and North America were designated autonomous under Metropolitan Evlogy and Metropolitan Platon (Rozhdestvensky) respectively. Later, the Synod of the Church Abroad attempted to strip away that autonomy, which led to rifts between Evlogy and Platon, on the one hand, and Antony and the Synod of the Church Abroad on the other.

Back in the Soviet Union, Patriarch Tikhon had, before his death, designated three bishops who would lead the church (as patriarchal *locum tenens*) until a Council could be convened to elect a new patriarch. The only one not already in exile at the time of Tikhon's death, Metropolitan Petr (Poliansky), designated Sergy (Stragorodsky) as his *locum tenens*. At the end of 1925, Petr was also arrested, leaving Sergy (as deputy *locum tenens*) in charge of the Church. After Patriarch Tikhon's death and Metropolitan Petr's arrest, the administration of the Church was in complete disarray. The only ecclesiastical administrative structures that were recognized by the state belonged to the Renovationists. Therefore, the activities of any clergy who did not belong to the Renovationists were considered illegal and as such could be arrested. Any kind of higher structures for the Church, such as a Synod of bishops, could not legally meet. In 1926, when the leadership of the Church fell to Sergy, he was prevented by the authorities from leaving his diocese (Nizhny Novgorod) or coming to Moscow.

The main task at this point was to regularize the Church's situation with the state, and Sergy entered into negotiations with government leaders.[4] The end result of these negotiations was the Declaration of July 1927, which became the most controversial statement in the history of twentieth-century Russian Orthodoxy. This declaration went further than Tikhon's declaration of political neutrality on his release from prison.

---

4. A particularly even-handed treatment of Sergy, who typically provokes intense polemics, is Ann Shukman, "Metropolitan Sergi Stragorodsky: The Case of the Representative Individual," *Religion, State and Society* 34, no. 1 (March 2006): 51–61.

The key phrase of Sergy's declaration was: "We want to be Orthodox and at the same time recognize the Soviet Union as our civil motherland, whose joys and successes are our joys and successes, whose failures are our failures."[5] Many regarded it as an unacceptable declaration of loyalty to an atheist government. Reactions within the Soviet Union were mixed: some rejected it outright—together with Sergy's further leadership of the Church—and formed underground "catacomb" churches. Others criticized some of its wording but recognized that some form of modus vivendi with the state was necessary. Still others accepted it as a necessary compromise to legalize and stabilize the situation of the Church in the Soviet Union. Despite all the controversy aroused by the Declaration, what caused even greater concern within the Soviet Union was that Sergy subjected episcopal appointments to the approval of the state security services, which then began to control the inner life of the Church in an unprecedented way.

Metropolitan Sergy demanded that the émigré clergy also make their own declarations of loyalty to the Soviet Union. Sergy's own declaration of loyalty to a godless state, combined with a demand for their loyalty to the Soviet Union, led to the decisive break between the Church Abroad under Metropolitan Antony (Khrapovitsky) and the Moscow Patriarchate under his former student and colleague Sergy—a schism that was only healed in 2007. At that time, the Church Abroad was in Serbia, but after World War II it relocated its headquarters to the United States and was effectively isolated from world Orthodoxy. Metropolitan Evlogy, by contrast, found a compromise. He wrote back to Sergy and informed him that it made no sense for his clergy to pledge loyalty to a state of which they were

5. Shukman, "Metropolitan Sergi Stragorodsky," 56.

not citizens; at the same time, he assured Sergy that neither he nor his clergy would speak against the Soviet Union "from the ambo" (the space in front of the altar from where a priest delivers the sermon).

Evlogy's compromise worked for several years to prevent rupture. In February 1930 Pope Pius XI called on Catholics to pray for the "persecuted Russian Church." As the Soviet Union was in negotiations to join the League of Nations, this international attention to its persecution of religion was particularly unwelcome. In response, Metropolitan Sergy supposedly gave an interview to the Soviet press, in which he asserted that there was no persecution of religion in the Soviet Union.[6] Such a public declaration of blatant falsehood caused a significant backlash nearly as serious as the 1927 declaration—most importantly among Evlogy's flock in Western Europe. A Russian historian only recently discovered that the entire interview was fabricated. In reality, Emel'ian Iaroslavsky (1878–1943), head of the League of Militant Godless, wrote the first draft of the entire interview—both the journalists' questions and Sergy's answers—and the entire text was significantly edited by Stalin himself. Soviet leaders and propagandists discovered decades ago the devastating power of "fake news."[7]

International attention to the Soviet persecution of religion continued, and the Archbishop of Canterbury organized an event in March 1930 to pray for the persecution's cessation. Evlogy participated in this event and distanced himself from Sergy after that "interview," stating that Sergy was forced to say such things under pressure from the Soviet authorities but

6. The text is in Philip Boobbyer, *The Stalin Era* (London: Routledge, 2000), 171–72, though here the authenticity of the text is still assumed.
7. Igor' Kurliandskii, "Stalin i 'interv'iu' mitropolita Sergiia sovetskim korrespondentam v 1930 g" ["Stalin and the 'Interview' of Metropolitan Sergy to Soviet Correspondents], *Rossiiskaia istoriia* 2 (2010).

that he, Evlogy, would not remain silent about Soviet religious persecution. As a consequence of the row, Evlogy broke with the Church in the Soviet Union. In order not to be set adrift, Evlogy brought his diocese in Western Europe under the jurisdiction of the Ecumenical Patriarch of Constantinople, who granted them a special autonomous status as an exarchate for Russian émigrés.

In 1934, Evlogy and Antony met in Belgrade, Serbia, for a personal reconciliation, although attempts at restoring relations between the two branches of the émigré church failed. Antony's health was already declining, and he passed away in 1936, though as the founding father of the Church Abroad he left a monumental legacy for Russians who remained devoted to the monarchy and Russian nationalism and adhered to a traditionalist view of Russian Orthodoxy.

Metropolitan Evlogy also left a monumental legacy, though it was of a very different character from his former teacher. By contrast with the conservative Russian émigrés who settled in interwar Germany and Yugoslavia, Paris attracted leading intellectuals and writers, especially the leading lights of the Russian religious renaissance (see chapter 5). Evlogy's greatest legacy was in fostering an incredibly creative and vibrant intellectual and religious flowering. He supported the establishment of the St. Serge Orthodox Theological Institute, with significant American Christian support, which became the leading Russian Orthodox center of theology in the interwar period.[8] Evlogy also defended Sergius Bulgakov as theologian and professor at St. Serge after the latter's teaching on "sophiology" was condemned by both Moscow and the Church Abroad. Finally, he developed positive ecumenical relations

---

8. Matthew Lee Miller, *The YMCA and Russian Culture: The Preservation and Expansion of Orthodox Christianity, 1900–1940* (New York: Lexington Books, 2015), chaps. 8–9.

with Western Christians (especially the Anglican Church) in the interwar period.

Back in the Soviet Union, Sergy was one of only four bishops of the Church to remain alive and free after the devastation of the Great Terror. Nevertheless, on the day of the Nazi invasion, June 22, 1941, Metropolitan Sergy issued an appeal to believers to defend the Motherland from the invaders, whereas Stalin did not address the nation until July 3. Sergy also encouraged churches to collect funds for the nation's defense, which led to the first legal recognition of the Russian Orthodox Church since 1918.

On September 4, 1943, in the midst of the war, a momentous meeting took place in the Kremlin, in which Stalin invited Sergy and two other leading hierarchs to meet with him and present him a list of the Church's needs. Sergy said that the most urgent matter was to hold a Church Council to elect a new patriarch. He also requested permission to reestablish theological education to train priests and the right to publish a journal, all of which Stalin granted. When Sergy had said the Church needed to train new priests to replenish its staff, Stalin reportedly asked him, "Why, where are your personnel?" Not touching on the fact that most had been repressed only a few years earlier, Sergy cleverly replied that "we train a man to be a priest, but he becomes a marshal of the Soviet Union"—a reference to the fact that Stalin himself had studied in seminary. He also asked if clergy could be amnestied to return to Church work; Stalin said to give him a list of names and he would consider it. Sergy submitted a list with twenty-five names, although it turned out that only one was still alive, the rest having been executed or died in the Gulag.[9]

---

9. Shukman, "Metropolitan Sergi Stragorodsky," 58.

Four days after this meeting, the Church was able to hold a bishops' council to elect a new patriarch, which resulted in the election of Sergy. Sergy would serve as patriarch for less than a year, however, before passing away on May 15, 1944. The following year, the Russian Church held another Council, which elected Aleksy (Simansky, 1877–1970) patriarch. This restoration of the Russian Orthodox Church was accompanied by the end of the Renovationist schism (which gradually dwindled after Tikhon's release from prison) as well as the reconciliation with some of the other groups, both within and outside the Soviet Union that had been in schism since 1927. Evlogy was one of those who sought reconciliation with the Moscow Patriarchate in 1945, though he passed away in August 1946 while negotiations were still ongoing. After his death, his diocese voted to stay under the jurisdiction of Constantinople rather than return to Moscow.

In sum, these four men were close in age and experience, their lives were interwoven from an early age, and they followed very similar career paths before the Revolution. Yet the Revolution drove them in radically different directions—quite literally in the sense that Tikhon and Sergy remained in the Soviet Union while Antony and Evlogy fled abroad. But they responded to the unprecedented challenge of the Russian Revolution in very different ways. Tikhon and Sergy did their best to lead the Church in impossible circumstances within the Soviet Union. Tikhon was very critical of Soviet assaults on religion, but he also believed it was necessary to keep the Church politically neutral and to negotiate with the regime. Tikhon was regarded by all sides as an exemplar and was canonized first by the Church Abroad in 1981 and then the Moscow Patriarchate in 1989. Sergy's role, by contrast, has been extremely controversial: Did he make the necessary compromises to ensure the Church's survival, or did he betray it, leaving the door open for the Soviets to control the Church from within?

By contrast, Evlogy and Antony fled the Soviet Union to preserve Russian Orthodox life elsewhere. Antony believed that religion and politics were inseparable, and continued to actively oppose Soviet communism and advocate the restoration of the monarchy. He sought to preserve Russian Orthodoxy unchanged and resisted any dialogue with Western Christians or modernity. Evlogy, by contrast, criticized the persecution of religion in the Soviet Union but avoided taking a broader political position. He believed that Orthodoxy abroad had a unique opportunity to witness to the West by engaging with it, so he supported unconventional approaches to Orthodoxy as well as fostered the greatest flowering of Russian religious thought.

Stalinist Persecution and the New Martyrs: Archimandrite Kronid (Liubimov), 1859–1937

Although the Soviet government repressed or restricted religion throughout its existence, the height of the repression was the Great Terror of 1937–1938. Although the Terror has been the subject of extensive scholarly literature in the West, Western historians have overlooked the fact that clergy and religious activists were a category specifically targeted for repression. The Russian Orthodox Church Abroad began canonizing some of these victims as "new martyrs" during the Soviet period, and the Moscow Patriarchate has actively sought to retrieve the stories, preserve the memory of those who suffered, and in appropriate cases, canonize them. The Bishops' Council in 2000 canonized over one thousand such new martyrs from the Soviet period, and hundreds more have been canonized since. We will tell the story of just one of these new martyrs as a representative case because of rare access to the secret police file against him.

Archimandrite Kronid became prior of Russia's most famous monastery, Trinity-St. Sergius Lavra, in 1915. The Bolsheviks closed the monastery in 1919, and the monks resettled in nearby monastic communities that had reformed themselves as agricultural collectives until being closed during collectivization. The monks were simply expelled, with no place to live or means of support (since clergy were deprived of rights by Soviet law). Kronid was given shelter by some of the faithful in a private apartment.[10]

On July 30, 1937, the security services, the NKVD (later KGB), issued an order about "anti-Soviet elements" and launched a "campaign of punitive measures" against them, known as the Great Terror. The order explicitly listed religious activists as one category of people that were blamed for "sabotage." The order directed that people deemed "anti-Soviet" be divided into two categories: the "most active" elements were to be executed immediately, and the "less active but hostile elements" were to be sent to the Gulag for eight to ten years. The order included target quotas for the estimated number of such "enemies" in each region, in effect striking out at entire categories of people rather than suspected individuals. It instructed that the investigations be carried out swiftly, and all "associates" of such "enemies" were to be discovered and arrested as well. The result was the most intense spiral of state violence and repression in the entire Soviet period.

The case against Kronid was initiated in October 1937. The

10. Kenworthy, *Heart of Russia*, chap. 9.

order for his arrest stated that he continued to have connections with former monks and "counterrevolutionary-minded" religious activists, that people respected him as a spiritual leader and continued to visit him. He was arrested on November 20. The investigation uncovered his other "associates," and fourteen other people—including monks, nuns, parish priests, and laypeople—were also arrested. The NKVD accused religious activists such as Kronid of two "crimes" (defined in article 58, paragraphs 10 and 11 of the Soviet criminal code): one was "counterrevolutionary activity," which in Kronid's case meant involvement in a "counterrevolutionary organization" that was the supposed continued existence of a secret monastery. The second crime was "anti-Soviet agitation," or publicly criticizing the regime. The investigation aimed to demonstrate that people who associated with Kronid viewed him as their "leader" and that they were his "followers" and "accomplices," thus amounting to a secret organization.

During his interrogation, the investigators asked Kronid about his political opinions; he stated openly that he thought monarchy was the best form of government but that he accepted the Soviet regime, "as a believer, as sent to the people as a trial of its faith in Divine Providence." The interrogation continued:

Question: From your testimony it is evident that you continue to lead the monks of the former Lavra, and therefore we demand from you truthful testimony.

Answer: The monks indeed visited me, but I exercised no leadership over them.

Question: You are accused of being a participant in a C[ounter]/R[evolutionary] grouping of religious activists; we demand [that you] give truthful testimony of your C/R activities.

> Answer: I repeat that by conviction I am a monarchist even now, and the monks of the former monastery were cultivated in the same spirit [by me], who are still followers of the true Orthodox Church. I confirm that monks of the former Lavra periodically visited me in Zagorsk [the Soviet name for the city], but I do not admit to being a part of a counterrevolutionary group.[11]

When the interrogators asked him about laypeople who visited him, he stated that they came mostly to help him and check on his health; he refused to name any, claiming he had forgotten their names. Kronid was convicted of being the "leader" of a "secret monastery" that the others, also convicted, were said to have belonged to. They were also found guilty of anti-Soviet agitation, which ironically included spreading "slanderous rumors about the 'persecution' of religion in the USSR." In other words, at this time, associating with other believers and speaking among themselves about what the regime was doing to fellow believers was enough to warrant a death sentence. Four of the accused, including a nun, a layman, and two parish priests, were sentenced to ten years in the Gulag. Eleven of the accused, mostly former monks of the Lavra along with Kronid, were sentenced to death; the sentence was carried out on December 10, 1937, at the NKVD's killing field at Butovo (near Moscow).[12]

Although he was seventy-eight years old, in failing health, and going blind, Archimandrite Kronid still held enough spiritual authority to be regarded as a threat twenty years after the Revolution. This is just one case among thousands. Solid research estimates the number Orthodox believers repressed for their faith in just those two years of the Terror at two hundred thousand, half of whom were sent to the Gulag and half

---

11. Russian State Historical Archive, fond 10035, opis' 1, delo P-59458, listi 106–107.
12. Kenworthy, *Heart of Russia*, 355–67.

of whom were executed. In other words, what happened in the Soviet Union was a scale of persecution of Christianity with few parallels in history—yet one about which Western Christians are barely aware, even though it took place in the recent past. Since the collapse of the Soviet Union, the Church has been one of the most successful organizations in drawing attention to the crimes of the Terror through canonizing the new martyrs, dedicating churches to them, and memorializing sites such as Butovo.[13]

An Unusual Saint and Popular Religiosity: Matrona Nikonova (d. 1952)

Although the Soviet attempts to eradicate Russian Orthodoxy in the 1930s succeeded in decimating the institution of the Church and its clergy, popular Orthodoxy survived at the grassroots level, outside the structures of the Church. This phenomenon can be seen in the story of Matrona. She was a simple, uneducated, blind, and crippled laywoman who gained a reputation for holiness and as a healer. Canonized only in 2004, she has become one of the most popular saints in contemporary Russia, and one must wait hours on any given day to visit the shrine devoted to her in Moscow. Matrona's story is less about her life and more about making an obscure peasant woman into one of Russia's most popular saints.

13. See John Burgess, *Holy Rus': The Rebirth of Orthodoxy in the New Russia* (New Haven: Yale University Press, 2017), chap. 5; Karin Christensen, *The Making of the New Martyrs of Russia: Soviet Repressions in Orthodox Memory* (New York: Routledge, 2017).

Icon of Matrona. *Photo copyright © 2020 Kamil Aisin. Reproduced by permission of the photographer.*

Matrona was born a peasant in a village in the 1880s. Only a few details of her life are known: she was born without eyes and therefore completely blind, and in her late teens she also lost the ability to walk. After the Revolution, she was unable to stay in the family home because her brothers had become Bolsheviks, so she moved to Moscow, where she would live for the rest of her life, sheltered by friends and supporters.

The first book about her was published in 1993, not long after the collapse of the Soviet Union. It was a short collection of stories written by Zinaida Zhdanova, in whose house in Moscow Matrona had lived in the 1940s. Most of the information about Matrona comes from this one source, which cannot be verified, so legend and fact can hardly be distinguished. Zinaida's mother was from the same village as Matrona, so the book collected stories from both the village and Moscow.

Because it was written by an ordinary woman and recounts many stories from the village, this life of Matrona is quite distinct as a saint's life in that it reflects popular religious belief and practice—a kind of folk Orthodoxy—much more than is typical of saints' lives produced by the Church. The book portrayed Matrona as undergoing great suffering, especially from her physical handicaps, but she accepted this with forbearance and without complaint. Her physical blindness was interpreted as giving her spiritual vision, and many of the stories centered on her clairvoyance, her ability to see into people's problems without even being told, and to understand the future. Reflecting a worldview of the village before the Revolution, the stories were filled with the supernatural, including battles against demons, witchcraft, and curses. Most, however, focused on the help that Matrona rendered to believers who came to her—help in very ordinary and daily concerns, griefs, and sufferings, from illness to marital, family, and work problems. Matrona is revered today, especially among Russian women, precisely because she is seen as rendering assistance and consolation in such daily concerns and sorrows.

Zhdanova's book was enormously popular, and within a few years the Russian Church began considering Matrona's case for canonization. However, because Matrona's first biography reflected aspects of popular Orthodoxy, there were elements to which the establishment Church objected. Particularly problematic was an apocryphal story about an encounter between Matrona and Stalin. According to the account that Zhdanova heard, in the fall of 1941 Stalin was concerned that the Nazis would take Moscow. Someone advised him to go to Matrona, who could predict the future and counsel him; Matrona assured him that "the Russian people will be victorious" and that Stalin alone among the Soviet leadership would not flee Moscow. Given that such an episode could not be verified, the Church's official versions of her life left out this episode, and either omitted, or "properly" explained questionable theological elements. Matrona was canonized as a "locally revered saint" in 1999 and for church-wide veneration in 2004.

A Russian anthropologist argues that the Stalin story was included in Zhdanova's account of Matrona's life to reinforce how important Matrona was. In the Putin era, however, the story has taken on a very different kind of significance. The story is used in nationalist-patriotic circles, and now that Matrona's popularity as a saint is well-established, it is paradoxically used in the process of rehabilitating Stalin's image. Stalin is viewed as a "great leader" in certain Russian patriotic circles especially because he is associated with victory in World War II, a defining moment in contemporary Russian national identity and patriotism. In this version of history, Stalin's visit to Matrona is seen as a kind of "conversion" moment for him that leads to both a reversal of Soviet policy toward the Church and to victory in World War II. Nationalist-patriotic circles even produced an icon of Stalin's visit to Matrona (Stalin, of course, is depicted without a halo), but the Church hierarchy swiftly prohibited this.[14]

Contemporary Russian Orthodox believers are divided in their approach to the Soviet past. The more active and educated segments regard Soviet ideology as antithetical to faith and focus on the Soviet persecution of the Church, such as in the canonization of the new martyrs. Matrona's story, however, represents a different approach: the Soviet system is understood neutrally as an assumed context in which Russians found themselves and attempted to live out their lives as best they could. The latter approach has a broader appeal among the vast majority of Russians who identify themselves as Russian Orthodox but are not active in church, especially in the atmosphere of Putin's Russia that seeks to reconcile Russia's conflicting pasts. Indeed, Matrona is a more popular saint than any of the new martyrs. But the main source of Matrona's popularity as a saint has little to do with politics; rather, she is venerated as an ordinary person who suffered and, through her faithfulness, became an instrument of God in the world to heal, console, work miracles, and help solve myriad daily problems and concerns. And in this respect, the ongoing story of Matrona's veneration in Russia is very revealing about the role that faith is playing in Russia today, especially among the vast majority of "unchurched" believers.

---

14. Jeanne Kormina, "Canonizing Soviet Pasts in Contemporary Russia: The Case of Saint Matrona of Moscow," in *A Companion to the Anthropology of Religion*, ed. Janice Boddy and Michael Lambek (Oxford: Wiley-Blackwell, 2013), 409–24.

An Unconventional Nun in Paris: Mother Maria (Skobtsova), 1891–1945

By contrast with the trauma and challenges of Christianity in the Soviet Union, Russian Orthodoxy experienced a parallel existence in exile that faced very different challenges and opportunities. Mother Maria was an extraordinary person in every respect; she was by no means a conventional saint. She devoted her life to serving poor Russian refugees in Paris, and during the Nazi occupation, she helped save the lives of Jews until she herself perished in the concentration camps.

Born Elizaveta Pilenko in Riga, she grew up on her family estate near Anapa, on the Black Sea. She was devastated by the sudden death of her father and lost faith in God. In St. Petersburg in the decade before the Revolution, she became a poet and moved in leading circles of Russia's Silver Age, a period of literary revival and spiritual experimentation (see chapter 5). She married, had one daughter, and divorced. After the fall of the monarchy she was elected mayor of Anapa for the Socialist Revolutionary party, a leftist peasant party that was not nearly as doctrinaire or antireligious as the Bolsheviks. During the Civil War she was put on trial by the Whites for being a Bolshevik sympathizer but was acquitted. She met Daniel Skobtsov, a local government representative involved in the case against her, fell in love, and married impulsively. The family fled Russia in 1920, and by the time they settled in Paris in 1923 they had a son and daughter.[15]

---

15. Sergei Hackel, *Pearl of Great Price: The Life of Mother Maria Skobtsova, 1891–1945* (Crestwood, NY: St. Vladimir's Seminary Press, 1982).

Mother Maria Skobtsova. *Photo courtesy of Orthodox Wiki (commons.orthodoxwiki.org).*

In 1926 her youngest daughter died of meningitis, and the tragedy proved a spiritual turning point. Before leaving her newly deceased daughter's side, Elizaveta wrote, "No amount of thought will ever result in any greater formulation than these three words, 'Love one another,' so long as it is love to the end and without exceptions. And then the whole of life is illumined, which is otherwise an abomination and a burden." Such a tragedy shattered the normal meaning of life but at the same time opened up the door to eternity. The experience drew her to a new sense of meaning in life and in mother-hood: "to be a mother for all, for all who need maternal care, assistance, or protection."[16] From that point on she devoted herself to social work as well as to theological writing with a social emphasis. In Paris she was connected to the St. Serge Theological Institute and the leading Paris émigré intellectuals; Fr. Sergius Bulgakov was her spiritual father (see chapter 5). After she and her second husband divorced, Metropolitan Evlogy tonsured her a nun with the name Maria in 1932. Her vision from the beginning, however, was of an entirely new kind of monasticism not of the cloister, but of service to those in need in the world.

Mother Maria rented a house on Rue de Lourmel in Paris, where she lived in one room and opened up the rest to impoverished Russian refugees, especially single women without jobs. She fed a hundred people a day. The house had stables in the back that were converted into a chapel, decorated by Mother Maria herself. She then rented other houses—one for men and another for families—and a rural property as a sanatorium for the ill. Sunday afternoons at the house on Rue de Lourmel were devoted to lectures and discussions, featuring speakers such as prominent theologians Bulgakov and Nikolai Berdyaev. For Mother Maria, social service and theology had to be tied together. She scandalized many traditional Orthodox by violating the conventional expectations of how an Orthodox nun should purport herself with her bohemian appearance and behavior. But, she wrote, recalling Matthew 25, "The way to God lies through love of people. At the Last Judgment I shall not be asked whether I was successful in my ascetic exercises, nor how many bows and prostrations I made. Instead I shall be

16. *Mother Maria Skobtsova: Essential Writings*, trans. Richard Pevear and Larissa Volokhonsky (Maryknoll, NY: Orbis, 2003), 19–20.

asked, Did I feed the hungry, clothe the naked, visit the sick and the prisoners. And that is all I shall be asked."[17]

During the Nazi occupation, Mother Maria stayed in Paris with the people who needed her. When the Nazis began to register Jews, many came to Mother Maria and her coworker, Fr. Dmitry Klepnin, who gave them fictive baptismal certificates.[18] In July 1942, over thirteen thousand Jews were arrested, including more than four thousand children, and most were held in a sports stadium without water, food, or sanitary facilities until they were shipped to Auschwitz. As a nun, Mother Maria was allowed to bring in food, and succeeded in smuggling out some children in trash cans. Jews began coming to the house on the Rue de Lourmel, and Mother Maria and Fr. Dmitry not only sheltered them but also helped to arrange their escape from Paris.

Finally, Fr. Dmitry, Mother Maria, and her son Yuri, who had joined his mother's work, were arrested in February 1943. The two men were sent to Buchenwald and then to the Dora camp, where they died in February 1944. Mother Maria was deported to the Ravensbrück camp. According to accounts of people who were with her, she was able to lift the spirits of those who surrounded her in the most horrible of conditions. In March 1945, as the Red Army was approaching, the Nazis stepped up their executions of camp detainees. On March 31, Mother Maria was sent to the gas chamber (according to one account, voluntarily going in place of another who had been chosen), a week before the camp was liberated. She and Fr. Dimitry Klepnin have been honored as Righteous Among the Nations for their

---

17. *Mother Maria Skobtsova*, 30.
18. On Fr. Dmitry, see Helen Klepnin Arjakovsky, *Dimitri's Cross: The Life and Letters of St. Dimitri Klepnin, Martyred During the Holocuast* (Ben Lomand, CA: Conciliar Press, 2008).

efforts to save Jews, and the two, together with Mother Maria's son Yuri, were canonized as saints by the Ecumenical Patriarch in 2004. Today she is better remembered and honored by Orthodox Christians in the West than in Russia.

Teacher of Prayer: Metropolitan Anthony Bloom of Sourozh, 1914–2003

The Russian experience in emigration after the Revolution was rich and diverse. We have already seen different currents represented by Antony (Khrapovitsky) and the Church Abroad on the one hand, and Metropolitan Evlogy and Parisian Orthodoxy on the other, including Mother Maria. Despite the traumas of dislocation, Russian Orthodox Christians took up the challenge of being outside of Russia by articulating the spiritual treasures of their tradition to non-Russian audiences. In the post-war period, one of the leading lights was Metropolitan Anthony, the bishop of the Russian Church in England for decades, who was a spiritual leader for many Orthodox abroad, for English Christians, and even Christians within the Soviet Union and post-Soviet Russia.

Andrei Bloom was born in 1914, in Lausanne, Switzerland. His mother was the sister of the famous composer Alexander Scriabin, and his father was a diplomat descended from Scots who settled in Russia. After the Russian Revolution the family became refugees, ending up in Paris in 1923. For years life was a struggle for survival for his family, though paradoxically, once life stabilized for the teenaged Andrei, he began to wonder if life had any meaning. He lost faith in God and became hostile to Christianity. He was disappointed by a talk he heard by Fr. Sergius Bulgakov and returned home to confirm his doubts by consulting the Gospels, expecting to find there what he found repulsive about Christianity. Instead, he encountered Christ. As he was reading, he felt that Christ was present with him; he experienced a "vivid sense that Christ was without any doubt standing there . . . [and] if the living Christ is standing here—it means that he is the risen Christ," and that what is written about him in the Gospel must be true.[19] His conversion experience was not an intellectual discovery but a personal encounter, which became the central experience shaping the rest of his life.

His experience and reading of the gospel convinced him of other things as well: that the God revealed in Christ is not the God of a particular nation or confession, but of all people. Moreover, he is a God who so loves his creation and humanity that he was willing to identify with it and its experience completely as the incarnate Son of God. It was particularly important for Russian refugees to identify with a God who became for them "defenseless, totally vulnerable, weak, powerless, and despised by those people who believe only in the triumph of might."[20] Andrei investigated various forms of Christianity and became convinced that Russian Orthodoxy most closely embodied Christ as he, Andrei, had experienced him. He decided he wanted to devote his life by taking monastic vows; at the same time, he wanted to put his Christian faith into practice by becoming a doctor so that he could help and heal people. He studied sciences at the Sorbonne and completed medical school. He served in the medical corps of the French Army and in hospitals in occupied Paris during the war, also

19. *Metropolitan Anthony of Sourozh: Essential Writings*, ed. Gillian Crow (Maryknoll, NY: Orbis, 2010), 34. This volume is an excellent collection of Metropolitan Anthony's writings. His life story is told in Gillian Crow, "*This Holy Man": Impressions of Metropolitan Anthony* (Crestwood, NY: St. Vladimir's Seminary Press, 2005). An archive of his sermons and talks (audio and video) is available at www.masarchive.org.

20. Crow, ed., *Metropolitan Anthony of Sourozh*, 35.

contributing to the French Resistance. He was tonsured a monk in 1943 and received the name Anthony, though he continued to serve in the French Army as a doctor and, after the war, in Parisian hospitals.

He was ordained as a priest in 1948, though he asserted that his medical and scientific training were crucial for his approach to pastoral work. After his ordination he visited England for the conference of the Fellowship of St. Alban and St. Sergius (an Orthodox-Anglican ecumenical organization); he was invited to return to England to work full time for the Fellowship. He served the Russian parish in London that was under the jurisdiction of the Moscow Patriarchate. He was consecrated bishop in 1957, and a new diocese was created to cover the territory of the British Isles. Though fluent in Russian, French, and German, he did not know English when he moved to London, but he quickly learned and began to preach and serve in English as well as in Russian.

Anthony's other vision was that Orthodoxy should not be constrained by ethnic confines but should reach out to all people. What began as a small congregation in London grew into an entire diocese, including many English converts. He gave regular talks broadcast on television and radio. British theologian Andrew Walker wrote that Metropolitan Anthony "indelibly stamped the spirituality and theology of the Orthodox tradition upon the British religious consciousness," and a leading BBC religious affairs correspondent once called him "the single most powerful Christian voice in the land."[21] He was the representative of the Moscow Patriarchate in England, but he managed to operate his diocese with substantial independence from any dictates from Moscow. His position also allowed him

21. Andrew Walker's obituary for Metropolitan Anthony in *The Independent*, August 8, 2003, https://tinyurl.com/uogn9z6.

to visit Russia frequently, where he was able to speak on spiritual matters much more forthrightly than clergy in the Soviet Union. His talks and sermons in Russian were also broadcast into the Soviet Union via the BBC World Service and Radio Liberty, which served as virtually the only spiritual nourishment for thousands in the Soviet Union.

He wrote a number of influential books on prayer. His interest was in the practical aspects of spiritual life rather than in abstract theological or exalted mystical concerns. For this reason, combined with his scientific background and because he acknowledged an important place for doubt and for the experience of the absence of God, he had a unique capacity for articulating the Orthodox tradition to a modern audience.

A Dynamic Priest in the Soviet Union: Father Alexander Men, 1935–1990

Russian Christian leaders like Metropolitan Anthony, though they had their challenges, were certainly much freer to teach and preach to the faithful than those in the Soviet Union. Yet despite the enormous obstacles in their path, devout and courageous clergy succeeded in providing spiritual guidance even within the Soviet Union. Father Alexander Men was a Russian Orthodox priest who offered an authentic Christian ministry for decades. He was able to capture widespread attention during the last years of the Soviet Union until he was murdered shortly before the Soviet Union collapsed.

Alexander Men. *Photo copyright © 1980 The Alexander Men Foundation. Reproduced by permission.*

Alexander Men was born in Moscow in 1935. His parents were Jewish, but his mother was drawn to Christianity, so that she and her son were baptized. Men's childhood had been deeply shaped by the spiritual circles his family associated with and so as a teenager in Moscow, he began to voraciously read books on philosophy and theology. Early influences included the key figures of the Russian religious renaissance (see chapter 5). He was also fascinated by nature, which he regarded as God's revelation alongside the Bible, and this drew him to study science. During an upswing in anti-Semitism in the late Stalin years, he was barred from Moscow University because of his Jewish heritage. Instead he entered the Institute of Fur in 1953, then located in Moscow before being relocated to Siberia in the midst of his studies.

Active as a churchgoer, he was blocked from completing his degree and pursuing a scientific career. Instead he was ordained in 1960 and served in a village outside Moscow. Fr. Men organized a group of young priests who served in nearby parishes. They represented a new generation, who wished not to follow the compromises made by the church hierarchy in the post-war period. This group included Fr. Gleb Iakunin (or Yakunin, 1936–2014), Men's roommate at the Institute; Fr. Dmitry Dudko (1924–2002), who had already spent time in the prison camps and who was known as an inspiring preacher; and Fr. Nikolai Eshliman (1929–1985), also an engaging priest. The group would meet to discuss theological questions and share pastoral experience. In 1965, Iakunin and Eshliman issued two open letters, one to the patriarch and the other to the leaders of the Soviet government, in which they criticized the state's interference in the life of the Church and the Church hierarchy's passivity toward this interference. Although Men agreed with the substance of the letters, he chose not to sign because he did not agree with the timing and approach. Both Iakunin and Eshliman were arrested and suspended. This moment marked the different paths Iakunin and Men would take: Iakunin was an activist in the international public eye, calling attention to abuses of human rights (especially freedom of religion) in the Soviet Union.[22] Fr. Men, by contrast, focused on his ministry. In order to accomplish that, he maintained cordial relations with local authorities and tried to stay below the radar. Though he and his parish were under constant KGB surveillance, he was largely successful. His reputation grew, and many people, especially intellectuals, made the trek from Moscow to visit his parish.

Fr. Alexander was a prolific author. He published articles in the *Journal of the Moscow Patriarchate* in the early 1960s, but most of his writings were published abroad and then smuggled back into the Soviet Union. He addressed an audience without any religious education but with a modern scientific mindset. He felt the need to present the Christian faith in a way that could speak to these people. One of his most important books was *The Son of Man*, a presentation of Christ and the gospel story to such an audience.[23] He also wrote extensively on the Bible and on the history of religion as culminating in Christianity. One thing that characterized Men's writing was his openness to dialogue with science and the modern world as well as various forms of Christianity in his effort to communicate the gospel.

A major turning point in the life of the Russian Orthodox Church came with the celebration of the millennium of the baptism of Rus in 1988, when suddenly it became permitted to speak publicly about Christianity. That summer brought an

---

22. Wallace Daniel, "'I Am a Fighter by Nature': Fr. Gleb Iakunin and the Defense of Religious Liberty," in *The Dangerous God: Christianity and the Soviet Experiment*, ed. Dominic Erdozain (DeKalb: Northern Illinois University Press, 2017), 74–96.
23. Alexander Men, *Son of Man: The Story of Christ and Christianity*, trans. Samuel Brown (Yonkers, NY: St. Vladimir's Seminary Press, 2012).

explosion of public interest together with radio and television appearances for Fr. Alexander. With *glasnost'* (the openness under Gorbachev), Men's popularity surged; in the next two years he would deliver over two hundred lectures in a variety of public venues on a range of topics.

With the new openness under Gorbachev, Fr. Men felt a sense of urgency. He was critical of the Church leadership for not casting off the Soviet past quickly enough and not being willing to engage society in an open way. He viewed it as trying to re-establish old patterns of Orthodox dominance over Russian society rather than preaching "the essentials of what we believe," the "authentic message of Christ," to people who were thirsting for it. Fr. Alexander, who greatly valued personal, spiritual, and political freedom, viewed the possibility of re-establishing a close alliance between the Church and an authoritarian state as a real danger. His openness was very attractive to many ordinary people but was opposed by entrenched interests in the Church as well as by contrary currents in Russian society. For ultra-nationalist groups, Men was a particular threat not only because of his openness, but also because of his Jewish roots. They viewed him as trying to undermine Orthodoxy from within.

Early Sunday morning, September 9, 1990, Fr. Men was walking to the station to take the train to his parish church. On his way through the woods an unknown assailant struck him on the back of the head with an axe; he managed to struggle back to his house, where he collapsed at the gate and died. His murder was never solved, the assassins never found. Speculation has focused either on ultra-nationalist and anti-semitic groups, or on forces within the Soviet government, and the KGB in particular, who opposed the challenge to their hold on Soviet society that Men represented.[24] His legacy is still important among more liberal currents in Russia, but he is looked upon with suspicion by the traditionalist or nationalist factions.

A Soviet Dissident: Alexander Ogorodnikov (b. 1950)

Western commentators frequently exaggerate the binary between the Church hierarchy compromised by the communist regime, on the one hand, and the dissidents who heroically stood against it on the other. There were many shades in between the extremes, many who sought to serve the Gospel but felt it necessary to make certain compromises in order to do so. At the same time, there were heroic individuals who stood up to the regime to draw international public attention to restrictions on religious freedom—and paid the price. Some, like Fr. Iakunin, were clergy, but others were laypeople. One such figure, Alexander Ogorodnikov, led a group of young seekers in discussions of Christian faith and society in the 1970s, as a consequence of which he spent nearly a decade in the Gulag.[25]

Ogorodnikov had a normal Soviet upbringing. His father was a factory engineer, his mother a teacher. An idealistic youth, Alexander was active in the Komsomol, the communist youth organization. He quickly began to realize that the realities of the Soviet system were far from its ideals. In 1970, he began

---

24. A fine recent biography is Wallace L. Daniel, *Russia's Uncommon Prophet: Father Aleksandr Men and His Times* (DeKalb: Northern Illinois University Press, 2016); an anthology of his writings is *Christianity for the Twenty-First Century: The Prophetic Writings of Alexander Men*, ed. Elizabeth Roberts and Ann Shukman (New York: Continuum, 1996).

25. Koenraad De Wolf, *Dissident for Life: Alexander Ogorodnikov and the Struggle for Religious Freedom in Russia* (Grand Rapids: Eerdmans, 2013).

studying philosophy at the Ural State University, but he was expelled because he had formed a group of students to discuss issues of Marxism, which was too free-thinking for the university administration. The following year he entered the Institute of Cinematography in Moscow. Both in the city and during trips he made throughout the Soviet Union, he interacted with youth who had become disillusioned with the Soviet system and were searching for spiritual truth. He attempted to make a film about this search, for which he was expelled from the Institute in 1973. He was drawn to Christianity through literature and film as well as through Voice of America radio programs broadcasting Metropolitan Anthony Bloom or Fr. Alexander Schmemann.

Ogorodnikov began going to church in 1973. He first took communion from Metropolitan Anthony Bloom, who was visiting Moscow. He also began attending the "Saturday evening talks" of Father Dmitry Dudko, the charismatic priest who held open discussions about faith with the youth in church—something virtually no other clergy were doing at the time, and soon Fr. Dmitry himself would be transferred to a village church far from Moscow as a consequence. Such open discussions with youth was not possible in churches, which were strictly monitored by the Soviet authorities.

Ogorodnikov and his friends, inspired by Fr. Dmitry, decided in 1974 to form a discussion group that became the Christian Seminar. Ogorodnikov was working as a janitor in a hospital, where he had a small apartment in which he held the seminars. Thirty to forty people took part in these meetings once a month with Ogorodnikov serving as the unofficial leader. Participants were of varying ages and different Christian confessions; they also came from across the Soviet Union, and in subsequent years set up branches of the Christian Seminar in other cities and reached hundreds of people. It was spread by word of mouth, and only those known and trusted by members would be included so as to prevent infiltration by the KGB. Participants believed that Soviet society was in a state of spiritual crisis and that the way out was through a revival of Christian faith; these issues were at the center of discussion. Seminars were devoted to Scripture, church history, and Russian religious thought. Ogorodnikov and another colleague attempted to launch a *samizdat* journal (self-published underground literature) titled *Obshchina* (Community), the first issue of which was confiscated by the KGB before it could be distributed. The second issue succeeded in circulating in 1978.

Ogorodnikov and other leaders of the Christian Seminar were followed and periodically harassed or subjected to searches by the KGB. Ogorodnikov began to send reports of these repressive measures abroad, including letters to the secretary of the World Council of Churches, which brought international attention to restrictions on religious freedom in the Soviet Union. Ogorodnikov was fired from his job and expelled from his apartment. Then in November 1978, he was arrested and convicted of "social parasitism" and sentenced to a labor camp for a year. The following year he was convicted of the more serious charge of "anti-Soviet agitation" and sentenced to six years in the Gulag; he was sent to Perm-36, a particularly harsh prison camp for political prisoners. He repeatedly went on hunger strikes to defend the rights of prisoners, including his right to possess a Bible. In 1985, when his sentence was up, he was convicted of violating camp rules.

His case, along with those of other dissidents, drew international attention, and finally in 1987, due to pressure from American President Ronald Reagan and British Prime Minister Margaret Thatcher, Ogorodnikov was released. In 1988, during the celebration of the millennium of the baptism of Rus Ogorodnikov staged an alternate millennium exhibition that displayed photographs of destroyed churches. The following year he established the Christian-Democratic Union, the first Christian political party in Russia. During these years he also spoke before international congresses and parliaments of numerous European countries as well as in the United States and Latin America. When the Christian-Democratic political movement began to fragment, Ogorodnikov decided to leave politics. He has spent the last quarter century primarily engaged in philanthropic activities, organizing a soup kitchen in Moscow and establishing a shelter called Island of Hope for young women who have been victims of drug abuse and domestic violence.

The First Post-Soviet Patriarch: Aleksy II (Ridiger), 1929–2008

After seven decades of religious repression, the Soviet Union unexpectedly collapsed. In the Soviet Union, the Orthodox Church had been restricted in every way: institutionally, in terms of the number of clergy, parishes, seminaries, monasteries, and so on, but also in its ability to teach and minister to the faithful. The regime also found ways of discouraging people from expressing their faith. When all the restrictions went away, the Church was faced with a new and unprecedented set of challenges in rebuilding the institution from the ground up. Other challenges came in the form of entrenched mentalities fostered by the Soviet system among the clergy themselves. There were deep divides among active clergy and believers themselves about how to reconstitute Russian Orthodoxy, which faced some of the same dilemmas and experienced the same divisions between traditionalist and progressive currents as the émigré churches already faced. Finally, the Church was challenged with trying to recapture the unchurched Russian people, who were mostly secular and who had been cut off from a living connection with the faith for several generations. With regard to the leadership of the Church, these challenges fell to the new patriarch Aleksy II, elected at the very twilight of the Soviet regime in 1990.

The future patriarch was born Aleksei M. Ridiger in Tallinn, Estonia, in 1929, to descendants of Baltic Germans. Aleksei's family was Orthodox and religiously inclined, and his father became a priest during World War II. The Baltic states were only annexed by the Soviet Union in 1939, so Aleksei did not grow up in a Soviet environment; he only became a Soviet citizen after World War II. In 1947, Aleksei entered the Leningrad Theological Seminary and continued his studies at the academy. He was ordained to the priesthood, serving a parish in Estonia. In 1961, he took monastic vows (with the name Aleksy) and was consecrated bishop of Tallinn. He would serve as bishop (and later as archbishop and metropolitan) of Tallinn until 1985.

From the moment of his episcopal consecration, Aleksy also began taking on important positions in the Moscow Patriarchate. In 1961, he became the vice-chairman of the Department of External Church Relations and was active in the World Council of Churches and the Conference of European Churches, which meant both that he had to travel abroad and also host international guests in the Soviet Union. Most importantly, at the end of 1964, Aleksy (age thirty-five) was appointed to the Holy Synod and made chancellor of the patriarchal administration, a very influential post he would hold for the next two decades.

Patriarch Aleksy II. *Photo by Alexander Volkov and Ilya Boryakov copyright ©
2011 Moscow Patriarchy. Reproduced under Creative Commons License 2.0.*

In December 1985, Aleksy wrote a letter to Gorbachev, the
young General Secretary of the Communist Party who had

recently ascended to power. Gorbachev had only tentatively indicated the need for reform in the Soviet Union, and Aleksy seized the opportunity, suggesting that if given more freedom, believers would be able to contribute positively to resolving the problems that plagued Soviet society. Although three years later Gorbachev himself would come to the same conclusion, the Soviet government was not ready to hear this, and in 1986 Aleksy was removed from his positions in the patriarchal administration and transferred to Leningrad.

After Patriarch Pimen's death in 1990, the Church held a Council that elected Aleksy as the new patriarch. This was the first Council since 1917 that was free of state interference. When hardline communists attempted a coup against Gorbachev in August 1991, Patriarch Aleksy questioned the legitimacy of those behind the coup and also called for the military not to use violence.[26] He thus stood on the side of reform and democratization that soon led to the collapse of the Soviet Union.

Although he was a successful bishop of Tallinn and a capable administrator, critics have questioned the degree of his cooperation with the Soviet government and the KGB.[27] Aleksy certainly did cooperate, as was unavoidable for someone in his position. The KGB regularly visited everyone in positions of high authority and also gave them code names for their own internal KGB usage, but this did not necessarily make one a

26. James Billington, "Orthodox Christianity and the Russian Transformation," in *Proselytism and Orthodoxy in Russia: The New War for Souls,* ed. John Witte Jr. and Michael Bourdeaux (Maryknoll, NY: Orbis Books, 1999), 51–65.

27. Unfortunately, the only book devoted to Aleksy in this period is unreliable: John and Carol Garrard, *Russian Orthodoxy Resurgent: Faith and Power in the New Russia* (Princeton: Princeton University Press, 2008), is marred by basic errors and misrepresentations of Orthodoxy in general as well as unsubstantiated claims about Aleksy. See Scott Kenworthy's review in *Journal of Church and State* 51 (2009): 700–02 and Alexander Agadjanian's review in *Journal of Religion in Europe* 4 (2011): 362–65.

KGB agent, as if one were working *for* the KGB, as many Western commentators assume. In 1991, Aleksy gave an interview to *Izvestia* (*The News*) one year after becoming patriarch in which he stated:

> Defending one thing, it was necessary to give somewhere else. Were there any other organizations, or any other people among those who had to carry responsibility not only for themselves but for thousands of other fates, who in those years in the Soviet Union were not compelled to act likewise? Before those people, however, to whom the compromises, silence, forced passivity or expressions of loyalty permitted by leaders of the church in those years caused pain, before these people, and not only before God, I ask forgiveness, understanding, and prayers.[28]

Though Aleksy certainly made compromises, the evidence of his life suggests that he made those compromises because he believed they were necessary to carry out the work of the Church, not to serve the interests of the state.

However compliant he may have been in the Soviet period, after becoming patriarch Aleksy devoted himself to building up the Russian Orthodox Church at a crucial period that witnessed its remarkable rebirth. The Church was confronted with severe shortages of funds, clergy, seminaries, and churches. Aleksy had always been very involved in ecumenical dialogue with other Christians, but he was frustrated when foreign (especially American) missionaries and evangelicals flooded into the country and, instead of helping the Orthodox Church rebuild, began competing for converts. Aleksy therefore supported the legislation that placed some restrictions on foreign missionary activity in 1997. Patriarch Aleksy stated that "the

---

28. Cited in Davis, *A Long Walk to Church.* Nathaniel Davis, *A Long Walk to Church: A Contemporary History of Russian Orthodoxy*, 2nd ed. (Boulder: Westview, 2003), 94. This book provides a balanced and reliable treatment of the late Soviet and early post-Soviet periods.

church is separate from the state, but it is not separate from society."[29] He also advocated the re-introduction of the Church into spheres such as chaplains in the military and in prisons, religious instruction in public schools, and the restitution of church properties. Aleksy rarely met with President Yeltsin; his relations with President Putin during the latter's first two terms (2000–2008) were warmer. Aleksy cooperated with the government in areas of mutual concern while not subordinating the Church to the interests of the state.

Patriarch Aleksy also faced deep divisions within Russian Orthodoxy itself between traditionalists and extreme nationalists on the one hand, and more open and progressive currents on the other. Aleksy was a centrist, and he successfully managed to prevent serious divisions within the Church, allowing these diverse currents a degree of freedom but within limitations. One significant accomplishment was the reconciliation of the Moscow Patriarchate with the Russian Orthodox Church Outside Russia in 2007. The Church experienced a phenomenal growth under his leadership. In his eighteen years as patriarch, Aleksy led the resurgence of Russian Orthodoxy from marginalization and repression in the Soviet era to playing a prominent role in contemporary Russian life.[30]

Church Leadership in Putin's Russia: Patriarch Kirill (Gundiaev) (b. 1946)

Patriarch Aleksy II made great strides in rebuilding the institution of the Russian Orthodox Church, and when he passed away

29. Cited in Irina Papkova, "Russian Orthodox Concordat? Church and State under Medvedev," *Nationalities Papers* 39 (2011): 667–83; citation at 669.
30. For a good overview, see Zoe Knox and Anastasia Mitrofanova, "The Russian Orthodox Church," in *Eastern Christianity and Politics in the Twenty-First Century*, ed. Lucian Leustean (New York: Routledge, 2017), 38–66.

the Church regularly scored as one of the institutions in which Russians had the most confidence. Aleksy's successor was faced with a more intangible challenge of bringing ordinary Russians back to church. It was as if the Church leadership confronted the question of whether to build support from the ground up by appealing to the ordinary people, or from the top down, by allying itself with the state. Perhaps because the former approach appeared to fail, Patriarch Kirill, who took the helm in 2009, has allied the church very closely with Putin since the latter's return to the presidency in 2012. Before becoming patriarch, Kirill was widely seen as one of the more progressive of the Church's high leadership, but since becoming patriarch he has allied himself with conservative, patriotic, anti-Western currents in Russia.

Patriarch Kirill was born Vladimir Gundiaev in 1946 in Leningrad. His grandfather (who came from peasant stock) and his father were both active in the Church for which they had done time in the Gulag; both were later ordained in the post-war period. Vladimir entered the Leningrad Theological Seminary in 1965. Recognizing his capabilities, the influential Metropolitan of Leningrad, Nikodim (Rotov), appointed Vladimir as his personal secretary. Nikodim convinced the state that it was useful to have educated clergy who could travel abroad to ecumenical meetings and promote world peace, and was therefore able to foster the next generation of the Church's leadership. With Nikodim at the helm, the Department of External Church Relations became the intellectual powerhouse of the Russian Church.

At a young age Vladimir took monastic vows and received the name Kirill, was ordained, and completed both seminary and the academy. He was a participant in the World Council of Churches and other ecumenical organizations for decades, which necessitated cooperation with Soviet authorities and the KGB. He was appointed rector of the Leningrad Theological Seminary and Academy at the age of twenty-eight. On the day of the celebration of his ten-year anniversary as rector of the Leningrad Academy, he unexpectedly received word of his transfer to the poor provincial diocese of Smolensk. This transfer came on the initiative of the Soviet authorities, because Kirill was too active and influential as rector, increasing the number and intellectual level of students and strengthening the seminary's contacts with both youth and intellectuals in Leningrad. He had also co-authored a statement by the World Council of Churches criticizing the Soviet invasion of Afghanistan in 1979.[31]

Kirill served as bishop of Smolensk until becoming patriarch. During Gorbachev's reforms he again assumed an influential position within the Church when, in 1989, he was appointed head of the Department of External Church Relations. Under Kirill, the department's energies were directed toward the relationship between the Orthodox Church and Russian society in the crucial transition period after the collapse of communism. This found expression in Kirill's regular television program, *The Pastor's Word*, held every week since 1994. Kirill and the department worked intensively on a key document, the "Basis of the Social Concept of the Russian Orthodox Church," adopted by the Bishops' Council in 2000, which articulated the Church's position on a whole range of issues concerning the its relationship to society. The document, on the whole, is a bal-

31. See Andrey Vandenko's interview with Patriarch Kirill: "Patriarch Kirill: By Denying God's Truth We Ruin the World," https://tinyurl.com/uo9lths.

anced and sophisticated expression of the Church's position on a wide range of modern issues.[32]

In the 2000s, Metropolitan Kirill focused on articulating a response to the rising discourse about individual rights and liberties stemming from the West. So long as human rights discourse focused on political and religious liberties, particularly during the Soviet period, the Russian Orthodox Church saw it as a positive force. But in the 2000s, when Western rights discourse began to focus especially on sexual identity, Kirill developed a counterargument that human rights discourse was not universal but rather an ideological expression of secular Western values that threatened traditional Christian and Russian values. He argued that individual rights and liberties needed to be balanced, on the one hand, by individual responsibilities and moral obligations, and on the other, by the rights of the family and society.[33] The argument has also been championed by President Putin since his re-election in 2012 and become a powerful force in Russia in the last years.

Kirill received the overwhelming number of votes by the Church Council in 2009 to become the next patriarch. As Patriarch, Kirill endeavored to strengthen the institution of the Church, substantially increasing the number of dioceses and bishops, and issuing a new church charter that strengthened the hierarchical authority within the Church. Another focus of his patriarchate has been on re-churching Russian society: although three-quarters of Russians identify as being Ortho-

32. Available in English at https://tinyurl.com/qgwvfk5, https://mospat.ru/en/documents/social-concepts/.
33. See in English, Patriarch Kirill, *Freedom and Responsibility: A Search for Harmony—Human Rights and Personal Dignity* (London: Darton, Longman and Todd, 2011), and *Patriarch Kirill in His Own Words* (Yonkers, NY: St. Vladimir's Seminary Press, 2016). See also Alfons Brüning, "'Freedom' vs. 'Morality': On Orthodox Anti-Westernism and Human Rights," in *Orthodox Christianity and Human Rights*, ed. Alfons Brüning and Evert van der Zweerde (Leuven: Peeters, 2012), 125–52.

dox, few are active in church life. He has attempted to convince believers, unbelievers, and state officials alike of the Church's view of the path Russia should follow. His efforts, for example, in introducing religious education into the schools or in banning abortion have not received widespread support. The Church's support for a 2013 law outlawing "propaganda" of homosexuality to minors received a lot of criticism from foreign observers as well as secularists in Russia, but was broadly supported by the general public.

Perhaps most complex are Kirill's relations to the state under Putin. Western observers and journalists frequently depict Kirill and the Church as giving unqualified support to Putin and the Russian state. To be sure, Kirill has developed certain concepts—such as the threat of globalization and Western liberal values to Russian traditional values, and the notion of the "Russian world"—that have been utilized by the Putin regime to bolster its authority and popularity.[34] The area of the greatest symbiosis has been in promoting Russian patriotism, which Kirill supports as a means of strengthening the tie between Russian identity and Orthodoxy.

At the same time, there have been tensions between Putin and Kirill. Putin is always careful to emphasize that the Russian state is secular and the Russian nation multi-confessional. Some scholars argue that Kirill is devoted to promoting the interests of the Church, and when cooperation with the state furthers the interests of the Church he is a very willing partner, but when their interests diverge, Kirill puts the interests of the Church first. Although there have been scandals and criticism of Kirill (allegations surrounding expensive watches

34. See Patriarch Kirill, "Address at the Grand Opening of the Third Assembly of the Russian World," *Russian Politics and Law* 49, no. 1 (2011): 57–64, as well as the other articles in this special issue.

and apartments), and his success at churching the unchurched majority remains questionable, the patriarch's approval ratings remain high.[35] In seeking to strengthen the Church's position by allying it with the Putin regime, however, Kirill runs an enormous risk both for himself and the Church if Putin loses popularity.

Orthodox Christians in Russia over the past century have faced challenges quite unlike those of Western Christians in the modern period. Many believers endured persecution and martyrdom at the hands of a militantly atheist state, while the Church's leadership had to navigate between options of resistance, negotiation, compromise, and collaboration, where the boundaries between them were often far from clear. Russian Christians abroad in the twentieth century encountered different challenges: as a minority in countries dominated by Western Christians, they chose either to preserve their faith unchanged by refusing to engage modernity, or to view the new circumstances as an opportunity to broaden the impact of Orthodoxy precisely through engagement. Finally, Russian Christians in the past several decades faced the collapse of the Soviet Union and the revival of the Orthodox Church, first in the chaotic but democratic 1990s, and since 2000 in an increasingly authoritarian but pro-Orthodox Russia under Putin.

35. Gregory L. Freeze, "Russian Orthodoxy and Politics in the Putin Era," Carnegie Endowment Task Force White Paper, February 9, 2017, https://tinyurl.com/wlwtkcc. See also Nicolai Petro, "The Russian Orthodox Church," in *Routledge Handbook of Russian Foreign Policy*, ed. Andrei Tsygankov (London: Routledge, 2018), 217–32.

5

Russian Orthodox Theology

During the first millennium of Christianity, the Eastern Church engaged in continuous, vigorous theological discussion. Indeed, the majority of the theological developments during the age of the Ecumenical Councils took place in the East, where there were a series of intellectual giants equaled only by Augustine of Hippo in the West (for an overview, see chapter 1). This theological energy was not transmitted to the Slavs, however, when they converted to Christianity in the ninth and tenth centuries. However one explains what Georges Florovsky referred to as the "intellectual silence of Old Russia," Russians effectively did not engage in theology until the early modern era.[1] Perhaps, coming after the age of the Ecumenical Councils, the Russians received Christianity as already completed and perfected, without need for further elaboration.

---

1. Georges Florovsky, "The Problem of Old Russian Culture," *Slavic Review* 21, no. 1 (1962): 1–15.

Russia had a weaker tradition of the type of learning that was common in Byzantium and in the high medieval West, and universities or theological schools did not exist until the modern period. Rather than engage in intellectual speculation or reflection on the faith, old Russia concentrated its energies on living and embodying Christianity. Therefore, it excelled at the religious arts, especially architecture and iconography. The literature it produced focused primarily on spirituality rather than theology, and perhaps the most developed genre was hagiography and the *patericon* (sayings and lives of monastic fathers)—the stories of those who lived exemplary Christian lives by their humility, prayer, or self-sacrifice.

Therefore, while speaking of theology, we should keep in mind this particular posture of the Russian Orthodox tradition whose intellectual energy was not primarily directed at rational theologizing in the same way as Byzantine or Western Christianity. It may, therefore, be artificial or inaccurate to speak of theology narrowly and divorced from lived spiritual experience, about which much more has been written in the course of the Russian tradition. For clarity's sake those developments are treated in chapter 3, while this chapter will focus on the intellectual reflection upon Christian belief. A second point to be made at the outset is that in the modern Russian tradition, the most interesting developments took place on the boundary between theology and philosophy as strictly understood in the West—something referred to as "Russian religious thought," which in fact was much more creative than developments in either theology or philosophy in Russia in the stricter sense of those terms. Moreover, these developments came generally not from churchmen trained by the Church's theological schools but rather from lay intellectuals.[2]

After the fall of the Byzantine Empire in 1453 (if not even earlier), when active theological development virtually disappeared from the entire Orthodox world, Orthodox leaders became extremely conservative. They regarded the true faith as having been articulated during the age of the Ecumenical Councils, especially as embodied in the Nicene-Constantinopolitan Creed, and either adding to that (as Catholics had done) or subtracting from it (as Protestants had done) was to stray from true Christianity. There was little room, in such a view, for creative theological expression; the task of theology was to preserve, defend, and pass on. Such an approach, however, left little opportunity for articulating the faith in ways that spoke to a changing world. This was the state of Orthodox theology in Russia until the middle of the nineteenth century.

Medieval Russian Orthodoxy certainly produced important intellectual reflections on the meaning of the Christian faith, beginning in the eleventh century with Metropolitan Hilarion's "Sermon on Grace and Law."[3] In later centuries, especially the late fifteenth and early sixteenth centuries, heresies such as the so-called Judaizers, as well as the debates between the Possessors and Non-Possessors, likewise produced important

2. See especially Randall Poole, George Pattison, and Carolyn Emerson, eds., *Oxford Handbook of Russian Religious Thought* (Oxford: Oxford University Press, 2020), which treats more fully virtually all the thinkers and movements discussed in this chapter; and G. M. Hamburg and Randall A. Poole, eds., *A History of Russian Philosophy, 1830-1930: Faith, Reason, and the Defense of Human Dignity* (Cambridge: Cambridge University Press, 2010). An anthology of texts by key thinkers in this tradition is Alexander Schmemann, ed., *Ultimate Questions: An Anthology of Modern Russian Religious Thought* (Crestwood, NY: St. Vladimir's Seminary Press, 1977); texts can also be found in John Witte Jr. and Frank S. Alexander, eds., *The Teachings of Modern Orthodox Christianity on Law, Politics, and Human Nature* (New York: Columbia University Press, 2007).

3. Serge Zenkovsky, ed., *Medieval Russia's Epics, Chronicles, and Tales* (New York: Penguin, 1974), 85-90.

articulations of the faith by Iosif Volotsky and Maximus the Greek. Paradoxically, the seventeenth-century Old Believers' schism did not result in important theological speculation, since theological issues were not primarily at stake.[4]

The first attempt at producing a systematic theology came not in Russia, but in Ukraine, in seventeenth-century Kiev. The key figure here was Peter Mogila, Metropolitan of Kiev from 1633 to 1647, at a time when Ukraine was part of the Polish-Lithuanian Commonwealth. Precisely in the context of competition between Protestants and Catholics, and particularly the pressures coming from the Catholic Church and the recently formed Uniate Church (that is, in union with Rome), the Orthodox were under enormous pressures to defend themselves. Metropolitan Peter did much to re-establish the Orthodox Church after the creation of the Unia and to strengthen it vis-à-vis the Catholic Church in the Commonwealth. One of his most important contributions was establishing a theological school, later known as the Kiev-Moglia Academy (Kyiv-Mohyla in Ukrainian), to train Orthodox elites. Another was to write the first *Confession of Faith*, a distinctly post-Reformation activity that Protestants and Catholics were also engaged in. Mogila's *Confession* received (in modified form) confirmation by a council of Orthodox bishops in Iaşi (Jassy), Moldavia, in 1642, and another council in Jerusalem in 1672, by which point it had become the standard catechism and definition of the faith throughout the Orthodox world.[5]

Although widely accepted and extremely influential, Mogila's *Confession* came under particular criticism in the

4. The discussion here and in what follows presupposes familiarity with the material discussed in chapter 3.

5. For Mogila's confession, see Jaroslav Pelikan and Valerie Hotchkiss, *Creeds and Confessions in the Christian Tradition* (New Haven: Yale University Press, 2003), 1:596–97.

twentieth century for its heavy reliance on Western, especially Roman Catholic, categories and language. Similarly, the Kiev Academy was modeled on Polish Catholic Jesuit schools. Students were taught Latin and Polish as well as Slavonic and Greek to prepare themselves for articulating Orthodoxy in the Commonwealth. This was natural, since Peter Mogila's goal was to defend the Orthodox Church in a Polish Catholic environment, where the latter had superior education at its disposal. In effect, he was using the enemy's weapons against them. But it left a legacy by which Orthodox theology became dominated by scholasticism, the method of academic systematic theology, based on logic and a dialectical method of analysis, developed in medieval Western universities, reaching its pinnacle with the Catholic theologian Thomas Aquinas (1225–1274). Although scholasticism was challenged during the Protestant Reformation, by the seventeenth century Protestant theology (both Lutheran and Reformed) had also come to be dominated by the scholastic approach; in effect, Peter Mogila was adapting Orthodox theology to pan-Christian trends.

Kiev, and with it the Kiev-Moglia Academy, became a part of the Russian Empire in the second half of the seventeenth century, where it effectively became the first institution of higher learning in the Russian Empire. As the Russian Church set out in the eighteenth century to establish a system of education for all future clergy as a result of Peter the Great's reforms, it drew upon the model of the Kiev-Moglia Academy—to the extent that theological education in Russia was conducted in Latin until well into the nineteenth century (paradoxically, since Latin was historically used by, and associated with, the Roman Catholic theological tradition!). In the late eighteenth century Russian Orthodox thought felt the imprint of the European

Enlightenment, for example, in the leading figure of Platon (Levshin, 1737–1812), who wrote an important catechism.[6] It took time for the Church's network of schools, seminaries, and academies to become established and produce Russian theologians capable of writing systematic theological works.

Theology and theological education underwent significant transformations in the second half of the nineteenth century. A central figure was Filaret (Drozdov, 1782–1867), who was Metropolitan of Moscow for more than forty-five years from 1821 until his death. Aside from producing a new catechism in 1823, which became standard, he was a leading figure in translating the New Testament into modern Russian—until that point, the Russian Church used the Bible in Old Church Slavonic. Filaret supported the renewal of Russian theology from its dependence on scholasticism by returning it to a fresh reflection upon the sources of Christian faith, especially the Scriptures and the early Church Fathers. As bishop of Moscow, he oversaw the reform of the Moscow Theological Academy and supported the serious development of various theological disciplines.[7]

Metropolitan Makary (Bulgakov, 1816–1882) wrote the first monumental systematic work of dogmatic theology (1849–1853), which then became the standard theology textbook in Russian seminaries for decades. As theological scholarship continued to develop in the second half of the century, however, Makary's work was widely seen as too dryly scholastic and rigidly conservative. The most significant changes in the theological schools came in the second half of the century,

6. Elise Wirtschafter, *Religion and Enlightenment in Catherinian Russia: The Teachings of Metropolitan Platon* (DeKalb: Northern Illinois University Press, 2013).
7. See Nicholas S. Racheotes, *The Life and Thought of Filaret Drozdov, 1782–1867: The Thorny Path to Sainthood* (Lanham, MD: Rowman and Littlefield, 2018).

when reforms promoted a much higher level of academic scholarship in all areas of study, resulting in much more sophisticated research on church history, liturgy, the study and translation of the Church Fathers, Scripture (though in this area they certainly lagged behind the Protestants), and other areas. By the end of the century, a new generation of theologians argued that simply repeating the old formulations from scholastic systematic theology was to deprive theology of its vitality. While adhering to the truths as formed especially in the age of the Ecumenical Councils, they believed that modern theologians needed to learn how to communicate those spiritual truths to their own audience, which necessitated following developments in philosophy as well as other disciplines, including science.[8]

Russian Religious Thought in the Nineteenth Century: The Slavophiles

At the same time that Metropolitan Filaret and others were taking steps for the renewal of Russian theology in the Church's theological schools, a group of lay intellectuals known as the Slavophiles gave birth to a creative tradition of modern Russian religious thought, something that developed outside the bounds of academic theology in the Church's institutions of theological learning. The Slavophiles were responding to a secular intellectual current known as the Westernizers,

8. The scholarship on Russian religious thought in the tradition of the Slavophiles, Vladimir Solovyov, and the Russian religious renaissance is much more developed than that on Russian academic theology. Two recent contributions have attempted to right that balance: Patrick Michelson and Judith Kornblatt, eds., *Thinking Orthodox in Modern Russia: Culture, History, Context* (Madison: University of Wisconsin Press, 2014); and Patrick Michelson, *Beyond the Monastery Walls: The Ascetic Revolution in Russian Orthodox Thought, 1814-1914* (Madison: University of Wisconsin Press, 2017).

which regarded Russia as backward by comparison with the West, especially in social and political terms because Russia had serfdom and autocracy rather than the rule of law and individual rights. Both sides drew from Western thought. The Slavophiles, especially Aleksei Khomiakov (1804–1860) and Ivan Kireevsky (1806–1856), argued that Russia was not inferior to the West, but in some ways even superior. Although the West, they agreed, was more technologically advanced, it had become too dominated by individualism and rationalistic strains of thought that resulted in the secularization of society. To be sure, the Slavophiles shared much with, and drew inspiration from, Romantic thinkers in the West such as Samuel Taylor Coleridge (1772–1834) in England and especially Friedrich Schelling (1775–1854) in Germany. However, they took that inspiration back to their own tradition to discover what was distinctive about it and came to emphasize that what distinguished Russia from the West was its Orthodox Christianity.

Khomiakov was interested in the question of religious authority and how to balance unity with freedom in view of that authority. He argued that the Roman Catholic Church maintained unity through the external authority of the papacy, which represented the final and infallible source of religious authority, but at the expense of freedom. The Protestants, in rejecting this authority in the name of freedom, had sacrificed unity. They claimed that Scripture was the only infallible source of authority; but since Scripture can be variously interpreted, the ultimate arbiter of the truth became the individual's interpretation of Scripture, and unity became impossible. According to Khomiakov, the Orthodox approach was exemplified in the Ecumenical Councils. Here the members of the church gathered together and, guided by the Holy Spirit, were brought to the truth unanimously. The individual's freedom is not subject to some external authority, but rather the individual voluntarily, through love, balances that freedom with the greater understanding that is reached by the group of which the individual is a part (i.e., the Church). The individual has the freedom to participate in the process of understanding and articulating the truth, but at the same time it would be seen as the height of arrogance to assert one's individual opinion over that of the entire body of believers. The Church is the body of Christ and therefore embodies the faith and its true teaching—but the Church in this view is not understood as an external institutional authority, represented by a magisterium, but rather as a body made up of all its individual members, including the laity. From this notion of truth arrived at in church councils (*sobor* in Russian), what ideally distinguishes Orthodoxy is *sobornost* (conciliarity) as the distinctive way of balancing unity and freedom through love. From these ideas about the Church, the Slavophiles also extended the notion of *sobornost* to refer to Russian society as a whole—denoting its solidarity in contrast with Western individualism.

Ivan Kireevsky was particularly concerned with ways of knowing. He argued that the West had become excessively rationalistic. This process had already begun in the age of medieval Latin scholasticism, when religious truth was approached as a system of logically demonstrable proofs that could be mastered intellectually through study—but was ultimately divorced from lived religious experience. Because analytical reason was accepted as the best way to approach the truth, the West embarked on a path that ended up in the split between theology and philosophy, between faith and reason. Kireevsky argued that the approach of the early Church Fathers had exemplified what he called "integral knowledge."

Scholasticism and rationalism turned the truths of the faith into external objects and into logical doctrine, whereas the patristic approach was to see them as living, and life-giving, truths. True faith was not to be reached either by thought or by feeling (as had come to characterize Western approaches), but by thought and feeling together. Because he believed that this holistic approach to theology was exemplified by the early Church Fathers, whose theology was vibrant and connected to spiritual life in ways that dry scholastic systematic theology was not, Kireevsky was important in promoting the rediscovery of the early Fathers in Russia. He cooperated with the key Russian monastery of Optina Hermitage in translating and publishing the Greek Church Fathers into Russian.

Two key ideas of the Slavophiles remained central themes in modern Russian theology: the first is *sobornost*, or the notion that religious truth is arrived at within the church as the whole body of believers. The second is integral knowledge, the notion that theology should be more than systems of abstract reasoning. They remain key elements in how Russian thinkers have understood Orthodoxy to be distinct from Western forms of Christianity.[9]

Vladimir Solovyov

In the second half of the nineteenth century, Vladimir Solovyov (1853–1900) was a particularly influential figure in the development of Russian religious thought.[10] Son of Sergei

9. A good collection of writings by Khomiakov and Kireevsky is *On Spiritual Unity: A Slavophile Reader*, ed. Boris Jakim and Robert Bird (Hudson, NY: Lindisfarne, 1998); see also Andrzej Walicki, *The Slavophile Controversy: History of a Conservative Utopia in Nineteenth-Century Russian Thought*, trans. Hilda Andrews-Rusiecka (Notre Dame: University of Notre Dame Press, 1989).

10. There is now a significant literature on Solovyov (also transliterated as Soloviev) in English, as well as translations of his key works. An excellent start-

Solovyov, the foremost historian of the age, Vladimir studied first mathematics and physics, and later history and philology at Moscow University. In what would become a common pattern for such religious thinkers, he went through a crisis of faith as a young man that, in the end, resulted precisely in its deepening. After finishing the university, he made an unusual decision for someone not from a clerical family and studied at the Moscow Theological Academy, while also pursuing graduate training in philosophy at the university. In 1873, at the age of twenty-one, he defended his master's thesis, *The Crisis of Western Philosophy,* a critique of positivism and the division in Western thought between theoretical and empirical knowledge. In 1878, he delivered a series of lectures on "Godmanhood" (*bogochelovechestvo,* alternately translated as "Divine Humanity" or "The Humanity of God") to an audience that included the great novelists Fyodor Dostoevsky and Leo Tolstoy (who were twice his age). He received his doctorate in philosophy from St. Petersburg University in 1880 with his thesis, *The Critique of Abstract Principles,* though he lost his university position because he appealed to Tsar Alexander III to show mercy on Tsar Alexander II's assassins.

The development of Solovyov's thought can be divided into three periods. In the 1870s, he focused his energies on developing a philosophical system that was intended to be a "critique of critiques" that sought the "unity of all things." He argued that Western philosophical systems were too narrow, being either empirical or rationalist; he sought a unity of knowledge that would link science, philosophy, and theology into a grand synthesis. As a young man, as he later described in poetical

ing point is Paul Valliere, *Modern Russian Theology: Bukharev, Soloviev, Bulgakov* (Grand Rapids: Eerdmans, 2000); see also S. L. Frank, ed., *A Solovyov Anthology* (New York: Saint Austin, 2001).

form, he had three visions of what he called "Sophia," Divine Wisdom, who appeared to him in female form. Sophia became a key component of his philosophy. He understood Sophia as an "eternal feminine," the world soul, God's "other." Sophia is a divine principle that links God with creation; it is the object of God's love, but the primordial unity was lost in the fall so that the world as we know it is characterized by fragmentation and separation from God and others. Salvation is the restoration of unity of all things in God, which is made possible by Christ as the God-man who unites Creator and creation.[11] Though the notion of Sophia would be taken up by later Russian thinkers, especially Florensky and Bulgakov, as we will discuss, it would also be one of the most controversial aspects of Solovyov's religious thought.

In the 1880s, Solovyov pursued the reunification of the Christian churches. He advocated Orthodox–Roman Catholic dialogue as a means to renew Christendom in a grand theocratic vision that would unite the universal Church with a universal empire under the leadership of the Roman pope and the Russian tsar. His ecumenical vision also included the Jews, and he attacked anti-semitism.[12] By the end of the decade, after publishing *Russia and the Universal Church* (1889, in French), he abandoned his project when he realized that it found little sympathy either in Russia or in the Catholic world.[13]

During the 1890s, Solovyov returned to philosophy, focusing more on concrete social, political, and ethical issues. In *The Justification of the Good* (1897) he developed a general theory of eco-

11. Vladimir Solovyov, *Divine Sophia: The Wisdom Writings of Vladimir Solovyov*, ed. and trans. Judith Deutsch Kornblatt (Ithaca: Cornell University Press, 2009).

12. Vladimir Solovyov, *The Burning Bush: Writings on Jews and Judaism*, ed. and trans. Gregory Glazov (Notre Dame: University of Notre Dame Press, 2016).

13. Vladimir Soloviev, *Russia and the Universal Church*, trans. Herbert Rees (London: G. Bles, 1948).

nomic and social welfare based on the principle that all human beings have the right to a dignified existence.[14] In politics he advocated constitutional monarchy, and his thought inspired the development of political liberalism in early twentieth century Russia that was an alternative to the extremes of autocracy and revolution. A poet as well as philosopher, his poetry was influential on the Silver Age of Russian literature, especially Symbolist poetry. His ideas had a profound impact on the Russian religious renaissance of the early twentieth century.

Christianity and Culture: The Russian Religious Renaissance

Nineteenth-century Russian thought was dominated by social and political concerns. As a rule, the Russian intelligentsia looked to the West for models of better social and political order than they found in Russia, though by no means necessarily the modes that were actually operative in the West (such as capitalism). In the mid-nineteenth century, the emphasis was particularly on individual rights and the rule of law. In the second half of the century, the intelligentsia grew more radicalized and were generally attracted to variations of materialist philosophies, particularly socialism, influenced by Western thinkers such as Ludwig Feuerbach and Charles Fourier. Marxism was not regarded by most as appropriate for Russia, which was still a predominantly agrarian society, and only began to attract a significant following in the 1890s. The challenges to Christianity that affected Western Europe in the nineteenth century were far less prevalent in Russia, and therefore so was

14. Vladimir Solovyov, *The Justification of the Good: An Essay on Moral Philosophy*, trans. Nathalie Duddington, ed. Boris Jakim (Grand Rapids: Eerdmans, 2005).

the spread of secularization and atheism. Indeed, the primary cause of atheism in Russia was neither the intellectual, rationalist challenges of the Enlightenment, nor the challenge presented by science. Rather, the cause of atheism was primarily political: the intelligentsia opposed Russia's political and social system, and because the Orthodox Church was tied to the state and seen as part of the system, opposition to the system meant rejecting the Church and, together with it, Christianity and belief in God.[15]

Literature in the nineteenth century was also dominated by the "cursed questions" of Russian identity and its relationship to the West, together with the sources of and solutions for the problems of Russian society. None of Russia's great authors was explicitly atheist; some, especially Nikolai Gogol (1809–1852) and Fyodor Dostoevsky (1821–1881), were devout Russian Orthodox believers. Indeed, Christian themes were central to Dostoevsky's major works, especially *The Brothers Karamazov*, and some consider Dostoevsky one of Russia's greatest religious thinkers for his profound exploration of existential spiritual and philosophical themes.[16] Leo Tolstoy (1828–1910), after completing his great novels *Anna Karenina* and *War and Peace*, underwent a spiritual crisis that led him ultimately to reject historical Christianity and effectively create his own version of it, stripped of all supernatural elements and focused exclusively on a radical, pacifist implementation of Christ's ethical teachings.[17]

By the early twentieth century, a new generation of literary

---

15. Victoria Frede, *Doubt, Atheism, and the Nineteenth-Century Russian Intelligentsia* (Madison: University of Wisconsin Press, 2011).

16. For a discussion of Dostoevsky by a prominent Western theologian, see Rowan Williams, *Dostoevsky: Language, Faith and Fiction* (Waco, TX: Baylor University Press, 2008).

17. See Jay Parini, ed., *Last Steps: The Late Writings of Leo Tolstoy* (London: Penguin, 2009).

and artistic figures in Russia rebelled against the dominance of realism and the necessity of dealing with the "cursed questions." They wished, for example, to explore the multiple valences of language; pursue art for art's sake; or explore inner, spiritual worlds for their own sake. They were attracted to various sorts of mystical, occult, and esoteric ideas (including theosophy) and apocalyptic visions. Since the realities of life were far too complex to be reduced to realism, the response in art was the Russian Avant-Garde, including key figures such as Kazimir Malevich, Wassily Kandindsky, and Marc Chagall. The early twentieth century is known as the Silver Age in Russian literature, which saw the revival of poetry as the central literary form; the Symbolists in particular were interested in the spiritual power of language and art.[18]

At the same time, members of the Russian intelligentsia, including several prominent Marxists, grew frustrated with the limitations of positivist and materialist forms of thought, likewise coming to the conclusion that reality was more complex than empirical knowledge could grasp. In particular, they concluded that Marxism did not protect the absolute value of each individual person. They first turned to philosophical idealism (especially the thought of Immanuel Kant and neo-Kantianism) and eventually made their way back to Christianity. This period has come to be known as the Russian religious renaissance.[19]

Virtually all—both the poets and the philosophers—were influenced by Vladimir Solovyov. Some Symbolist thinkers, such as Dmitry Merezhkovsky, rejected traditional Christianity

---

18. See Sibelan E. S. Forrester and Martha M. F. Kelly, *Russian Silver Age Poetry: Texts and Contexts* (Boston: Academic Studies Press, 2015).

19. Nicholas Zernov, *The Russian Religious Renaissance of the Twentieth Century* (New York: Harper and Row, 1963).

and embraced instead what they saw as a future Christianity of the "Third Testament" inspired by the Holy Spirit. Some, such as Lev Shestov and Semyon Frank, were Jews (though the latter converted to Christianity). The poet and philosopher Viacheslav Ivanov was drawn first to the mysteries of classical antiquity and after the Revolution became a Catholic in Rome. Others, such as Vasily Rozanov and Nikolai Berdyaev, remained members of the Russian Orthodox Church but felt free to criticize not only the Church but elements of historic Christianity. Berdyaev (1874–1948), who emigrated after the Revolution, became particularly well-known in the West for his Christian personalist existentialism that championed spiritual freedom and creativity.[20] Though by no means a theologian in the narrow sense of the word, he still remains an influential Christian thinker inside and outside Russia. Finally, still others, such as Pavel Florensky and Sergius Bulgakov, embraced the Orthodox Church in an explicit way, becoming Orthodox clergy and influential theologians. After the Bolshevik Revolution, most of these figures either fled or were expelled from Russia, so the Russian religious renaissance continued to flourish in Paris in the inter-war period.[21]

The Name Glorifiers Controversy

One of the few outright theological controversies in Russian Orthodox history erupted in the early twentieth century over the name of God. This controversy was sparked by a book on prayer and spirituality (with reference to the Jesus Prayer)

20. A key text of Berdyaev's is *The Destiny of Man* (New York: Harper & Row, 1960).
21. A very fine survey of modern Orthodox theology, including key figures discussed in the remainder of this chapter as well as other, non-Russian theologians, is Andrew Louth, *Modern Orthodox Thinkers: From the Philokalia to the Present* (Downers Grove, IL: IVP Academic, 2015).

which claimed that "the Name of God *is* God Himself"—meaning that God is present when invoked in prayer. Some thought that, as a dogmatic statement, this went too far. In the ensuing dispute, the teaching of the so-called "Name Glorifiers" was condemned by both the Ecumenical Patriarch of Constantinople and the Russian Holy Synod. The majority of Russian monks on Mount Athos refused to recant, and the episode was "resolved" in 1913 when the Russian authorities sent in naval ships that carted off hundreds of monks by force and returned them to Russia.

Despite being condemned by the official church structures, many Russian Orthodox thinkers did not accept the condemnation as some authoritative "magisterium" of the Church so long as the teaching was not considered by a Church Council. Florensky and Bulgakov continued to reflect on the issue in the 1920s, writing treatises devoted to the philosophy of language and the theology of the divine names. Both asserted the basic correctness of the claim that "the Name of God is God"—but also argued that the converse (i.e., God is his Name) was not true. They drew upon the theology of the fourteenth-century Byzantine theologian Gregory Palamas and his distinction between the "essence" and the "energies," or operations, of God, and maintained that the Divine Names are manifestations of the energies of God. Because the controversy itself erupted on the eve of World War I and the Revolution, the dispute effectively remained unresolved and even largely forgotten, though there has been a revival of interest since the collapse of the Soviet Union.[22]

22. Scott Kenworthy, "The Name Glorifiers Controversy," in *Oxford Handbook of Russian Religious Thought* (see n. 2 above); Paul Ladouceur, *Modern Orthodox Theology* (London: Bloomsbury, 2019), chap. 15.

Pavel Florensky and Sergei Bulgakov, painting by Mikhail Nesterov (1917). *Photo courtesy of Wikimedia Commons.*

Pavel Florensky (1882–1937)

Pavel Florensky is one of the most fascinating and tragic figures of the twentieth century; a recent biography justly calls him "Russia's unknown da Vinci."[23] His father was an engineer and his mother, an Armenian, was artistic, thus shaping Florensky's own abiding interests in both science and art. As a youth, he underwent an intellectual crisis that challenged his

23. Avril Pyman, *Pavel Florensky, a Quiet Genius: The Tragic and Extraordinary Life of Russia's Unknown da Vinci* (New York: Continuum, 2010).

absolute confidence in science. He studied mathematics and physics at Moscow University; one of his professors, the prominent mathematician Nikolai Bugaev, was the father of Andrei Bely, who would become one of the leading Symbolist poets and theoreticians. Through Bely, Florensky came to know the leading Symbolists and figures of the Silver Age. In 1904, he entered the Moscow Theological Academy, where he followed the full course of study, and after completing his graduate training he remained as professor of philosophy and editor of the academy's theological journal until the academy's closure in 1919. He married in 1910 (and had five children), and was ordained a priest in 1911. His magnum opus was *The Pillar and Ground of the Truth*, published in 1914.

Unlike most other figures of the Russian religious renaissance, Florensky remained in the Soviet Union. After the Revolution he turned his attention to spiritual dimensions of art and language. As it became clear by the mid-1920s that he would not be able to publish theological works in the Soviet Union, Florensky returned to his scientific pursuits. For the next decade he worked for the State Experimental Electrotechnical Institute, patented numerous scientific inventions (such as a non-coagulating machine oil), and published a monograph and over one hundred articles in electro-chemistry and other scientific fields. Because of his scientific expertise, he was tolerated by the Soviet authorities for a surprisingly long time. He was finally arrested in 1933 and sentenced to ten years in the Gulag. Even in the Gulag he continued to conduct important research in chemistry and botany. He received a martyr's death, executed by the security services in 1937.

Florensky was highly critical of scholastic and formal methods of theology and theological education, which found expression in the unusual way in which he presented his major work. *The Pillar and Ground of the Truth* is a series of letters and unfolds in a conversational style; rather than follow the traditional structure of a systematic theology text, the second letter is on the theme of doubt. Truth, for Florensky, is not to be exposited in a logical way so much as to be discovered and experienced through encounter. That is because truth transcends reason. Reality is not what it appears, as Florensky was learning from non-Euclidean geometry, higher mathematics, and Einstein's relativity. Florensky was as aware as any of the immense powers of human reason and therefore also acutely aware of its limitations. Kant had already demonstrated that certain questions, such as the existence of God, were beyond the power of reason to demonstrate or refute, but for Kant, this meant that the existence of God was unknowable. If one remains limited to reason, Florensky argued, one must remain in the realm of doubt and unknowing. Truth, because it transcends reason, is antinomic; it appears contradictory or paradoxical to the human mind. The only way out of the dilemma of doubt and unknowing is offered by Christianity, hence the nature of all the core Christian doctrines is antinomic: God is one yet three; Christ is God yet man; Mary is virgin yet mother; the Eucharist is bread and wine yet also Christ's body and blood. If truth were demonstrable, it would be necessary, and there would be no room for freedom; one would simply have to accept it. But such is not the nature of reality. Christian dogma forces one to surrender the ego-self and the control asserted by reason; only through faith can a person be open to encounter with God, which is made possible through love.

According to Florensky, a person encounters the transcendent God above all through symbols. A symbol does not merely represent something else; rather, it is something of one realm that participates in or in some way embodies another realm, and therefore acts as a point of intersection or bridge between them. For this reason, Florensky became intensely interested in worship, in icons, and in language because all of these are symbols that mediate God, that become points of encounter with God. For the Orthodox, the Eucharist is understood in this way: it is bread and wine that becomes the body and blood of Christ without ceasing to be bread and wine. According to Florensky, an icon plays a similar role, as does language in prayer—especially when invoking the Divine Names, particularly the name of Christ. Orthodox icons are not somehow more primitive or less developed than Western art after the Renaissance. Western art, using linear perspective, tries to create an illusion of the reality of this world of sense perception. The icon, by contrast, is "on the boundary of heaven and earth, belonging to one, disclosing the other."[24] In the icon, the believer encounters the person depicted and is drawn into a relationship with Christ, the Mother of God, or one of the saints who belongs to heaven—so that the believer is, in effect, drawn up to touch heaven.[25]

For Florensky, Christianity cannot be demonstrated through intellectual argument; it has to be lived. "Orthodoxy is shown, not proved. That is why there is only one way to understand Orthodoxy: through direct Orthodox experience.... To become Orthodox, it is necessary to immerse oneself all at once in the very element of Orthodoxy, to begin living in an Orthodox way. There is no other way."[26] The way to truth is the way of asceticism, to follow the path to holiness.

Florensky also asserted that knowing and being are ulti-

24. Louth, *Modern Orthodox Thinkers*, 40.
25. Pavel Florensky, *Iconostasis*, trans. Olga Andrejev and Donald Sheehan (Crestwood, NY: St. Vladimir's Seminary Press, 1996).
26. Pavel Florensky, *The Pillar and Ground of the Truth*, trans. Boris Jakim(Princeton: Princeton University Press, 1997), 9.

mately inseparable. The only way to know God is to become, through ascetic effort, less ego-centered and more God-centered. Florensky developed the key Orthodox notions of salvation as synergy and deification (see chapter 1). The spiritual journey requires the cooperation of the human and divine wills together ("operation" being understood quite literally): as the person, through effort of the will, opens him- or herself up to God's will, then God's will "operates" within the person. The more a person allows God's energies or grace to operate within him- or herself, the more the person is conformed to God, is transformed to become more godlike or holy (deification). Therefore, according to Florensky, it is in this way that one comes to know God: it is a process by which the knower and the known become one, but a oneness that is an encounter of persons.

Sergius Bulgakov (1871–1944)

Sergius Bulgakov was one of the greatest Orthodox theologians of the twentieth century. Born in provincial Russia, his father was a parish priest. Sergius lost his faith while studying at the seminary because no one there was able to answer his questions and doubts, so he transferred to a secular school and became attracted to Marxism. After finishing Moscow University, he went on to teach political economy (first in Kiev, and later in Moscow) and published two major books in the field. His research brought him to doubt the rigidity of Marxist schemes, and, together with Nikolai Berdyaev, Peter Struve, and Semen Frank, he made the journey from Marxism to philosophical idealism under Solovyov's influence. Like Solovyov, he believed that modern philosophical systems contained important insights as well as limitations; each one, however, failed to admit its limitations but rather presented itself as the only correct philosophy. Indeed, Bulgakov did not reject socialism altogether; on the contrary, he was open to the idea of Christian socialism as the most just economic system. The problem was not socialism per se, but Marxism specifically, because Marxism was not just an economic model but a totalizing ideology that sought to explain all aspects of life, a kind of surrogate religion, and thereby undermined its own pretensions of being scientific.[27] After the Revolution of 1905, Bulgakov, together with Berdyaev, Struve, Frank, and others, contributed a very important collection of essays called *Landmarks* in which they prophetically argued that the ideals of the revolutionary intelligentsia, without being rooted in a spiritual-moral foundation, could easily justify coercion and violence against individuals in the name of a utopian future. By 1917, Bulgakov had completed his journey from Marxism to idealism to Orthodox Christianity in what he described as the prodigal's return to the Father's house. He would become an important participant in the Russian Church Council of 1917–1918, and in 1918 was ordained to the priesthood.[28]

In the winter of 1922–1923, Bulgakov was deported from the Soviet Union along with other leading intellectuals, and by 1925 settled in Paris, where he served as professor of theology and dean of the St. Serge Orthodox Theological Institute for nearly two decades until his death. Bulgakov and others faced a new situation for Russian theology—the aftermath of the Bolshevik Revolution, when Russia itself was controlled

---

27. Sergei Bulgakov, "An Urgent Task," in *A Revolution of the Spirit: Crisis of Value in Russia, 1890-1924*, ed. Bernice Rosenthal and Martha Bohachevsky-Chomiak (New York: Fordham University Press, 1990), 107-33.
28. On Bulgakov, see Valliere, *Modern Russian Theology*; Poole et al., *Oxford Handbook*; Sergius Bulgakov, *A Bulgakov Anthology*, ed. Nicholas Zernov (Eugene, OR: Wipf and Stock, 2012).

by a militant atheist regime, and Russian theologians were transplanted to a context in which Orthodox Christians were a minority.

Russian theology in the emigration, broadly speaking, followed three currents: The first was ultra conservative and saw the task of theology to be the preservation without any change or innovation in what was strictly Orthodox. Effectively, this meant continuing the tradition of pre-revolutionary Russian dogmatic theology. This current found expression primarily in the Russian Church Abroad. The second, exemplified by Bulgakov, continued the line of the Russian religious renaissance and the inspiration of Vladimir Solovyov, in a way that was open to engagement with Western philosophy and theology. The third was the "neo-patristic synthesis," considered below, which argued that the starting point for Orthodox theology must be a return to the Church Fathers. The latter two currents were located in Paris and later New York, and in general both were open to engagement with the ecumenical movement. Paris theology was centered especially at the St. Serge Theological Institute, and included many great theologians such as Nicholas Afanasiev, Cyprian Kern, Pavel Evdokimov, and others.[29]

Bulgakov was the dominant figure in Paris and was also an important Orthodox participant in the nascent ecumenical movement. Bulgakov asserted that the Church's dogmas, as defined by the Ecumenical Councils, were obligatory for all Orthodox Christians—but were in fact few in number, constituting effectively only the doctrines of the Trinity and Christology. Other questions belonged to realm of *theologoumena,*

29. For essays by each of these thinkers and more, see Michael Plekon, ed., *Tradition Alive: On the Church and the Christian Life in Our Time* (Lanham, MD: Rowan and Littlefield, 2003).

that is, theological opinions that were still open for discussion—and Bulgakov believed that there remained a great many unresolved issues, which he approached in an open-ended way. His own theology centered on the notion of Sophia (Divine Wisdom), first developed by Vladimir Solovyov. Bulgakov's Sophiology was controversial; although he was at pains to show that Sophia existed in the tradition (especially churches dedicated to the Holy Wisdom), it had never been developed in Orthodox theology, and therefore many regarded it as an innovation. Indeed, it was criticized by other Russian theologians, especially by Vladimir Lossky (see below), and condemned by both the Church Abroad and the Moscow Patriarchate. However, Bulgakov's own bishop, Metropolitan Evlogy (see chapter 4), defended and protected Bulgakov and permitted him to continue his theology and teaching.

Bulgakov developed the notion of Sophia to explain the gulf that separated God from his creation, and how that gulf can be bridged. Sophia represents the "in between," between God and creation. God relates to creation through wisdom, and through wisdom human beings seek God. As Andrew Louth put it, wisdom "is the face that God turns towards his Creation, and the face that Creation, in humankind, turns toward God." This relatedness of creation and humanity toward God, and of God toward creation and humanity, is at the center of all Bulgakov's theology.[30]

Bulgakov's major theological treatises, grouped in the "minor trilogy" and the "major trilogy," can be understood as developing these ideas. In the minor trilogy—*The Burning Bush* (1927), *The Friend of the Bridegroom* (1927), and *Jacob's Ladder* (1929)—he reflected on Mary the Mother of God, John the Bap-

---

30. Louth, *Modern Orthodox Thinkers*, 58.

tist, and the angels as humanity and creation turned toward God. In the major trilogy on "Divine Humanity" (or Godman-hood), he explored God as turned toward creation in the incar-nate Son of God (*The Lamb of God*, 1933), the Holy Spirit (*The Comforter*, 1936), and culminating in the Church and eschatol-ogy (*The Bride of the Lamb*, 1945).[31] For Bulgakov, if God is capa-ble of becoming human, this says much about human nature and its capacity for, and ultimate destiny in, deification. If God becomes human in Christ, then humanity becomes deified in the Church, the new humanity. Eschatologically, Bulgakov hoped this would ultimately include all humanity, and he defended the theological opinion held by some of the Greek Fathers such as Gregory of Nyssa that, at the end of time, all would be reconciled to God (*apokatastasis*). The controversy over Sophiology and criticisms from the neo-patristic theolo-gians undercut much of Bulgakov's influence in the remainder of the twentieth century, but in the twenty-first century there has been a more open and appreciative re-evaluation of his theology among contemporary theologians both in Russia and the West, where his major theological works have finally appeared in translation.

Return to the Fathers: Neo-Patristic Synthesis

Georges Florovsky (1893–1979) undoubtedly had the most pro-found impact during the twentieth century on the whole of Orthodox theology—except in Russia, where none of the émi-gré theologians had an impact during the Soviet period. Recent assessments of Florovsky have been more critical, though his construction of the history of Orthodox theology has been so

---

31. All of these works (and others) have been translated into English and published by Eerdmans.

influential it has become hard to escape. Florovsky was the son of an Orthodox priest and grew up in Odessa, where he studied philosophy and history at the university. His family fled during the Revolution and by 1925 he ended up in Paris, where Bulgakov invited him to come and teach patristics; he was ordained in 1932. His criticism of Bulgakov and the thought of the Russian religious renaissance in general led to his estrangement from other émigrés in Paris, so in 1949 he moved to the United States, where he became Dean of St. Vladimir's Orthodox Theological Seminary in New York until 1955. From 1956 to 1964 he taught at Harvard University, and from 1964 until his death in 1979, at Princeton University. He was also one of the founding fathers of the World Council of Churches in 1948. His theology had a most profound impact on reshaping all Orthodox theology (not just Russian) in the second half of the twentieth century.

Florovsky's core argument was that the purest expression of Christian theology was to be found in the Church Fathers. Contra Protestant theologians such as Adolf von Harnack, who asserted that Christianity became corrupted when it became "Hellenized," Florovsky maintained that Christian Hellenism, which was a consequence of the Christianization of the gentiles, was providential and therefore of lasting significance. But whereas the theology of the Fathers had vitality because it responded to concrete living issues, Western scholasticism, by trying to create a logical system of thought, had become dry and lifeless. Therefore, Christian theology was truest when it was in keeping with the spirit of the Fathers. His monumental book *The Ways of Russian Theology* (1937) was the story of how Russian theology progressively strayed from the patristic roots of Christian Hellenism. Although this was a gradual process, a key moment was when Peter Mogila constructed both his own theology and his own educational program (later adopted in Russia) following Roman Catholic scholastic models. This, according to Florovsky, resulted in the "Babylonian captivity" of Orthodox thought, which, divorced from its roots, underwent a "pseudomorphosis," losing its true character. However, the modern attempt to revitalize Orthodox thought inspired by Vladimir Solovyov and continued especially by Bulgakov had only replaced Western scholastic theology with German idealist philosophy as its intellectual root, and therefore was equally alien to a true Orthodox theology. What Florovsky advocated was a "return to the Fathers," though in a creative, not rigid, way. It was not sufficient merely to repeat or imitate what the Fathers had written; rather, one had to acquire the "mind of the Fathers" as a whole, enter into their way of thinking, and from that standpoint creatively address current theological concerns so as to construct a "neo-patristic synthesis."

Perhaps paradoxically, Florovsky himself never attempted such a synthesis. His major books—surveys of patristic thought and the *Ways of Russian Theology*—were written in Russian in the inter-war period; after he came to the United States, his seminal works were all occasional essays (in English, German, and French). Some of his individual arguments, such as the understanding of tradition and the relationship of tradition to Scripture, were certainly important. But Florovsky's greatest influence was more programmatic than in terms of the content of his theology itself: the call to "return to the Fathers" as the root of all authentic Orthodox theology, the critique of Western theology and philosophy, and the skepticism toward all Orthodox theology that was dependent on Western categories (be it scholasticism or idealism). Recent scholarship has demonstrated the extent to which Florovsky's thought developed in a polemical relationship with Russian theology from

Solovyov to Bulgakov, though it had a significant impact on subsequent theologians in constructing Orthodox theology in opposition to the West and the Western theological and philosophical traditions.[32]

Other theologians contributed more to the construction of a neo-patristic synthesis, and in the second half of the twentieth century a fairly coherent picture was formed. Though these theologians were mostly Russian émigrés, they were no longer writing in Russian, but in French (such as Vladimir Lossky) and/or English (such as John Meyendorff). Lossky (1903–1958) sketched the main outlines in an influential book titled *The Mystical Theology of the Eastern Church*, in which he argued that, by contrast with the West, the Eastern Church made no sharp distinction between mysticism and theology, "between personal experience of the divine mysteries and the dogma affirmed by the Church." By this he meant an ineffable experience of communion with God in the depths of the soul, one that brought about a profound change in the human person. For Lossky, such an experience is only possible because Christ has already bridged the gap between human and divine. In the Church, "our humanity becomes consubstantial with the deified humanity, united with the Person of Christ."[33] Theology and the mystical are inseparable because theology serves as the correct guide to a true experience with God, on the one hand, and, on the other, because theology itself grows out of direct personal experience of God. Lossky wrote, "We must live the dogma expressing a revealed truth, which appears to us

---

32. Paul Gavrilyuk, *Georges Florovsky and the Russian Religious Renaissance* (Oxford: Oxford University Press, 2014); for a collection of his seminal essays, see Brandon Gallaher and Paul Ladouceur, eds., *The Patristic Witness of Georges Florovsky: Essential Theological Writings* (New York: Bloomsbury, 2019).

33. Vladimir Lossky, *The Mystical Theology of the Eastern Church* (Crestwood, NY: St. Vladimir's Seminary Press, 1976), 181.

as an unfathomable mystery, in such a fashion that instead of assimilating the mystery to our mode of understanding, we should, on the contrary, look for profound change, an inner transformation of the spirit, enabling us to experience it mystically."[34]

Because God is a mystery beyond our comprehension, Eastern theology is at its root *apophatic*, that is, a negative theology that emphasizes that God is beyond all human language and concepts. Apophatic theology "excludes all abstract and purely intellectual theology which would adapt the mysteries of the wisdom of God to human ways of thought. It is an existential attitude which involves the whole person: there is no theology apart from experience; it is necessary to change, to become a new person. To know God one must draw near to Him. No one who does not follow the path of union with God can be a theologian."[35] Therefore dogmas are true not in the sense that they express in a verbal formula the fullness of the divine truth, which is not possible, but as accurate and necessary signposts for the spiritual journey.

The culmination of the neo-patristic theology came with the rediscovery of the Byzantine theologian Gregory Palamas by John Meyendorff (1926–1992). If God in his essence is completely transcendent and unknowable, then how is it possible for humans to experience God directly as the Orthodox mystics claimed they had? Palamas's key contribution was to make a distinction between God's essence—which is indeed transcendent and unknowable—and God's "energies" or actions and grace that he directs toward creation, but while distinct from his essence, God's energies are still truly God. It was a defense and justification of Orthodox spiritual traditions, but equally

34. Lossky, *Mystical Theology*, 8.
35. Lossky, *Mystical Theology*, 39.

applied to how the believer was transformed through worship and the sacraments. All the threads of modern Orthodox theology were brought together in this revival of Palamism and became the sine qua non of theology through much of the Orthodox world (including especially the West as articulated by Timothy Ware and John Meyendorff) by the end of the twentieth century. Orthodox theology was not an abstract logical system of thought; it was existential, a reflection of and guide to direct encounter with God, who, though ineffable, can be experienced directly because of the outpouring of his energies that transforms the believer and deifies him.

Whereas proponents of the neo-patristic synthesis emphasized the existential, experiential nature of theology, another major Russian émigré theologian, Alexander Schmemann (1921–1983), emphasized the inseparability of theology and worship. Both Schmemann and Meyendorff were born of emigrés, educated in Paris before coming to the United States to teach at St. Vladimir's Seminary. Central to Schmemann's theology was the understanding of the Eucharist, which, he argued, is not merely one of the sacraments or a means of grace that the church has the power to make possible. Rather, the church has its very source, being, and end precisely as the body of believers gathered together in eucharistic celebration, giving thanks to Christ who makes himself present. In the Eucharist, the faithful commune with Christ and with each other, thereby becoming the body of Christ. Schmemann advocated a liturgical revival through certain reforms to make worship services more comprehensible for believers and through frequent communion.[36] Seen as a reformer, Schmemann's

---

36. Alexander Schmemann, *For the Life of the World: Sacraments and Orthodoxy* (Crestwood, NY: St. Vladimir's Seminary Press, 1995).

legacy has been very influential on American Orthodoxy but remains controversial in Russia.

Theology in Soviet and Post-Soviet Russia

The greatest flowering of modern Russian theology took place outside Russia, in the Russian emigration after the Bolshevik Revolution. The Revolution, as we saw in chapter 3, was totally hostile to religion, and Russian Orthodox Christians were forced into survival mode. The Moscow and Leningrad Theological Academies were reopened shortly after World War II, and it took time for them to develop an academic staff capable of serious scholarship; in the meantime, theology was strictly conservative. Things began to open up when, under Metropolitan Nikodim (Rotov), the Leningrad Theological Academy achieved a relatively high level by the 1960s and 1970s, with some of its theologians embracing surprisingly open and even modernist positions. Of course the scope of questions they could ask was severely restricted within the atheist state, as was the distribution of their ideas given the limitations on religious publishing, but it was especially important in training the next generation of leadership (including Patriarch Kirill).[37]

Alexander Men (see chapter 4) was the most notable religious writer of the Soviet period. Men was not a traditional theologian, and he did not have formal theological education; rather, he was mostly self-taught in theology. Vladimir Solovyov and other figures of the Russian religious renaissance were key influences, and he read very widely in theology, history, and the sciences, even familiarizing himself with the

37. L. E. Shaposhnikov, *Osnovnye techenie v russkoi pravoslavnoi mysli XIX–XXI vekov* [The Basic Currents in Russian Orthodox Thought, 19th–21st Centuries] (St. Petersburg: RKhGA, 2016). There is almost no literature on Russian theology during or after the Soviet period.

works of leading Western theologians. The main thrust of Men's theology was finding a way to communicate with his audience—that is, modern, secular people with a scientific education and little familiarity with religion. He wrote on a wide range of topics, including the interpretation of the Scriptures and the liturgy, but his monumental work *The History of Religion: In Search of the Way, the Truth, and the Life,* in seven volumes, is an exploration of the human search for meaning through history with the overarching argument that this search culminates in Christ.[38] The project was intended to speak in a context in which the official Marxist ideology (indoctrinated in public education) depicted religion as a byproduct of obsolete exploitative socioeconomic structures that was destined to disappear. Men, like Mircea Eliade, sought rather to show that the search for spiritual meaning was a persistent feature of human history and therefore a core part of what it means to be human. Men's vision of Orthodoxy was open, ecumenical, and engaged with the concerns of the contemporary world, which has made him popular in some circles and suspect in others.

Gradually, after the late 1980s, higher religious education in the theological academies, especially in Moscow and St. Petersburg, started a recovery in the new conditions of religious freedom. In 1993, the Moscow Patriarchate created a special Synodal Biblical-Theological Commission—an official body to develop Orthodox theology and to coordinate dialogue with other Christian churches worldwide. Regular discussions with Roman Catholics, Lutherans, and other Protestants through the ecumenical World Council of Churches, stimulated theological thought. The legacy of Russian pre-revolutionary and

38. The first volume has appeared in English: Alexander Men, *The Wellsprings of Religion,* trans. Alasdair Macnaughton (Yonkers, NY: St. Vladimir's Seminary Press, 2017).

émigré theology of the twentieth century, which became fully available only in the 1990s, was another major stimulus.

A new type of institution for Russia developed in the post-Soviet period, namely Orthodox universities, institutions of higher education that provided a general education rather than being theological schools only for training clergy. The first and the biggest was St. Tikhon's Orthodox University founded in Moscow in 1992 and funded partly by the Moscow Patriarchate. The university has numerous religious-related fields of study but also some general programs such as history and education, which are designed for everybody; there is also a Theological Institute, linked to the university, which is uniquely designed for training future priests.

In the same year, the St. John the Theologian University was created (now—the Russian Orthodox University). In addition to these, there is the Russian Christian Academy of the Humanities in St. Petersburg, which was co-founded by the Orthodox Church and other Christian denominations, being, therefore, more "pan-Christian" and ecumenical in orientation. In 2009, the Patriarchate established another major academic institution—SS. Cyril and Methodius Theological Institute of Graduate Studies—an attempt to create an up-to-date intellectual elite center beyond the traditional theological academies and seminaries.

By the 2010s, theology suddenly became one of the central issues of the Church's public profile: now the Church decided to promote theology *outside* ecclesiastic institutions, trying to make it a part of public secular higher education, and this initiative was supported by the state. A few theological departments were launched in state universities, and theology was legally approved as a full-fledged educational field of study similar to other academic subjects. This move was controversial, as critics vehemently labeled it as a trend toward clericalism, denied theology a status of an academic discipline, and declared the move a violation of the constitutional principle of separation of church and state. Why would not theology stay within private religious academies and schools, as before, and similar to a few Protestant or Catholic colleges, or Muslim madrasas, created across Russia after the end of the Soviet Union? The supporters of this innovation, in their turn, would refer to denominational theological departments in the public universities of some European countries, such as Germany, and the fact that Western theology tends to be an open intellectual enterprise compatible with current human and social sciences. They also argue that public universities were free to open parallel departments of Islamic, Judaic, Protestant, or Catholic theologies, in addition to Eastern Orthodox.

How can we assess this controversy? Will Orthodoxy's domination in the religious field allow this ideal of religious plurality to be sustained? Moreover, will the current level of theology allow it to be considered as a solid academic discipline similar to history or sociology?

The main issue, in the final analysis, is not so much the institutional status but the real intellectual level and content of Russian Christian theology. Since the intellectual opening after the end of the Soviet Union, some old and solid traditions have been restored, and some have been received from the émigré legacy described earlier in this chapter. There are books, journal articles, and courses with sophisticated analyses of such disciplines as patristics, liturgics, and church history. Such priorities now reflect some inherited predispositions: early Church Fathers, mostly Greek, have been an intellectual pillar of the Orthodox legacy, and the liturgical life of the church constituted the bulwark of the tradition in its broader sense.

Some other branches of Christian theology are, however, less developed. Although a solid church dogmatic handbook is available for students,[39] as well a series of undergraduate-level textbooks on various standard theological subjects, there are still few original works on particular branches—especially those highly requested and elaborated in Western Christianity such as anthropology, Christology, or ecclesiology. However, there is certainly a revived interest in some controversial theological issues that reflect the current sensitivities within the church and the society at large.

One example of such sensitivity is an esteemed senior professor of the Moscow Theological Academy, Alexey Osipov, whose lectures were sharply criticized in 2015 by the aforementioned Biblical-Theological Commission for containing ideas allegedly contradicting canonical dogmas. There were at least three such controversial issues. One was Osipov's emphasis, with reference to God's infinite mercy, on *apokatastasis*—the doctrine of eventual universal salvation of all, and thus the denial of eternal sufferings for sinners. This more open and inclusive interpretation that we have earlier referred to as supported by Sergius Bulgakov was challenged by the official critiques as not grounded in true Orthodox tradition. Another sensitive issue was Osipov's interpretation of the main Christian mystery, the Eucharist, as *not* implying the real transformation of bread and wine into Christ's flesh and blood but rather containing a "mystery of unification" of Christ with the "holy gifts." This interpretation was criticized as too close to the Protestant understanding of communion.[40] Yet another issue

---

39. Oleg Davydenkov, *Dogmaticheskoe bogoslovie* [Dogmatic theology] (Moscow: St. Tikhon's Orthodox University, 2013).
40. The issue of Eucharist, in many ways, has been central to the Russian discussions, and the case of Osipov was preceded by a few other debates publicly held throughout the last decades.

was Osipov's denial of obligatory baptism of infants, which in his view neared magic and was meaningless without consciously chosen faith. In all these cases Osipov started with opposing Roman Catholic teaching but apparently moved too far into the direction of Protestantism and, therefore, as the critics would say, came on the verge of heresy in Eastern Orthodox terms (though the word *heresy* was not pronounced and the whole statement of the Theology Commission was presented as "unofficial" criticism). Osipov passionately responded to accusations drawing upon a variety of early Christian sources. He was not fired from the theological academy and acquired some supporters. Overall, the debate revealed some new sensitivities within the understanding of core Christian concepts but also showed that the Church wanted to stay firm to protect its theological identity with an authoritarian discipline, although not going so far as to really punish the author of controversial theological ideas.

There were other theological debates with a lower profile but that revealed deeper significance. For example, theologians argued about what constitutes the very essence of Eastern Orthodox tradition, in particular, whether the teaching of Gregory Palamas about the divine energies can be qualified as a major foundation of Eastern Christian identity and not another form of deviation. A major contribution to the revival of the interest to Palamite theology has been the writings of Sergey Horujy (b. 1941), who, in the pre-revolutionary tradition, is a lay thinker, trained as physicist, then became a philosopher, and finally evolved into a self-fashioned but respected Orthodox theologian. His central concern has been anthropology. He started by criticizing the Western anthropological tradition as rationalistically limited and proposed an alternative "synergetic anthropology," in which he combined modern scientific concepts with a strong emphasis on Palamas's teaching about divine energies and *hesychasm* (the practice of contemplative prayer). In fact, Horujy's project has been one of a synthesis of science and theology; while remaining a secular philosopher in no way inclined to the mystical side of hesychasm, he has sought to appropriate some Orthodox theological ideas with the purpose to expand the human potential with spiritual experience.[41]

There have been other debates about particular issues in Christian eschatology, sacramental theology, and Christology, though these have been narrow issues limited to a group of elite theologians. In the field of twenty-first-century theology, a major enterprise must be mentioned, which has strongly stimulated Christian thought in Russia. This project was the new *Orthodox Encyclopedia*—a huge Russian-language publication with seventy-five planned volumes, over fifty of which have appeared by 2020, both in print and online, which brought together the best scholars and theologians (www.pravenc.ru/). Although the magnitude of the project was such that one cannot expect the same consistent quality in all entries, many of them contained fine scholarship and authentic reflections. This is true, for example, of the encyclopedia's entries related to biblical studies.

Characteristically, biblical studies has never been a strong priority in Russia as compared to its central place in Protestant theology, and this relative weakness remains. However, in addition to a few collections of essays,[42] there is another pro-

41. Sergey S. Horujy, *Practices of the Self and Spiritual Practices: Michel Foucault and the Eastern Christian Discourse*, ed. Kristina Stoeckl, trans. Boris Jakim (Grand Rapids: Eerdmans, 2015); Kristina Stoeckl, "New Frontiers in Russian Religious Philosophy: The Philosophical Anthropology of Sergey S. Horujy," *Russian Studies in Philosophy* 57 (2019): 3–16, and Horujy's articles translated for that special issue devoted to him.

42. Metropolitan Ilarion Alfeev, ed., *Sovremennaia bibleistika i predanie tserkvi* [Cur-

ject that is particularly important and crucial—the translation of the Bible into contemporary Russian language. The task of translation, which needs to be accurate, transparent, and spiritual, inevitably raises multiple disputes and interpretations, and requires in-depth research. As the translation issue was controversial in the nineteenth century, with competing projects sponsored by the Church itself and the Russian Bible Society,[43] so it remains now, with a number of new attempts made in the twentieth and twenty-first centuries. The question of linguistic modernization came up vigorously with the post-Soviet religious revival, and a few groups started enthusiastically to promote a current-language Russian version of both Scripture and liturgy. These reforms were, however, rejected by Church authorities in the 1990s as an inappropriately radical innovation. Therefore, the 1876 version of the Russian Bible, the so-called Synodal Bible, is still the official text of the Church; as for the liturgy, it is still officially served in old Church Slavonic.[44]

Yet, the Church needs the text written in current spoken Russian language to be available for the purpose of mission and for the believers. At the same time, the new translation cannot be just a simplified adaptation; it needs to be up-to-date in terms of academic accuracy, confirmed against current studies of archeology, history, exegesis (critical textual analysis), and other disciplines. The Russian Bible Society, a revived heir of the pre-revolutionary one, with its strong academic background, has become in the twenty-first century the central

rent Biblical Studies and Church Tradition] (Moscow: St. Cyril and Methodius Theological Institute of Post-Graduate Studies, 2017).

43. Stephen Batalden, *Russian Bible Wars: Modern Spiritual Translation and Cultural Authority* (Cambridge: Cambridge University Press, 2013).

44. On the issue of language in contemporary Russian Church, see B. Bennett, *Religion and Language in Post-Soviet Russia* (London: Routledge, 2011).

player in this work. In addition to a new Russian translation of the entire Bible, the Bible Society has continued the Scripture's translation into many languages of Russian minorities and neighboring peoples. It is also noteworthy that while the Bible Society maintained a close relationship with the Patriarchate of the Russian Orthodox Church, it also collaborated with other Christian groups, including Western, thus positioning itself as an ecumenical Christian enterprise.

Let us now have a look at how Russian Christian thought, in its broadest sense, is being developed in today's Russia—beyond the realm of theology produced by the academic elite. The central core of this thought is ecclesiology writ large, implying reflections about the meaning of the Church within the new, secular frame of modern culture, and about how the Church as an institution relates to modern societies built on new conceptions of individual autonomy.

This broad field of communicating with the changing world is relatively unexplored in Russian Christianity. It is still struggling with the sense of a certain exclusivity and with a particular tradition trying to preserve its special ethos, flavor, and aesthetic purity by protecting itself against other religions, cultures, and most importantly, against the "global secular culture" that is said to contradict Christianity's core values. This position, although it is based on strong traditional arguments, sometimes creates a model of a besieged fortress and prevents creativity. Controversial contemporary issues are largely avoided as irrelevant to the Russian context or treated with a staunch conservatism, such as issues surrounding gender equality: a Russian Orthodox feminist theology is nonexistent.

At the same time, the Church wants and needs to be *in* the world and *with* the world, and is cognizant of its mission. To succeed in keeping its high profile in society, it needs relevance and more inclusivity. It needs to appeal to broader social groups of actual and potential believers, most importantly the younger ones, who might find old ways obsolete and irrelevant.

Yet these social groups are diverse, and so is the Christian message. There are clerics and thinkers who develop openness and pastoral care appealing to modern individuals—those who start as "religiously unmusical" and seek "new birth" in the Church. The famous Russian Metropolitan Anthony Bloom of Sourozh, who served in England (see chapter 4), developed a practical, pastoral theology based on a worldview that was called "a theology of encounter"—meaning the encounter with God that dramatically defines personal being, while never creating a wall with the world. There is now beginning to emerge a younger generation of theologians who build on the legacy of twentieth-century Russian theology while also creatively engaged with current trends in Christian theology broadly speaking.[45]

Another highly sensitive issue where Christian intellectual energy has been invested in the first decades of the twenty-first century is that of historical memory—memory of the trauma of communist persecutions and memory about the significance of 1917 Revolution and the entire Soviet period. The Nazi experience and the extermination of the Jews led to a deep reinterpretation of Christian identity and made possible an elaborated post-Holocaust theology in the West. Although the context and experience of the Orthodox Church under Stalin's Terror was very different, it has developed no theo-

---

45. Antony Bloom, *Encounter* (London: Darton, Longman and Todd, 2005). Two representatives of the younger generation of creative theologians include Alexander Filonenko (from Kharkiv, Ukraine) and Oleg Davydov (Moscow Theological Academy). Their major works are published in Russian.

logical comprehension of this historical trauma; nothing like a "post-Gulag" theology has yet developed. Rather, it has explored this painful memory more through the remembering of those who suffered, writing their lives, and canonizing them as saints. In a way, hagiography—narratives about the saints—became a language of Russian Christian thought.

In this mapping of current Russian Christian thought, where do we place the Church leadership—the patriarchs and the upper hierarchy? They tended to distance themselves from ultra-conservatives who fought "apocalyptic" modernization, as well as from the radical revivalists (see chapter 6). They have been trying to develop a moderate conservative agenda, supporting up-to-date theological language (as they were well-versed in it and had constant communications with Western churches), but also promoting a largely protective stance against global secular liberalism.

Kirill Gundiaev, patriarch since 2009, has played an important role (see chapter 4). He mobilized his followers to create several interesting official documents, a sort of "official theology," particularly in the realm of social doctrine, with the help of the Synodal Theological Commission. These documents became milestones in history of Eastern Christianity—which had never before produced any such documents in this form, which is more typical of Roman Catholicism. In fact, this endeavor was an attempt to officially solve the controversies that existed in all topical issues of contemporary life. The most important such document was the Social Doctrine (more precisely called "The Bases of the Social Concept"); another one—the document on Christianity and human rights; and a few shorter documents on various issues such as euthanasia, juvenile courts, surrogate motherhood, ecology, blasphemy, and so on.[46] These texts were written in contemporary language and show the active involvement in the issues of the current world; they all contain elements of theological reasoning and in many ways may be seen as an Orthodox reaction to thousands of similar documents produced by Catholic and Protestant theologians in the course of the last century. Although their overall position is conservative, "The Bases of the Social Concept" is a carefully worded document that seeks to engage tradition with very contemporary problems.

In the Social Doctrine, the Church theologians promote the idea of a nation as a legitimate Christian community; justify political neutrality, non-interference, but close collaboration in Church-state relations; justify protest against rulers in case they blatantly violate Christian values; condemn homosexuality as a malaise and abortion as murder; fail to unambiguously condemn the death penalty; endorse traditional gender differences; endorse private property but call for a socially oriented economy; affirm the human causes of the ecological crisis, asserting that it is ultimately a spiritual problem of selfishness and "irresponsible consumption"; reject secular liberalism and globalism; and articulate an active involvement of the Church in public life (in contrast with isolationist Christian world-renouncement). Human rights, in the document devoted to the topic, was characterized as a secular Western invention that has some resemblances with Christian values but is contrary to them on key points. In other documents, the issue of protecting "traditional values" has become central.

One of the most prominent and prolific voices of the official intellectual elite of the Moscow Patriarchate has been Metropolitan Hilarion Alfeyev (b. 1966). Hilarion came of age in

46. English-language versions of the key documents can be found at https://mospat.ru/en/documents.

the late Soviet period and received his doctorate in Patristics at Oxford University under Metropolitan Kallistos (Ware). He has served as the chair of the Department of External Church Relations, the position Patriarch Kirill held before his election as patriarch, and he is a musical composer as well as theologian. In addition to participating in the above projects (e.g., the Social Doctrine), he wrote a number of studies on Eastern Christian Church Fathers (Isaac the Syrian, Gregory the Theologian, Simeon the New Theologian). A prolific author, he produced a general brief introduction to Orthodox theology as well as a multi-volume introduction to Orthodoxy that treats history, theology, and liturgy, aiming to represent the contemporary vision of the entire teaching and practice of the Orthodox Church. Finally, he has also written a six-volume study of the life and teaching of Jesus Christ. Much of his work is translated into English.[47]

Some of the positions expressed in Metropolitan Hilarion's writings have been criticized from two sides: as too liberal and innovative for some or, conversely, too fundamentalist and reactionary for others. Overall, this constitutes, in fact, what is called pragmatic moderate conservatism. These teachings cannot be enforced as mandatory for all parishes, priests, and believers because, no matter how prominent Hilarion is, he is still just an individual theologian whose writings do not have the same level of authority as documents adopted by the Councils or issued by the ruling Synod. Nevertheless, Hilarion's work provides a certain reference point to bring together the

47. Hilarion Alfeyev, *The Mystery of Faith: An Introduction to the Teaching and Spirituality of the Orthodox Church* (London: Darton, Longman and Todd, 2002); *The Spiritual World of Isaac the Syrian* (Kalamazoo, MI: Cistercian Publications, 2000); *Christ the Conqueror of Hell* (Crestwood, NY: St. Vladimir's Seminary Press, 2009); *Orthodox Christianity,* 5 vols. (Crestwood, NY: St. Vladimir's Seminary Press, 2011–2019); and so far two volumes of *Jesus Christ: His Life and Teaching* (Crestwood, NY: St. Vladimir's Seminary Press, 2018–).

diversity of views and tastes within the Russian Christian community.

In conclusion, an original Russian Orthodox theology began in the mid-nineteenth century. It began within the Church's academies, where scholars developed a variety of fields of study such as that of the liturgy and the Church Fathers, but this theological legacy did not have much influence outside Russia and mostly stopped in 1917. At the same time, lay intellectuals began a parallel tradition, stemming from the Slavophiles to Solovyov, which flourished after the Russian Revolution, especially with Sergius Bulgakov. This approach, which was rooted in the Eastern Church Fathers but also engaged with modern philosophy, was challenged by proponents of the "neo-patristic synthesis," which claimed greater legitimacy by ostensibly basing itself on the authentically Orthodox sources. This view of Orthodox theology was profoundly influential among Russian émigrés and other Orthodox Christians. Since the collapse of communism, Orthodox theologians in Russia have sought to reconcile these three divergent traditions—the pre-revolutionary academic one, the lineage of Solovyov and Bulgakov, and that of the neo-patristic synthesis, while also engaging with recent intellectual trends in the West. While many foundational works have been produced, such as those of Hilarion Alfeyev and the *Orthodox Encyclopedia*, many younger Russian theologians themselves would admit that Russian theology has thus far been playing a game of catch-up for the time lost during the Soviet period and are only now beginning to develop new creative articulations of their faith for the modern world.

6

Russian Christianity in Twenty-First Century: Post-Soviet Plurality and Sociopolitical Significance

Christ the Savior cathedral, the main sacred building of Russian Christianity today, dominates the landscape of downtown Moscow. It is situated not far from the Kremlin, on the bank of the Moscow River, and its massive gilded domes dominate the skyline of central Moscow. The huge building was restored in the 1990s literally out of nothing—or, rather, by the power of memory.

The enormous cathedral was first conceived in the aftermath and in commemoration of the victory over Napoleon in the war of 1812, and its purpose was to glorify the Orthodox Russian nation's historical triumph. It took decades for the construction to be approved, designed, and completed, and the cathedral was finally consecrated in the 1880s. After the 1917

Revolution, it continued to dominate the landscape and thus became a challenge to the communist visual propaganda. The communist ideology could not tolerate a powerful structure reflecting competing values.

Christ the Savior Cathedral, Moscow (c. 1903). *Image courtesy of the Library of Congress.*

Thus the Soviet authorities decided to blow up the building completely and to replace it with a gigantic monument to communism, the Palace of the Soviets, designed in terms of the then hegemonic constructivist architectural style, with an enormous statue of Vladimir Lenin on the top of it. This change would be a blatant symbol of an epic turn of history, a powerful metaphor of the victory of reason over the "opiate" of religion, according to Karl Marx's famous saying, and also a metaphor of a cardinal change in the nature of the political regime. The old regime and the old culture were to be destroyed, and the cathedral was thus both physically and symbolically demolished in 1931 by a few blasts. The terrain was completely cleaned up. However, the ambitious construction plans on the spot proved to be unrealistic and were dropped. Eventually, a huge open-air swimming pool was opened at the cleared site. The communist government destroyed hundreds of churches across the country, but the case of Christ the Savior church was certainly the most spectacular and symbolic of all.[1]

In a powerfully symbolic act soon after the collapse of the Soviet Union in 1991, the Church and the new rulers decided to restore the cathedral. The restoration, carefully based on original plans and consecrated by the patriarch in 1996, was indeed the central event symbolizing a historical closure of one era and a significant return to the past—or, maybe to a totally new era. Thanks to massive investments by both the government and new private businesses, the cathedral reappeared, as from a dream, on exactly the same place where it stood before the demolition, and became again one of Moscow's major landmarks. While it yields in beauty, as the experts say, to many other churches, it is striking in its grandeur and magnificence. Its status as the main national cathedral is uncontested, and the patriarchal services are conducted there on Christmas and Easter in the presence of the highest state dignitaries. It therefore works again as a symbol of the "official" Russian Chris-

---

1. Konstantin Akinsha and Grigorij Kozlov, *The Holy Place: Architecture, Ideology, and History in Russia* (New Haven: Yale University Press, 2007).

tianity—a particular mode of religion that combines canonical orthodoxy and political influence. In a way, this was an attempt to revive the old model of the Church's place in society. In many other ways, though, as we shall see, the situation was quite new. The status and the sacral splendor of the Moscow Christ the Savior cathedral acquired new meanings.

Post-Soviet Growth and New Challenges

As discussed in chapter 3, 1988 was the millennial anniversary of the Baptism of Rus by Prince Vladimir. By that time, the Soviet empire was already in deep crisis, and the liberal policies of the last communist party leader, Mikhail Gorbachev, already undermined the ideological sway of atheism. Gradually, religion became more and more welcome and even fashionable. Christianity was recognized, at least, as a formative source of culture, national consciousness, social morality, and, finally, some "spiritual values" alternative to the outgoing communist ideology.

The 1988 celebrations made obvious and completed the semi-hidden evolution of the last Soviet decades. Patriarch Pimen (1970–1990) and the members of the Holy Synod, the ruling ecclesiastical body, met with Gorbachev at the Kremlin, and the press was full of triumphant glorifications of the national religious tradition. This moment started a new period, which was a period of revival, renewal, and, in some sense, of the reinvention of religion. Another milestone event in this line was a reunification of the Moscow Patriarchate with the Church Abroad in 2007, which had broken communion with the Moscow Patriarchate eighty years earlier over its compromise with the Soviet regime (see chapter 4). This act of reunification looked like an inspiring symbolic closure of a period of schisms and troubles.

The Church had to come to terms with the Soviet past in many ways. It was a hard, tragic, and contradictory memory—memory of persecution, resistance, and collaboration at the same time. Above all, the Church had to fathom the depth of the trauma and the amount of loss. This was perceived in Christian terms as martyrdom. The Church made an enormous effort to make known the names of those Christians—bishops, priests, monks, nuns, and laity—who were murdered by the communists or perished in Stalin's camps. After a careful investigation of each case, some of the persecuted people were canonized as "new martyrs and confessors." The number of the new martyrs—close to 1,800 as of the end of 2010s—is far fewer than the number of those persecuted, and yet such a number of fully canonized saints was unprecedented in the history of Christianity.[2]

The Russian Orthodox Church was said to have been resurrected on the blood of the martyrs. Indeed, the post-Soviet period showed fascinating statistics concerning the institutional growth of the Church. In 1988, the date of de facto cardinal turn in government policy (three years before the official collapse of the Soviet Union), there were 76 dioceses, 6,893 parishes, 6,674 priests, and 22 monasteries in the Russian Orthodox Church (including the Soviet Union and all other

2. See Karin Christensen, *The Making of the New Martyrs of Russia: Soviet Repressions in Orthodox Memory* (London: Routledge, 2017). The themes in this chapter are developed in Alexander Agadjanian, *Turns of Faith, Search for Meaning: Orthodox Christianity and Post-Soviet Experience* (Frankfurt am Main: Peter Lang, 2014). See also Zoe Knox and Anasasia Mitrofanova, "The Russian Orthodox Church," in *Eastern Christianity and Politics in the Twenty-First Century*, ed. Lucian Leustean (New York: Routledge, 2014), 38-66; Geraldine Fagan, *Believing in Russia: Religious Policies after Communism* (London: Routledge, 2014).

countries).[3] By the mid-2010s, the Moscow Patriarchate (including Central Asia and the post-Soviet countries of Ukraine, Belarus, Moldova, and some other places) had grown to include 303 dioceses (partly by reducing the size of large ones), 36,878 churches and other places where liturgy is held, 34,774 priests, and 944 monasteries.[4]

In a quarter century after the collapse of communism, the institutional structures and personnel of the Russian Orthodox Church have grown at least four to six times, and forty times in the case of monasteries. Some skeptics would find these official figures, coming from the Patriarchate, inflated. Some of the parishes or monasteries might be too small or existing just "on paper" (which certainly happens), and the multiplication of the dioceses may be interpreted as reflecting ambitious ecclesiastical politics (which is partly true). Overall, however, one cannot deny that the growth has been truly remarkable. The Church became a powerful administrative body spreading across Russia, within its new borders, and beyond them—especially in the former Soviet lands.

Another visible and palpable fact of the post-Soviet resurgence was the growth of church property. First, there was a large-scale restitution of old estates, buildings, and facilities that used to belong to the Church and had been confiscated by the Soviet government in the twentieth century. Under the Soviets, many old church buildings that were not destroyed but served as storehouses, clubs, or government agencies were now returned to the Church. The Church also reclaimed other buildings that had been turned into museums. Hundreds of

3. Figures appear in the speech by Kirill, the patriarchal *locum tenens*, on January 27, 2009, with reference to the report of the Council of 1988, https://tinyurl.com/saqu6dd.

4. Report by Patriarch Kirill at the Bishops Council, on November 29, 2017, https://tinyurl.com/rk49mok.

churches were restored or renovated. Most of these renovations were because of local donations—either by many ordinary donors or by a few or single wealthy supporters or businesses; economic liberalization produced this new capitalist type of people and firms.[5] However, the state, in most cases local authorities, was also active, either in coordinating massive support or even in contributing directly, as in the case of the Christ the Savior cathedral, which was partially funded by the office of Moscow mayor, or through the special funds allocated to the restoration of churches as historical monuments.

Restitution became law in 2010: the Church's claim for old real estate became fully legitimate, though this move was criticized by many because the Church's lobbying pressure was seen to be motivated by economic interests. Since many of the church buildings were turned into museums during the Soviet Union, the restitution cases produced disputes between the secular museums and the Church and their respective supporters among the population. The Christ the Savior cathedral was not such a case, obviously; it was newly rebuilt from nothing. But a great number of monasteries—like the Solovki fortress-monastery in the Far North or the New Jerusalem outside Moscow—became the cases of real contestation; both Solovki and New Jerusalem turned completely into monasteries administered by the Church, while the museums were built (or supposed to be built) outside the monastic space, in separate buildings.

There were other cases where these contestations occurred and became high-profile public events. In 2017, St. Isaac's cathedral, built in the nineteenth century and a central architectural landmark of St. Petersburg, made the news when the

5. Tobias Koellner, *Practicing Without Belonging? Entrepreneurship, Morality, and Religion in Contemporary Russia* (Berlin: LIT, 2012).

government decided to transfer it from a status of "state museum and monument" to the Church. This case became a *cause célèbre* as thousands of local people and organizations mobilized against such a decision while thousands of others came to the streets in support of it. The row in Russia's "northern capital" was so great that the authorities decided to freeze (at least, for a time) the process of restitution. The argument of museums, in this and other cases, was that the Church would not be able to properly maintain the religious buildings. Also, the restitution would mean privatization and therefore reduce access to objects of cultural heritage for those who do not consider themselves as belonging to the Church.

Similar debates emerged when the Church claimed some famous ancient icons now displayed in museums. Icons play a central role in Eastern Orthodox worship, but would the Church be able to preserve them in the way a professional museum would? The debates, in how they were framed, touched upon the very deep issue of religion's place in today's secular society: What is the link between Christianity and the culture at large? How is this link perceived by today's Russians, after a century of forced, most outrageous secularism? Is Russian culture still traditionally Christian by roots and essence, or is Christianity just a part of a broad, plural, and predominantly secular culture? Even though the common feeling has been that religion should receive back what was taken by force, the issue of post-communist religious resurgence was far from straightforward. There were cases of reconciliation when museums and the Church could avoid conflict and find a mutual solution. Such was the case of a former St. Nicholas church that was turned long ago into the reserve stock of the famous Tretiakov gallery—the biggest collection of Russian art in Moscow. The church held the highly revered Vladimir icon of the Mother of God (see chapter 1). The Patriarchate and the gallery agreed to reopen the church with regular services and a parish while the space continues to serve as part of the museum. The famous icon thus combined both functions—a museum artifact and the object of religious devotion.

Besides restorations and restitutions, the post-Soviet period saw hundreds of new church buildings, big and small, sprung up everywhere. To be sure, this construction took place at the same time as the emergence of new or restored mosques, synagogues, Buddhist temples and monasteries, and churches of various Christian denominations, although the latter happened less in the capital or major cities, but mostly in regions where people of different faiths lived. At the same time, the new Orthodox structures outnumbered all the rest taken together. As the Church's public voice became stronger, there was a widely promoted program of creating as many small church buildings as needed to be available within walking distance of where people live. This ambition was strongly criticized as utopian but supported in some cities including Moscow, where two hundred new churches were set to be built under a special program cosponsored by the Church, the state, and businesses.[6]

And again, as in the case of the restitution, there were a number of challenges and arguments for and against. Some of the ecological activists and local denizens resisted the plan of church construction in the suburbs, in the middle of parks or next to apartment buildings. In one such case, in 2015, at the Torfianka Park at Moscow's northern outskirts, one rivalry over the plans to build a new church mobilized activists from both Orthodox and secular groups; the police had to be

6. See this story on "Orthodox Christianity" website at: http://orthochristian.com/107926.html.

involved, and finally, as a compromise, an alternative place was allocated. Another contested case was the rebuilding of the landmark St. Catherine's church in the city of Ekaterinburg. Similar to Moscow's Christ the Savior, the church was completely destroyed by the Soviets in the 1930s. When, in 2019, the decision was made to restore the church in a different place (the original place was inaccessible) in a downtown park, thousands of local citizens mobilized against the plan in the name of protecting the park and the urban space. After the clashes between the protesters and the supporters of the construction, the city authorities decided to stop the original plans and find a different location.

We see that the post-Soviet revival of religion is a complex phenomenon. The contestations prove that the place of religion in today's Russia is not a mechanical return to the old times of the Orthodox empire; at the same time, the revival does not reflect a picture of religious indifference or a completely secular, pluralistic society. Surely, the boom in restitution and construction can be understood as a truly symbolic marker of a religious revival and, therefore, of a new period of history of Russian Christianity. We can say that history struck back, the pendulum moved in the direction opposite to the long era of Soviet persecutions, and a substantial symbolic demand for religion legitimated the growing visibility of religious structures.

For many, this new era resonated as a direct return to the past. Practically all new church buildings, in their exterior design and interior layout and decoration, replicated traditional pre-Revolutionary architectural styles, almost completely ignoring new trends developed worldwide during the twentieth century in both secular and religious architecture. This fact explains the meaning of the revival as it was perceived: Orthodoxy is a millennial tradition, and we must return back to this tradition; therefore it should be revived in a supposedly "unchanged" form, as it should be the return to the moment when it was cruelly stopped by the 1917 Revolution. "Restoration" was the true name of this project. The time between then and now—the Soviet period of 1917 to 1991—was perceived as a dark interlude, a black hole to be memorialized only as a period of sufferings and martyrdom.

To assess the real significance of the post-Soviet revival, however, we need to turn to other facts and impressions beyond the fascinating and flamboyant construction of new buildings or the growth of church properties. How did the weight of the Church in the public square change beyond the reappearance of traditional onion-shaped domes in architectural profiles of the cities and the countryside? Do we live now in a new era that cannot be seen as a simple restoration of a supposedly pious Christian past? This is the main question to which we will now turn.

By all evidence, the *political* profile of the Church also became visible and omnipresent. According to all surveys, the Church was among the most trusted institutions in Russia, Ukraine, Belarus, Moldova, Georgia, and Armenia, the six countries of the former Soviet Union with dominant Eastern Christian traditions. The high level of trust in religion was similar in all post-Soviet lands, whether Christian or Muslim. As restoration of the old or the construction of the new buildings could be seen across the former Union, so was the growth of the religions' real cultural profile and political impact. For example, the Georgian Orthodox Church became the leading identity-forming institution in the post-Soviet Republic of Georgia and the Armenian Apostolic Church in Armenia.[7] The Roman Catholic Church played a somewhat similar role in Lithuania, as did the Lutheran churches in Latvia and Estonia, although these Baltic countries, which soon became members of the European Union, are much more secularized and have adopted a more neutral, distanced model of church-state relationships. In the Muslim countries of Central Asia and in Azerbaijan, Islam flourished as a source of culture and identity, but the ruling elites were quite determined to prevent the uncontrolled growth of Islam's political role, promoting an "allowed," docile Islam and crushing any kind of Muslim opposition that was labeled as "extremist."[8] Within Russia proper, in regions with large Muslim populations, such as Tatarstan and Bashkortostan, in the Middle Volga, and in the Northern Caucasus, the situation was similar: mosques were being built (some of the same stature as the Christ the Savior cathedral in Moscow), the role of Muslim institutions and clerics has been high, and religion has been a major source of ethnic identity, but there has been a cautious promotion of "traditional" Islam and resistance to forms of Islam that can be radicalized.[9]

But let us return back to Russian Orthodoxy. With substantial economic power, the Church, if taken as a social institution, became one of the biggest land and real estate owners, an influential ideological institution, and, therefore, a prominent political player. The patriarch has always been listed among the top ten members of the ruling elite and influential political

7. On the religious developments in the Caucasus, see A. Agadjanian, A. Jodicke, and E. van der Zweerde, eds., *Religion, Nation and Democracy in the South Caucasus* (London: Routledge, 2014).

8. Adeeb Khalid, *Islam after Communism: Religion and Politics in Central Asia* (Berkeley: University of California Press, 2007).

9. Shireen Hunter, *Islam in Russia: The Politics of Identity and Security* (London: Routledge, 2004); Galina Yemelianova, *Radical Islam in the Former Soviet Union* (London: Routledge, 2009).

figures, even though the Church officially abstained from politics. In the provinces, Orthodox bishops are influential local leaders whom the local governments cannot ignore. Private Christian academies, seminaries, and schools grew swiftly. The introduction of religion-related classes in public schools turned into law in 2012, although students and parents have the right to choose among a few options including the "secular ethics." Public universities started introducing theology as a recognized academic discipline.

The news about Orthodox hierarchs, bishops councils, the moral debates with references to "Orthodox values" or "Orthodox morality," have been constantly present on TV and the internet.[10] The circulation of Orthodox canonical and historical books as well as numerous booklets, newspapers, and websites has been incredible. Although this growing public influence has been controversial and in some cases might have contradicted the constitutional principle of separation of church and state (we will return to this issue later), the fact of such new visibility cannot be contested.

The international presence of the Church is another dimension of this new visibility. The Church retains an old imperial outreach and a massive following in former Soviet lands. The Russian Orthodox Church of the Moscow Patriarchate dominates the religious landscape in Belarus and Moldova. (Below we will turn to the special case of Ukraine.) The Church also holds a significant presence in Western Europe, although a number of communities remained under the Patriarchate of Constantinople instead of Moscow. The Moscow Patriarchate has only a handful of parishes in North America, but there is a significant presence of churches of the Russian tradition

---

10. The Orthodox TV channel "Spas" (*Savior*) got the status of a national free channel, officially funded by private donations and with no advertising.

through the Russian Church Abroad (now semi-autonomous under the Moscow Patriarchate) and the Orthodox Church in America (granted autocephaly by Moscow in 1970). The Russian Church has parishes across Asia and Australia. It keeps real estate and a residence in the Holy Land. All this endows Russian Orthodoxy with a significant international agency. This agency may be used by the Russian state in its international relations, becoming an important part of Russia's "soft power" that promotes Russian interests and cultural legacy. At the same time, the Church has its own interests beyond being the state's agent. It is very active in interchurch networks, such as the World Council of Churches, the Inter-Orthodox meetings, and bilateral communications with other religious bodies worldwide.

Such is, overall, the undeniable if not uncontested revival of the Russian Orthodox Christianity in post-Soviet times.

Going in Depth: Mentality and Behavior of Today's Christians

The revival of the Orthodox Church in post-Soviet Russia can only partly be told in terms of numbers of church buildings or the patriarch's political weight. What happened behind this striking visibility—behind multiplying churches, news references, religiously staged political ceremonies, and the omnipresence of religious symbols? How did the masses of the population react to this tectonic shift from official atheism to religious resurgence? While we speak primarily of the Russians, we also keep in mind, of course, the Ukrainians, Belarusians, Moldovans, and all other Orthodox followers scattered across the former Soviet Union. What have been the changes in their beliefs and practices? The main question can be worded as follows: Was the revival just a project staged "from above," in a search for strong national symbols that were supposed to replace the disintegrating Marxist-Leninist ideology, or was it buttressed "from below," at the level of popular ideas and behavior?

It goes without saying that the promotion of Orthodoxy as a national religion could not be simply "staged" without a powerful popular quest. The late 1980s to early 1990s was, indeed, a profound turning point in mass consciousness. The communist ideology crumbled quickly. For sure, the process was complex: the ideology had already lost some relevance throughout the course of Soviet rule, while, at the same time, its particular and important fragments survived the Union here and there. However, as a comprehensive, cohesive system, supported by the apparatus of the state, it disappeared in just a few months. The liberalization brought about an explosion of openness and information, as many old ideological taboos were removed.

The taboo on religion was one of the strongest. For millions of Soviet people, the Bible, the Quran, and other religious literature were completely unavailable. Now they swamped people's homes. Earlier censored or forbidden books of all kinds followed; symbols and images poured into the public space—bookstores, TV screens, institutions, then on the internet—and this explosion created a totally new communicative environment providing a plethora of things with the irresistible lure of formerly prohibited truths. People were rediscovering the spiritual dimension of life, in contrast to a rueful routine of formerly official Marxist materialism.

After all, religion was considered as a means of reconnecting to what has been lost, forgotten, or blocked before. Reconnecting with "the lost culture of the past" became a powerful mechanism of identity construction. Yet we know that the past is always manifold, and the "reconnected truths" might vary and sometimes be contradictory. For example, for some people religion was the tool to be reconnected with world culture, from which the Soviet Union was cut off by the Iron Curtain. World culture presumed "universal human values"—one of the most circulated expressions in the public debates of the early 1990s. The universal human values, were an antithesis to the Marxist "class values," or specific, idiosyncratic "socialist values" or "communist values" as opposed to all the rest, as they were promoted in the Soviet Union. Religion—in an unspecified, non-denominational, cross-cultural sense—was now considered a repository of these human, humane values, with a special emphasis on individual, personal needs—something that was desperately lacking in the Soviet class-ridden, militant, collectivistic worldview.

The association of religion with universal values and universal spirituality was, however, only one possible version of the new interest in religion. It was fitting to urban intellectuals who reacted against the rigid communist materialism—and this process started long before in the Soviet underground. A contrary and perhaps more powerful motive of religious sensibility was nationalism, the national nostalgia that needed a strong spiritual and emotional underpinning. The wreckage of the Union was accompanied and largely provoked by the rise of strong nationalisms in all Soviet republics and in smaller ethnic communities. The centrifugal impulse started in peripheral regions that wanted independence from the imperial center, and this center was firmly associated with Moscow and Russia as a colonial power. Therefore, national religious traditions became prominent parts of anti-Soviet nationalism everywhere—in the Baltic States, Ukraine, the Caucasus, and other parts of the Soviet Empire. This national-religious link was not just an invention of the nation-building elites but a general feeling. Across the Soviet Union, before and after its formal collapse, millions of people associated themselves symbolically with the ethnic and national past to support their individual and collective identity.

Russian Orthodox Christianity also acquired such symbolic agency of national empowerment. In the case of Russia, this process was more reactive—Russian nationalism was a response to local nationalisms tearing the Russia-led Union apart. It might seem that Russian Orthodoxy, associated with the imperial center, was comfortable with the imperial structure of the Union and would be distant from nationalism. Indeed, the Soviet Kremlin continuously propagated internationalist, transnational communist ideology. Yet the matter was more complex; in fact, within Russia proper, a stream of Russian ethnoreligious nationalism emerged in the latter decades of Soviet history as a semi-hidden opposition to Soviet official internationalism. This Russian nationalism with Orthodox references was muted by official propaganda, although it received support from a part of the ruling elite.[11] It also manifested in the rising interest to old Russian churches, seen as a sort of ethnography museum. An organization called the Society of Protection of the Places of Memory, then *Pamiat'* Society (Memory Society) was created as a channel of this latent, semi-hidden Russian nostalgia; the association's function was to keep and restore the cultural and religious legacy of pre-Soviet Russia.

The end of the Union and the explosion of anti-Soviet and anti-Russian movements across the empire made Russian

11. Nikolai Mitrokhin, *Russkaia partiia: Dvizhenie russkikh natsionalistov v SSSR. 1953-1985* [The Russian Party: Russian Nationalism in the USSR, 1953–1985] (Moscow: Novoe literaturnoe obozrenie, 2003).

nationalism a thriving and now emancipated cultural force, and Orthodox religious nationalism became a strong part of it. In a critical time of wreckage and transition, religious nationalism became a strong underpinning of identity. The *Pamiat'* society evolved into a militant nationalist group with anti-liberal and anti-Semitic overtones. New groups of religious nationalists emerged promoting strong anti-Catholic and anti-Protestant sentiments, but also rejected what was perceived as anti-Christian liberal Western values. They were also strongly anti-Muslim, responding to the rise of Muslim separatism and militancy, as well as the growth of immigration from Muslim areas of the former Soviet Union to Russia. The Orthodox nationalists created a nostalgic image of a perfect Orthodox society that they placed back into the seventeenth or the nineteenth century. These groups "nationalized" Christianity, making of it a sort of purely Russian spirituality, asserting that Russia remained the last stronghold of true Christian spirituality.[12] Some extreme ideologues went as far as to proclaim Jesus Christ and Virgin Mary ethnic Russians.[13]

A famous event that emboldened Russian patriotism was the canonization of the last tsar, Nicholas II, in 2000. The Church canonized the Tsar and his entire family who were murdered by the Bolsheviks in Ekaterinburg in the midst of the Civil War, on the night of July 16, 1918. The official canonization took place at the Bishops Council, and the royal family was canonized at the same time as the "new martyrs." The royal family, however, was not canonized as martyrs since they were

12. Such nationalist ideology had already developed before the 1917 Revolution; see John Strickland, *The Making of Holy Russia: The Orthodox Church and Russian Nationalism before the Revolution* (Jordanville, NY: Holy Trinity, 2013).

13. On the merger of ethnic and religious identities, see Vyacheslav Karpov, Elena Lisovskaya, and David Barry, "Ethnodoxy: How Popular Ideologies Fuse Religious and Ethnic Identities," *Journal for the Scientific Study of Religion* 41 (2012): 638–55.

killed for political, not religious reasons; they were canonized as "passion bearers," like Russia's first saints Boris and Gleb, for the Christ-like way in which they bore their suffering and death. In the process, the Bishops Council sought to ensure the canonization was neither perceived as sanctifying monarchy as such, nor Nicholas II as a ruler. Overall, the celebration of the "new martyrs" as Orthodox saints was the Church's response to the communist persecutions. Yet the tsar and his family's case was special. Despite the Church's efforts, the canonization of the royal family inspired the right-wing monarchists who vehemently rejected both the communist past and the liberal-democratic prospects of Russia.

The militant nationalist groups might be a marginal phenomenon by itself. Yet they were quite visible and prominent in the media. They also revealed a less aggressive and yet widespread feeling of natural, endemic, or even genetic religious belonging to Orthodox Christianity among millions of Russians or Ukrainians (although "national" meant different things in these two cases). The "national"—though not necessarily "nationalist"—motive was central, indeed, in the people's identification; the massive interest in religion was not deeply spiritual or "purely religious." According to many surveys throughout the post-Soviet period, 70 to 80 percent of the Russian population would call themselves "Orthodox Christians." These figures exceeded the share of Russians who, according to the same polls, "believed in God." This paradox—having more "Orthodox Christians" than "believers"—can be explained sociologically: for most of the people the national faith responds, above all, to cultural identity needs, rather than religious needs. The seven decades of official atheism—coupled with a more global trend toward secularization—had its deep impact. Most people could not really engage in religious ideas or practices they had never heard of from their parents or even grandparents, but they easily identified with religion as a "marker" presumably defining national identity.[14]

How can we define millions of people who shared this mindset? We can call them "heritage Orthodox" or "cultural Orthodox"—in the same way as when we speak of "cultural Catholics," such as in France. Would this be an appropriate comparison? What can we say of the "religion" of such people? We can say that the statistics of religious revival reflected, overall, this type of religiosity that sociologists call "minimal" or "thin"—without a deeper knowledge or a stronger commitment, and mostly animated by the feeling of belonging to a loosely held national collectivity. It is what can be called belonging without believing.[15]

Thus, looking over the religious landscape, three trends have been identified: those described as universalist religious seekers, the marginal but active religious nationalists, and the mass of "nominal" believers. We now should add a fourth group after the first decade of the post-Soviet history and well into the twenty-first century: people who really care about observing Christian practices, who feel themselves deeply committed, who are trying to follow commandments seriously and without reducing faith to nation or loosely defined cultural tradition. This is only a minority—maybe no more than 5 percent—who are more or less active religiously: reading and discussing the Scripture, fasting, observing feasts, coming to

14. For the sociological analysis of the post-Soviet Russian Orthodox identity, see, for example, Zoe Knox, *Russian Society and the Orthodox Church: Religion in Russia after Communism* (London: Routledge, 2009); Katja Richters, *The Post-Soviet Russian Orthodox Church: Politics, Culture and Greater Russia* (London: Routledge, 2012).

15. Opposite to the notion of "believing without belonging" that some sociologists have used to characterize religion in Western Europe, see Grace Davie, *Religion in Britain: A Persistent Paradox,* 2nd ed. (Oxford: Wiley-Blackwell, 2015).

communion on Sundays, and contributing regular donations to their congregations.[16]

The observant minority—what is called "in-churched" (*votserkovlennye*) in Russia—is not a single group or type. It may include people of different temper and behavior: some more liberal and open, and some—perhaps, most of them—rather conservative and forming a special church subculture. They usually come from two groups of people. One group is traditional believers who kept the faith through the atheist times and are usually linked to rural folk or urban environments, relatively less educated. Another group is made of more educated recent converts, similar to those "born-again" who can be found elsewhere, who re-discovered deep Christian spirituality both in books and in their own hearts; they chose to join the Church and observe practices or even take monastic vows rather than staying outside of it and loosely associating with it. In today's Russia, the real churchgoers from one of these two groups, or sometimes, their combination, define the typical parish or congregation.

It is true, however, that well beyond this practicing minority, there was a massive upsurge of people's involvement in so called life-cycle religious rituals, such as baptisms, weddings, and funerals. These rituals may be massively observed by those "minimal" Christians who otherwise are not very involved in the Church. They would also participate—less frequently, however—at the two major Christian holidays, Christmas and Easter. The participation in life-cycle rituals and holidays—in contrast to the regular performance of communion, prayers,

16. The percentage of those really deeply involved and *always* observing are still smaller, perhaps, not more than 2 to 4 percent in Russia. The figures are higher in Ukraine, which was more religiously active even in Soviet times for historical reasons.

or fasting—reflects in most cases not so much a deep religious commitment but rather a symbolic tribute to collective national feelings and tradition. In the Russian Church, the formal membership in congregations is loose and voluntary, and most of the people who partake of life-cycle rituals and occasional holidays are not permanent members of congregations.

Another form of mass expression of post-Soviet Christianity has been pilgrimages. As discussed in chapter 1, they grew exponentially and became a common feature of religious life. As old churches and monasteries across the country have been returned to the Church, a dense network of pious itineraries covered the entire nation's territory and poured beyond, into the Holy Land, Mount Athos, Italian Bari (with the highly revered relics of St. Nicholas), and many other holy places. Practicing believers were the driving force of the pilgrimages, but again, the millions of less-active people would follow, reflecting the overall growth of mobility, tourism, and cultural curiosity.[17] Some major pilgrimages bear a strong symbolic and even political message. The most striking and relatively new example is the so-called Tsar's Days in the area of Ekaterinburg—a massive pilgrimage each July to the place of the murder of the last tsar and his family in 1918. During the Tsar's Days, pilgrimage from across Russia turns into a sequence of mourning processions and commemorative liturgies with a clear message of celebrating Russian Orthodox monarchical tradition and old Russian Christian values.

Regarding the nature of Russian Christian religiosity, there was another less obvious, less spectacular, and probably less

---

17. See Jeanne Kormina, "Inhabiting Orthodox Russia: Religious Nomadism and the Puzzle of Belonging," in *Praying with the Senses: Contemporary Orthodox Christian Spirituality in Practice*, ed. Sonja Luehrmann (Bloomington: Indiana University Press, 2018), 143–62.

massive necessity that triggered the interest in religion: the need for social cohesion or the longing for sociality in a general sense. Late Soviet society was a special case of the lack of middle-rank associations between the family/kinship ties and the state-run apparatus; there was nothing similar to free private enterprises, volunteer societies, or autonomous charities—in other words, neither for-profit nor nonprofit associations were out of government tutelage or control. There was no such thing as a civil society within what we call a totalitarian regime. Religions, as we remember, were under strong pressure and completely withdrawn from public life; the state kept religions, reluctantly, within the "ghettoes of the temples," but never let them outside the temples.

The end of the Soviet Union saw an upsurge of middle-sized associations in society. The market and private property were legalized, free enterprise and capitalism flourished, and civil society activism grew exponentially. Although Vladimir Putin's long presidency has marked a reversion back to a more assertive control of the state over society, the contrast with the Soviet system was still obvious. The religious field was free to develop, and thousands of religious and faith-based communities emerged—charitable, cultural, educational, nationalist, and so on. The Russian Orthodox Church started to restore its formerly reduced, curtailed associational structure, and there was a period of reconstruction of not just church buildings but also of local congregations, parishes, brotherhoods, charities, and religious nongovernmental organizations. In most cases, these associations, as well as nonprofit religious associations of all kinds, were formed not so much from above by the ecclesiastical hierarchy but rather by local, bottom-up initiatives, and they brought together people who were looking for a new type of free sociality. To be sure, this quest for stronger

271

civil community life was a more general trend in society, but religion provided a strong energizing ferment for the quest's satisfaction. In the transitional time of shattered institutional structures, in the time of uncertainties and rapid change, in the time of dramatic reevaluation of long-unquestioned values, religious communities provided small oases of certainty and trust.

This sense of community belonging was especially important for those lower and poorer classes who, with the collapse of the Soviet Union, lost more or less foreseeable economic stability and social guarantees. The Russian Church has been traditionally seen, among other things, as a sort of welfare institution, as it used to be in pre-Revolutionary Russia. It ceased to be so in the Soviet times; it reemerged as such in the aftermath. The newly reopened monasteries became, as they were centuries ago, shelter for disadvantaged people; the churches attracted, among others, socially and psychologically vulnerable people of middle or older age; parishes were often reopened and churches reconstructed by the joint efforts of local non-wealthy enthusiasts, who were seeking a new support for their uncertain identities and a relative material security in the times of economic crisis.[18]

This does not mean, however, that the entire search for religious sociality was just a compensatory impulse of "elderly, lonely women"—the most predictable group of churchgoers, as they used to be characterized. The three quests we have described—for social cohesion, for spiritual fulfillment, and for national identity—were much more universal. All three might merge into one, but not necessarily. In any case, there was

18. See a painstaking analysis of the parish moral economy in Detelina Tocheva, *Intimate Divisions: Street-Level Orthodoxy in Post-Soviet Russia* (Berlin: LIT Verlag, 2017).

also a deep need for sociality among younger people, who, for one reason or another, chose the spiritual version of community to a pragmatic or material one. Some educated and relatively well-to-do urbanites would become fervent Orthodox neophytes trying to construct a committed, tightly held communal life. Their versions of what they believed to be the true Orthodoxy might have strongly varied (for example, in the degree of national feelings or in the degree of openness to secular culture) and differ from the official or mass media presentation of Orthodoxy, but what they were looking for, above all, was this strong sense of commitment and identity, which were sorely lacking.

Spiritual and Sacred in Everyday Practices

When we speak of the causes and real underpinnings of religious revival, we should stay for a moment and decipher what we have called the "spiritual quest." As said above, this social and cultural thirst for things spiritual was an initial incentive that turned people to religion—but "religion" in a very broad and elastic sense. Russian Orthodoxy might have been the most expected and natural version of it for Russians, but by no means was it the only one. We saw an interest in universal values related to an imagined universal religion, or for a universal Christianity as many in the opinion polls called the faith with which they associated themselves. For some, this might mean going global and becoming ecumenical, to even transnationally, spiritual. Yet, being drawn to the biggest, "national" church—the Russian Orthodox—was something quite natural for the majority.

Many of those individuals we call "universal seekers," who were in search of a new experience, were not attracted by the

Big Old Church that seemed obsolete and non-revivable. They associated the old Church with the past, especially because the general trend was restoration, not renewal. The almost total lack of congregational experience and religious knowledge made many feel awkward in the reopened temples. Or, they simply needed another form of communal experience than the one reconstructed in the old Church.

What happened was a massive, overwhelming interest in anything spiritual, sacred, mystical, magical, or occult—beyond and outside the old religious institutions. The 1990s, the first post-Soviet decade, was an amazing time when millions of Russians, who might have paid lip service to Russian Orthodoxy, would go to thousands of self-proclaimed psychics, magicians, spiritists, healers, clairvoyants, and wizards. Millions would put small vessels with water before their TV screens to get the water "energized" by a famous wizard, Alan Chumak, and millions watched the séances of televised healing by a famous psychic, Anatoly Kashpirovsky. The degree of mass credulity was astonishing and could only be explained by the previously forbidden interest in things mysterious, the overall crisis of worldviews, a total lack of knowledge about religious matters, and, plainly, the economic hardships of the first post-Soviet decade.

Russia in the late 1980s and 1990s was indeed a place of spiritual experiments, of rapid opening, and the start of globalization, which coincided with similar trends in the rest of the world. As the Iron Curtain fell, a huge variety of new spiritualities poured into Russia and other post-Soviet lands. The Russian Christian tradition faced powerful new competition from New Age communities, yoga and meditation centers, Sufi and Buddhist groups, neo-pagans, energetic foreign evangelical Protestants, and ambitious new religious movements, Russian and foreign, more or less self-assertive and some aggressively apocalyptic.

The Russian native faith—dubbed "paganism" in Christian parlance and in the media—can be seen as a special, interesting alternative. It resonated with Slavic nativism and nationalism, and in this sense some groups of this kind could come close to Christian nationalism. Yet the native religion was in principle anti-Christian, calling for the rejection of Christianity as foreign deviation and a return back to ancient Slavic polytheism. Some of the neo-pagans were agitating for the joy of life (that Christianity allegedly suppressed) and some practices similar to what the Western Wiccan do, with the only difference that they celebrated not Celtic or Germanic but ethnic Russian folk culture. The associations and groups they created were quite small and did not have much impact, but the image of their ancient traditions was attractive. Finally, however, the loosely tolerant popular Orthodoxy did not harshly contradict the native faith and even included some "native" elements from church practices.[19]

All these groups of different kinds would emerge, blossom, disappear, and then reemerge in a sort of circulation; some lingered and became a part of the cultural landscape mostly at the turning period of the 1990s, during the dismantling of the Soviet system. In many ways, diffused, fragmented, informal beliefs were projected onto what people would expect from regular Orthodox priests and regular Orthodox rituals. People would go back to their Church, but rather than looking for "cold rituals," they would look for some kind of miraculous power. And many Orthodox sites do provide this kind of spirituality. Two such spiritual places in Russian Orthodoxy are

19. Kaarina Aitamurto, *Paganism, Traditionalism, Nationalism: Narratives of Russian Rodnoverie* (London: Routledge, 2016).

a famous Diveyevo monastery not far from Nizhny Novgorod (see chapter 1) and the relics of St. Matrona of Moscow in the Pokrovsky monastery in the Russian capital (see chapter 4). In both cases the relics are expected to produce miraculous power, and they attract thousands of pilgrims daily.

As a matter of fact, there was nothing new in this: for centuries, popular Christianity's authority rested on the faith in miracles produced by icons, relics, sanctified waters, or intense prayer. This faith weakened with the growing knowledge provided by science. Conversely, the dissatisfaction with Soviet ideological materialism might have revitalized the quest for miracles. These fluctuations were galvanized by the cognitive chaos produced by the fall of this materialist ideology. The healing relics of popular saints have been rediscovered; the holy springs were venerated; the wonder-working icons were the foci of flourishing pilgrimages and religious processions; and in many cases, people saw the rituals of communion, baptism, and wedding in terms of their miraculous material effects. Rejecting old Soviet official materialism does not preclude people from being materialistic in another sense—interpreting Orthodox practices as the source of bodily and mundane welfare.

All these multiple forms of popular Christianity are widespread, and they are sometimes mixed up with beliefs that rigorous priests and zealous recent converts would criticize as either pagan superstitions or heresies. However, there are various vantage points to see where purity and authenticity starts and ends. There is a lot of disagreement within the Church and even more outside of it, among the "minimal" believers who decide by themselves the amount and the rigidity of traditional practices or whether to combine them with Zen meditation or yoga, similar to what can be found in the West.

Therefore, in this era of postmodern pluralism and individual spiritual experimentations, Christian Orthodoxy is becoming, indeed, less orthodox, and operates as a certain imagined reality. However, if we take together all the elements, beliefs, and symbols associated with it, it looks quite ubiquitous, ambient, as a part of the cultural atmosphere, especially in combination with the Russian national identity. Thus, when the media announced Virgin Mary's belt or St. Nicholas's relics coming on display for veneration in Moscow (from Mount Athos and the Italian town of Bari, respectively), hundreds of thousands of Muscovites and pilgrims from elsewhere stood in line for ten hours or more, under any weather, to see and touch the relic and to kneel and pray for a few seconds while passing by. The phenomenon is sometimes called "flashmob religion," for the crowd gathers quickly as a snowball, with people various social classes, genders and ages, many of them not members of congregations or even loosely observing believers. A few weeks later, the precious relics were packed up to go to another city where crowds were already waiting to feel a special emotional involvement in a collective feeling linked, in their mind, with a sense of spiritual tradition.

This kind of post-modern mixture with popular devotional elements is rejected by more rigorous Christian groups found in big cities and composed of educated Christians who are referring back to early Christian ideals. They might be skeptical about both the magic of "holy icons" and too much power of the hierarchy in the Church. For them, the exaltation of saints' relics (bringing water or flowers sanctified by the presence of a popular saint's remains) seems too magical. Such groups may face certain distrust both from simpler believers and from the patriarchal institutions.

One such group is a reform-minded Orthodox network, who

are followers of Fr. Alexander Men (see chapter 4). Another one is a network of communities founded by Fr. Georgy Kochetkov. For the latter, the central issue was practical ecclesiology, what exactly "the Church" should mean today. An energetic and learned man, Kochetkov converted to Orthodoxy in the communist times and built a network of recent convert followers. His idea was to revive the spirit of the apostolic brotherhood of the first Christian centuries, and so he created the Brotherhood of the Holy Transfiguration, based not so much on ecclesiastical hierarchy (which he criticized as formal and cold) but on his theology of a love-based Christian brotherly community, *koinonia* in Greek. This ecclesial project drew in many ways on sacramental theology of émigré theologians such as Alexander Schmemann but also resonated with the tradition of *sobornost'* (conciliarity) emphasized by the nineteenth-century Slavophiles, and it was practically realized in a few parishes across Russia. Fr. Georgy also founded the St. Filaret Institute—named after the famous Moscow metropolitan of the nineteenth century—another private theological center for study and research, with a special emphasis on the phenomenon of Christian community.

Fr. Georgy received harsh criticism from conservative quarters, however: he was accused of "Protestant sectarian heresy" and "renovationism." In the mid-1990s, the official ecclesiastical hierarchy reacted harshly by removing him from his parish and even forbidding him from serving at all, and then pressing him to renounce some of the practices that went outside established tradition, including the liturgy in modern Russian language. This conflict was gradually resolved, and Fr. Georgy was restored to his office. The overall reformist project was left aside, but the theology of communion through community remained an important precedent in the recent history of Russian Christianity.[20]

A radically different type of Orthodoxy from these more reformist and relatively liberal groups can be found in the religious landscape. For traditionalist-nationalist currents, the fusion between Christianity and Russianness is a matter of principle. These currents believe that Russian Christianity is the core of a distinctive national tradition. A charismatic figure on this side was Metropolitan of St. Petersburg Ioann Snychev (1927–1995). His writings were a passionate theo-ideology of the Russian nation, its natural link to monarchy, and its global mission, both sacrificial and redemptive, with militant rebukes against the "foreign enemies"; in particular, he linked both liberalism and Bolshevism with Jewish influence. The zealous consistency and ascetic life of Metropolitan Ioann, in combination with his monarchism and nationalism, attracted many from a certain circle of conservative believers. Many of them shared a belief in Russian religious nationalism, which continues to be galvanized by both Muslim immigration and the conflict in Ukraine in the 2010s. A few assertive activist groups such as the Union of Orthodox Banner-Bearers or the so-called Christian State (by analogy to the Islamic State); these extreme nationalists are rather marginal but publicly visible.

Close to this circle were those who created much public resonance on a topic that might seem curious. In the 1990s many conservative clergy and laity resisted the introduction of individual tax numbers (ITN)—or electronic IDs or chips or other high-tech innovations—as they feared these numbers contained the Number of the Beast, the devil's 666 sign men-

20. See Alexander Agadjanian, "Reform and Revival in Moscow Orthodox Communities: Two Types of Religious Modernity," *Archives des sciences sociales de religions* 163 (2013): 75–94.

tioned in the biblical book of Revelation. The naïve popular theology mobilized many and reflected a fear of what they thought of as control over Christian souls imposed by the secular state and, through it, by the globalist machinations anticipating doomsday. The official Theological Commission of the Moscow Patriarchate had to step in and seriously refute these views as superstitions. Although the group of ITN fighters consisted of only a small minority of believers, the case produced a lot of media noise and revealed the amazing diversity of sentiments and worldviews within the Church.[21]

As we can see, there is a large spectrum of forms Christianity is taking in the twenty-first century in a society that is deeply secularized but always in search of stronger spiritual and moral pillars; that is deeply engaged with the rest of the world and yet is always concerned with its special path. State politics have been traditionally involved in these processes.

Russian Christianity, the State, and Politics

How does this new profile of Russian Christianity affect the public and political realm of Russia and other post-Soviet societies? The new Constitution of the Russian Federation, in its article 14, clearly proclaims the secular character of the state. Article 28 of the Constitution guarantees religious freedom and the freedom of conscience—the right to belong to any religion or to have none. We find similar norms in the Constitutions of Ukraine, Belarus, and Moldova, the countries with strong Eastern Christian traditions. This double norm of separation and religious freedom is not, theoretically, dissimilar from the

---

21. See. A. Agadjanian and K. Rousselet, "Globalization and Identity Discourse in Russian Orthodoxy," in *Eastern Orthodoxy in a Global Age. Tradition Faces the Twenty-First Century*, ed. V. Roudometov, A. Agadjanian, and J. Pankhurst (Ithaca: Altamira, 2006), 29–59.

common arrangements in the Western countries. At the same time, it goes without saying, as we have seen earlier in this chapter, that the Orthodox Church dominates and enjoys a high public profile in Russia and in some other post-Soviet states.

Even before the collapse of the Soviet Union, the Russian Federation adopted a new law on religion in 1990 that was very liberal, effectively ending complete state control over religious organizations. After the collapse of communism, a significant number of foreign missionaries came to Russia to convert the "atheists." However, this flood of foreign missionaries—especially American evangelicals, who came with substantial financial resources but very little understanding of Russian culture and history—generated intense resentment among the Russian Orthodox Church in particular and many in Russian society more generally. The Russian Orthodox Church felt that after decades of persecution and control by an atheist state, Western Christians came not to help it recover and rebuild, but to steal their flock away by aggressive proselytization. In response, the Orthodox Church and other religious groups began pressuring the state to provide some protection. This stance found enough support in the State Duma, the Russian parliament, that a new law was finally passed in 1997.

The 1997 law guaranteed freedom of worship for all but distinguished between types of religious organizations. Russian Orthodoxy was named first as having a special historical significance for Russia. Then came a list of four religions recognized as religions of "historical heritage"—in the public discussions this term was rendered as "traditional religions": the list included "Christianity, Islam, Buddhism and Judaism." (Interestingly, "Christianity" and "Russian Orthodoxy" were both distinguished and overlapping.) The organizations belonging to these religions were given full rights. Those religious organizations that were not registered for fifteen years before the law passed—that is, those that were newly introduced ones—were treated differently. They were allowed freedom of worship but had more limited rights in terms of owning property, accessing the media, and inviting foreign guests. The notion was to give a fifteen-year grace period, as it were, for traditional religions to re-establish themselves. Though the law was sharply criticized for contradicting freedom of religion, the real restrictions were initially were quite limited. However, in the 2010s the legislation has been used to restrict the activity of such groups as the Salvation Army, Scientology, and especially Jehovah's Witnesses, who were completely banned from Russia in 2017.[22]

The situation in which the Orthodox Church dominates in Russia creates political, legal, and cultural problems. The first problem is how to reconcile the overwhelming dominance of one faith over others with the principle of religious freedom and legal equality of all religions. Such an issue is less problematic in countries with an initial religious pluralism and the absence of one religion, seen unofficially as "national," but Russia is certainly not unique in having one historically dominant religious tradition. In spite of the vibrant religious pluralization in the early 1990s, when hundreds of Christian and other communities, many of them from the West, found their way to the formerly forbidden territory, the Russian Orthodox Church headed by the Moscow Patriarchate, with a high level of mass approval, has inevitably acquired a immense political prestige and influence, and many official and unofficial privi-

---

22. The legal ban of the Jehovah's Witnesses in 2017 drew on charges of "extremism," and this was the most controversial case. The verdict was upheld by the Supreme Court and caused a storm of criticism worldwide.

leges over other religions. This exclusive status has gradually risen in the 2000s and 2010s.

Given this new political profile and significance of the Russian patriarchal Church, and it is no wonder that this dominant Church received much more direct and indirect financial support from local and central authorities and private businesses than other communities. Minorities were not that lucky. Some of them were contested in the courts and eventually banned. Small Protestant, Pentecostal, and other Christian communities struggled to survive legally under pressure of local authorities. The Roman Catholic Church, a millennium-long rival of Eastern Orthodoxy, faced some pressure as well.[23] With the rise of religious terrorism in the 2000s, when religious issues started to be seen in connection with public security, the new anti-extremist laws hit some Muslim and other religious groups usually not at all related to violence or threat.

It is important to understand, however, that in the country with such a predominant, ambient Orthodox culture, one would expect such problems with minorities, unless the state develops a fine-tuned regulatory system. For the political class, the strong image of revived Orthodox Christianity is a powerful source of legitimacy, which outweighs the liberal principle of religious liberty. The state has, however, another challenge: the fact that there are regions, relatively small but significant, with predominantly non-Christian populations. The Russian Northern Caucasus, with its strong separatist trends, is predominantly Muslim, with some people sympathetic to transnational Islamism. The regions along the Volga River, such as Tatarstan and Bashkortostan, are mostly Muslim too, although the population is mixed. Three regions are populated by the

23. See Forum 18, a Nordic human rights watch group that monitors religious freedom in Russia and former Soviet lands, at www.forum18.org.

followers of Buddhism of the Tibetan tradition—Republics of Kalmykia, Buriatia, and Tuva. Some other regions, especially big cities full of migrants, have mixed populations ethnically and religiously. The Russian state cannot ignore these facts and presents the country, in the official rhetoric, as "multi-ethnic" and "multiconfessional." In different circumstances the rhetoric varies between models—the Orthodox nation and the multiconfessional nation.

In fact, we have just mentioned the two main obstacles, or limits, on the way of making Orthodox Christianity, either legally or de facto, *the* established religion: one is secular legislation and norms, and another, the pragmatism of the state policy, given the multireligious identities of the population. To this we should add yet another, third limit—the overall high level of secular attitudes and the pluralistic composition of society at various levels—from the globally oriented millennials to the political elite itself, with their deeply held secular instincts.

The Orthodox Church nevertheless remains a strong ideological resource used by the political regime. Many leading politicians, including Vladimir Putin, who has been in power since 2000, have declared themselves Orthodox and showed, from time to time, their involvement in some practices or links with some revered clergy.[24] The Church is a powerful economic proprietor and political player affecting local and international policies.

This tandem of church and state echoes the ideal of *symphonia*, the Byzantine principle of a harmonious cooperation

---

24. Thus, there have been rumors (which might be regulated or spontaneous) that Vladimir Putin had special spiritual links with a late revered *starets* (elder), Ioann Krestiankin, and later with a powerful Moscow cleric, Metropolitan Tikhon Shevkunov.

between the two institutions (see chapter 1). To be sure, this ideal can only be used as a metaphor: in no way can the Russian State be called "Christian," and there is no monarch whose power is sacralized as God-given. Even the 2020 amendment to the Constitution that introduced a reference to God ("keeping the memory of the ancestors who transferred to us ideals and faith in God") did not technically cancel the separation principle. Yet the ideal of *symphonia* is frequently invoked by observers and high clerics themselves to stress that the ideological agenda of the Russian state and the Russian Church are, indeed, common.

As a matter of fact, the agenda seems to be common, and it includes a few fundamental elements: a strong authoritarian state; patriotism promoted by both the state and the Church; the importance of Orthodoxy as a historically proven and uncontested spiritual foundation (in a pragmatic alliance with other old, "traditional" religions of the land, such as Islam, Judaism, and Buddhism); and the domination of conservative "traditional values" viewed as based upon Christian morality.

This last point—the so-called traditional values—has been an especially strong discourse in the 2010s, referenced frequently by state bodies and religious activists. Traditional values included the rejection of same-sex relationships, surrogate motherhood, and in-vitro fertilization; criticism of the gender equality agenda; active pro-life stance in abortion issues; and questioning human rights and liberal agenda as a whole as Western and foreign invention unsuitable for Russia. At the same time, a patriotic glorification of a powerful Russia, cemented together by Christian faith, is a common official discourse. Christian moral teaching, in its conservative form, was in line with a conservative turn of the Russian state power and the Russian media in the beginning of the twenty-first century.

The Russian ruling elite has used the notions of "traditional Christian values," with Russia as their defender and preserver, as a way to boost their legitimacy by using a nationalist-patriotic and anti-Western discourse. In this way, the Church and the state were moving close to each other, without losing autonomy.

This tandem relationship has been strongly criticized from different corners. In Russia, such a rapprochement between the Church and the state elicited opposition from liberal groups who considered "clericalization" as anti-constitutional and see the Church as an ideological instrument of the ruling conservative power. These groups reject religion classes in public school, property restitution claims, and the Church's criticism of the human rights agenda. The critique of the Church has also become a political critique. These critical groups claim to be either religious but anti-clerical or simply atheist.

The critique is clearly manifested through what we can call humanistic activism. For example, scientists in universities mobilize against the claims of theology to be publicly accepted as an academic discipline. Some artistic events are filled with controversy. Contemporary art exhibits may be attacked by religious activists for being too blasphemous in their view. The opera *Tannhäuser* by Richard Wagner (in 2015) was banned because it portrayed Jesus in a frivolous context. The *Mathilde* movie screening (2017) was obstructed because it showed the love affair of the last Russian tsar, Nicholas, now a canonized saint, with a ballet dancer. Since such a depiction contradicts the image the Church is trying to portray of him as an ideal family man, many clergy and religious activists demonstrably objected to the film.

The most famous case was the defiant performance of Pussy

Riot, a punk feminist group, titled "Mother of God, Rid Us of Putin!" right in front of the altar of the Moscow Christ the Savior cathedral in February 2012. Even before this event, the group had staged a series of protest performances surrounding Vladimir Putin's re-election campaign in early 2012. None, however, garnered the attention of the one they performed within the cathedral, especially after their video went viral on the internet. Wearing balaclavas and making mock prostrations with their backs turned to the altar, the song criticized Patriarch Kirill's support for Putin and defended feminism and gay rights. Two members of the group were later arrested, convicted of "hooliganism motivated by religious hatred," and sentenced to two years in prison. (A third member was also arrested, but her sentence was commuted.)

The episode received colossal international attention and was interpreted in the West primarily as an attack on free speech and confirmation of Russia's authoritarian drift. Pussy Riot's act was decoded in the West in a way that resonated with the current cultural trend toward identity politics. In Russia, however, the episode was perceived very differently. Although the majority of Russians thought the punishment too severe, only a very small percentage (6 percent) supported or sympathized with Pussy Riot. A much larger percentage understood that they were being prosecuted for "offending the religious feelings of believers" rather than for political protest against Putin (42 percent vs. 17 percent).[25] Western interpretations, both journalistic and academic, failed to understand what Pussy Riot's act meant to most Russians because they did not

25. According to the independent Levada polling agency, which is generally agreed upon even by Western scholars as the most objective and reliable source for public opinion in Russia: "Rossiane o dele Pussy Riot" [Russians on the Pussy Riot Case], July 31, 2012, https://tinyurl.com/tqwqrxz.

take into account the significance of religion in Russian society and view Orthodoxy only as a propaganda tool for the Putin regime. As a result, most Western analysis tended to miss the full cultural picture, particularly the historical context that shaped Russian perceptions—for example, that this very cathedral, as discussed at the beginning of the chapter, symbolizing the rebirth of Orthodoxy after the destruction of the Soviet period. To the majority of Russians, the patriotic association of Orthodoxy, the Russian nation, and the Russian state all seemed to be under attack in the name of "decadent" and "liberal Western" values (such as radical feminism and gay rights). This perception was reinforced by the enthusiastic way Pussy Riot was lauded in the West. In this way, Pussy Riot "offended the religious feelings" even of non-practicing Orthodox because it was perceived as "offending Russia." The polarization over Pussy Riot aligned the political opposition with those who support Western against Russian values in a way that helped bolster support for Putin rather than challenge it.[26]

There have been many cases of this kind, and subsequent heated public discussions. Although the term *blasphemy* has long disappeared in the language of the law, "offending the feelings of believers," however fuzzy and unclear the norm sounds, became a crime in 2013 after the Pussy Riot episode. The very fact of introducing and debating such a norm shows

26. Samuel Greene and Graeme Robertson, *Putin v. the People: The Perilous Politics of a Divided Russia* (New Haven: Yale University Press, 2019), chap. 2. The literature on Pussy Riot is enormous; a typical account that lionizes Pussy Riot is Masha Gessen, *Words Will Break Cement: The Passion of Pussy Riot* (New York: Riverhead, 2014). For interpretations that are more sensitive to the Russian religious context, see the special issues of the journals *Religion and Gender* 4:2 (2014) and *Popular Music and Society* 39:4 (2016); Dmitry Uzlaner and Kristina Stoeckl, "From Pussy Riot's 'Punk Prayer' to Matilda: Orthodox Believers, Critique, and Religious Freedom in Russia," *Journal of Contemporary Religion* 34 (2019): 427–445; John Burgess, "Church, State, and Punk: The Pussy Riot Protest," *The Christian Century*, September 17, 2012.

how sensitive the issues of Christian identity are in today's Russia, and how highly acknowledged Christianity is as a political resource—even though everyday piety is relatively low and there are no political parties or movements openly claiming Christian loyalty.

As we said before, the Russian Church, as a Russian soft power, has been increasingly present outside the Russian Federation. But the Moscow Patriarchate's largest presence has been in Ukraine. Ukraine posed the biggest challenge overall to the political and religious prestige of the Russian Church. The Moscow Patriarchate sought to keep intact its "canonical" boundaries, which included all of the Soviet Union, even after its collapse and the emergence of new independent nations such as Ukraine, Belarus, and Moldova. Ukraine was a particularly complicated region because there were movements dating back to the time of the Russian Revolution for autocephaly of the Ukrainian Church, and Ukraine has been politically torn between pro- and anti-Russian currents within its own society. Much is at stake for the Moscow Patriarchate, however, because nearly one-third of its parishes (some twelve thousand out of thirty-seven thousand at least until 2018) were in Ukraine, and rates of religious participation are higher in Ukraine than Russia.

The problem emerged in the very beginning of Ukraine's independence in 1991 and especially after the Maidan revolution of 2014.[27] In 2018, a part of the Ukrainian Church, backed

27. For a more in-depth look at the Ukrainian case of church-state politics, see Nicholas Denysenko, *The Orthodox Church in Ukraine: A Century of Separation* (DeKalb: Northern Illinois University Press, 2018); Michał Wawrzonek, *Religion and Politics in Ukraine: The Orthodox and Greek Catholic Churches as Elements of Ukraine's Political System* (Cambridge: Cambridge Scholars, 2014); Andrii Krawchuk and Thomas Bremer, eds., *Churches in the Ukrainian Crisis* (New York: Palgrave Macmillan, 2016); Thomas Bremer and Sophie Senyk, "The Current

by the Ukrainian government, applied to Bartholomew I, the Patriarch of Constantinople, with a petition to approve complete independence from the Moscow Patriarchate and to proclaim the full-right Ukrainian Orthodox Church as equal to all others. The response was positive, and Bartholomew granted autocephaly to the Ukrainian Church in January 2019. Moscow was outraged in part because the act was seen as an intrusion by the Constantinople prelate in its internal affairs (since it concerned granting autocephaly to a branch that was seen as a canonical part of the Moscow Patriarchate) and carried out against its wishes. As a result, Moscow broke communion with Constantinople. The whole affair was deeply politicized because of the hostility between the Russian and Ukrainian governments and because of the implied nationalism from both sides. Overall, for Russian Orthodoxy, this was the biggest institutional challenge since the end of the Soviet Union.

Let us briefly reiterate the basic shifts in the post-Soviet developments in Russian Christianity. This was a totally new historical era. Religion became one of the underpinnings of the new sociopolitical setting. After the communist suppression and quasi-oblivion, the Russian Orthodox tradition became tightly linked to the major national narrative as a perennial spiritual tradition. It saw a tremendous return to the public sphere and into the everyday visibility. It recovered its splendid artistic heritage, formerly kept behind the ideological veil. It worked on restoring charitable and other social engagement. It became a common reference in people's search for identity. It was used in a variety of ways—from being a focus of strict observance or high spirituality for some, to being a source of loose and mostly

Ecclesial Situation in Ukraine: Critical Remarks," *St Vladimir's Theological Quarterly* 63 (2019): 27–58.

nominal identity for many. The Russian Orthodox Church as an institution became more powerful in many senses.

This does not mean that the societies where it operated became necessarily more religious. These societies have definitely become more plural, with many new secular options, and traditional Orthodox Christianity was just one of many possible individual choices, although it was quite attractive and strong as a recourse of identity. Christianity retained its pervasive presence in the cultural heritage, old arts, literature, and language, but its constitutive dominance in today's dynamic cultural atmosphere is contested. In spite of administrative unifying efforts of the official ecclesiastical leadership, Russian Christianity is far from monolithic and includes a variety of styles, from right-wing patriots to ecumenical-oriented reformers; from pious miracle-seekers to pursuers of authentic monastic spirituality.

Concluding Remarks

Over the past century, the experience of Russia's Christians has been dramatically different than that of other Christians around the world. The United States, a land characterized by religious pluralism from the beginning, experienced a resurgence of religion in the public sphere over the past four decades, but in the past decade or so it has also experienced a sharp rise in the number of the "nones," the religiously unaffiliated. Western Europe has undergone steady secularization, what sociologists refer to as "believing without belonging," where the majority retains some residual religious identity but participation in religious communities has gradually but continually declined. The Global South, by contrast, has seen a continual rise in the number of Christians over the past century, driven both by conversions (especially in Africa) and demographic factors (in Latin America). No other Christians in Christian-majority countries, however, suffered such a concerted effort by the state to eradicate religion as in the Soviet Union and, for less time and with less intensity, elsewhere in Eastern Europe. As we have seen, during communism not only was the Russian Orthodox Church disestablished and stripped of its property, and not only were the vast majority of churches closed, but in the 1930s clergy and active believers were systematically rounded up and either executed or sent to the Gulag.

Yet Russian Orthodoxy survived; it flowered, especially theologically, among émigrés. In the Soviet Union it adapted, taking new forms among the believers. World War II—still referred to in Russia as "the Great Patriotic War"—renewed the link between Russian Orthodoxy and the Russian nation, securing the former a place, restricted as it was, in the collective imaginary of the post-war Soviet Union. Since the collapse of communism and the demise of the Soviet Union, Russian Orthodoxy became once more a sign of collective, ethnonational belonging, which contributed to a massive revival of Christianity in Russia. This "de-secularization" is quite different from the experience of Western Europe and surprising to those who accepted the model of secularization as inevitable.

At the same time, although the decades of state-enforced secularization have ended, its effects on society and even on the Church have not, and it continues to shape the way in which religion has returned to the post-Soviet public sphere. Secularization has continued, despite the high political profile of Russian Christianity. Yet the secular worldview continues not in its old aggressive form but rather as a more or less plural environment of free choice. At the moment of writing this book, the new environment of religious pluralism and religious freedom is still in process; it is a far cry from Soviet totalitarian secularity. This environment offers plural possibilities, including not only secular choices but also a broad variety of religious options—from a sense of identitarian belonging to a deep individual, faith-based Christian spirituality to cultivated forms of revived spiritual heritage that are both Russian and universally meaningful.

The resurgence of Christianity in post-Soviet Russia has therefore been ripe with paradoxes. When the revival began in the waning years of the Soviet Union, ecclesiastical officials and lay believers alike had great hope in the possibilities of a renewed Christian faith, Church, and culture in Russia. There have been particular clergy and movements that have had profound impacts on particular communities. Yet for many, those hopes have been disappointed. The Russian Orthodox Church has not succeeded in "churching" the majority, whose lifestyle remains largely secular. At the same time, many activist believers hoped for a renewal of the institution of the Russian Orthodox Church itself, which, after decades of restrictions and forced compromises, had taken on many characteristics of Soviet institutional culture. However, the promise of a return to a democratized Church, in the spirit of the 1917 Church Council, never materialized; the Church remains a rigidly hierarchical institution and it has once again allied itself closely with the state, allowing the popular associations of Orthodoxy with Russianness to be weaponized by nationalist rhetoric in order to bolster support for the Putin regime. Only time will tell whether political shifts in Russia might result in widespread disaffection with the Church and its alliance with the state, or whether those who have created vibrant communities will succeed in bringing about a broader renewal of church life.

Further Reading

Adams, Amy Singleton, and Vera Shevzov, eds. *Framing Mary: The Mother of God in Modern, Revolutionary, and Post-Soviet Russian Culture*. DeKalb: Northern Illinois University Press, 2018.

Agadjanian, Alexander, ed. *Armenian Christianity Today: Identity Politics and Popular Practices*. London: Routledge, 2014.

Agadjanian, Alexander. *Turns of Faith, Search for Meaning: Orthodox Christianity and Post-Soviet Experience*. Frankfurt am Main: Peter Lang, 2014.

Alfeyev, Hilarion. *The Mystery of Faith: An Introduction to the Teaching and Spirituality of the Orthodox Church*. London: Darton, Longman and Todd, 2002.

———. *Orthodox Christianity*. 5 vols. Crestwood, NY: St. Vladimir's Seminary Press, 2011–2019.

Angold, Michael, ed. *The Cambridge History of Christianity*. Vol. 5, *Eastern Christianity*. Cambridge: Cambridge University Press, 2014.

Bartholomew (Patriarch). *Encountering the Mystery: Understanding Orthodox Christianity Today*. New York: Doubleday, 2008.

Batalden, Stephen. *Russian Bible Wars: Modern Spiritual Translation and Cultural Authority*. Cambridge: Cambridge University Press, 2013.

Bennett, Brian. *Religion and Language in Post-Soviet Russia*. London: Routledge, 2011.

Billington, James. "Orthodox Christianity and the Russian Transformation." In *Proselytism and Orthodoxy in Russia: The New War for Souls,* edited by John Witte Jr. and Michael Bourdeaux, 51–65. Maryknoll, NY: Orbis, 1999.

Bremer, Thomas. *Cross and Kremlin: A Brief History of the Orthodox Church in Russia.* Translated by Eric Gritsch. Grand Rapids: Eerdmans, 2013.

Breyfogle, Nicholas. *Heretics and Colonizers: Forging Russia's Empire in the South Caucasus.* Ithaca, NY: Cornell University Press, 2005.

Bulgakov, Sergius. *A Bulgakov Anthology.* Edited by Nicholas Zernov. Eugene, OR: Wipf and Stock, 2012.

Burgess, John. *Holy Rus': The Rebirth of Orthodoxy in the New Russia.* New Haven: Yale University Press, 2017.

Casiday, Agustine, ed. *The Orthodox Christian World.* New York: Routledge, 2012.

Christensen, Karin. *The Making of the New Martyrs of Russia: Soviet Repressions in Orthodox Memory.* New York: Routledge, 2017.

Chryssavgis, John. *Creation as Sacrament: Reflections on Ecology and Spirituality.* Edinburgh: T&T Clark, 2019.

———. *Light through Darkness: The Orthodox Tradition.* London: Darton, Longman and Todd, 2004.

Coleman, Heather, ed. *Orthodox Christianity in Imperial Russia: A Source Book on Lived Religion.* Bloomington: Indiana University Press, 2014.

Coleman, Heather. *Russian Baptists and the Spiritual Revolution, 1905-1929.* Bloomington: Indiana University Press, 2005.

Corley, Felix. *Religion in the Soviet Union: An Archival Reader.* New York: NYU Press, 1996.

Crow, Gillian, ed. *Metropolitan Anthony of Sourozh: Essential Writings.* Maryknoll, NY: Orbis, 2010.

Crow, Gillian. *"This Holy Man": Impressions of Metropolitan Anthony.* Crestwood, NY: St. Vladimir's Seminary Press, 2005.

———. *Orthodoxy for Today.* London: SPCK, 2008.

Cunningham, Mary, and Elizabeth Theokritoff, eds. *The Cambridge Companion to Orthodox Christian Theology.* Cambridge: Cambridge University Press, 2010.

Daniel, Wallace L. *Russia's Uncommon Prophet: Father Aleksandr Men and His Times.* DeKalb: Northern Illinois University Press, 2016.

Davis, Nathaniel. *A Long Walk to Church: A Contemporary History of Russian Orthodoxy.* 2nd ed. Cambridge, MA: Westview, 2003.

Denysenko, Nicholas. *The Orthodox Church in Ukraine: A Century of Separation.* DeKalb: Northern Illinois University Press, 2018.

Destivelle, Hyacinthe. *The Moscow Council (1917–1918): The Creation of the Conciliar Institutions of the Russian Orthodox Church.* Translated by Jerry Ryan. Notre Dame: University of Notre Dame Press, 2015.

Dunn, Dennis. *The Catholic Church and Russia: Popes, Patriarchs, Tsars and Commissars.* Burlington, VT: Ashgate, 2004.

Erdozain, Dominic, ed. *The Dangerous God: Christianity and the Soviet Experiment.* DeKalb: Northern Illinois University Press, 2017.

Evlogy (Georgievsky), and Tatiana Manukhina. *My Life's Journey: The Memoirs of Metropolitan Evlogy.* Translated by Alexander Lisenko. Yonkers, NY: St. Vladimir's Seminary Press, 2014.

Fagan, Geraldine. *Believing in Russia. Religious Policies after Communism.* London: Routledge, 2014.

Fedotov, G. P., ed. *The Way of a Pilgrim and Other Classics of Russian Spirituality.* Mineoloa, NY: Dover, 2003.

Fedotov, G. P. *The Russian Religious Mind.* 2 vols. Cambridge, MA: Harvard University Press, 1966.

Florensky, Pavel. *Iconostasis.* Translated by Olga Andrejev and Donald Sheehan. Crestwood, NY: St. Vladimir's Seminary Press, 1996.

———. *The Pillar and Ground of the Truth.* Translated by Boris Jakim. Princeton: Princeton University Press, 1997.

Freeze, Gregory. "Russian Orthodoxy: Church, People and Politics in Imperial Russia." In *The Cambridge History of Russia.* Vol. 2, *Imperial*

Russia, 1689-1917, edited by Dominic Lieven, 284–305. Cambridge: Cambridge University Press, 2015.

———. "Russian Orthodoxy and Politics in the Putin Era." Carnegie Endowment Task Force White Paper, https://tiny url.com/ wlwtkcc.

Friesen, Aileen. *Colonizing Russia's Promised Land: Orthodoxy and Community on the Siberian Steppe.* Toronto: University of Toronto Press, 2020.

Gallaher, Brandon, and Paul Ladouceur, eds. *The Patristic Witness of Georges Florovsky: Essential Theological Writings.* New York: Bloomsbury, 2019.

Gavrilyuk, Paul. *Georges Florovsky and the Russian Religious Renaissance.* Oxford: Oxford University Press, 2014.

Geraci, Robert, and Michael Khodarkovsky, eds. *Of Religion and Empire: Missions, Conversion, and Tolerance in Tsarist Russia.* Ithaca, NY: Cornell University Press, 2001.

Goldfrank, David, trans. and ed. *Nil Sorsky: The Authentic Writings.* Kalamazoo, MI: Cistercian Publications, 2008.

——— trans. and ed. *The Monastic Rule of Iosif Volotsky.* 2nd ed. Kalamazoo, MI: Cistercian Publications, 2000.

Greene, Robert. *Bodies like Bright Stars: Saints and Relics in Orthodox Russia.* DeKalb: Northern Illinois University Press, 2010.

Hackel, Sergei. *Pearl of Great Price: The Life of Mother Maria Skobtsova, 1891-1945.* Crestwood, NY: St. Vladimir's Seminary Press, 1982.

Hamburg, G. M., and Randall A. Poole, eds. *A History of Russian Philosophy, 1830-1930: Faith, Reason, and the Defense of Human Dignity.* Cambridge: Cambridge University Press, 2010.

Horujy, Sergey S. *Practices of the Self and Spiritual Practices: Michel Foucault and the Eastern Christian Discourse.* Edited by Kristina Stoeckl. Translated by Boris Jakim. Grand Rapids: Eerdmans, 2015.

Hovorun, Cyril. *Political Orthodoxies: The Unorthodoxies of the Church Coerced.* Minneapolis: Fortress Press, 2018.

Karpov, Vycheslav, Elena Lisovskaya, and David Barry. "Ethnodoxy: How Popular Ideologies Fuse Religious and Ethnic Identities." *Journal of the Scientific Study of Religion* 51 (2012): 638–55.

Kenworthy, Scott M. "Monasticism in Modern Russia." In *Monasticism in Eastern Europe and the Former Soviet Republics*, edited by Ines Angeli Murzaku, 265–84. London: Routledge, 2015.

———. "Rethinking the Orthodox Church and the Bolshevik Revolution." *Revolutionary Russia* 31, no. 1 (2018): 1–23.

———. *The Heart of Russia: Trinity-Sergius, Monasticism, and Society after 1825.* Oxford: Oxford University Press, 2010.

———. "To Save the World or to Renounce It: Modes of Moral Action in Russian Orthodoxy." In *Religion, Community, and Morality after Communism,* edited by Mark Steinberg and Catherine Wanner, 21–54. Bloomington: Indiana University Press, 2008.

Khomiakov, A. S. *On Spiritual Unity: A Slavophile Reader.* Edited by Boris Jakim and Robert Bird. Hudson, NY: Lindisfarne, 1998.

Kirill (Patriarch). *Freedom and Responsibility: A Search for Harmony —Human Rights and Personal Dignity.* London: Darton, Longman and Todd, 2011.

Kirill, (Patriarch). *Patriarch Kirill in His Own Words.* Yonkers, NY: St. Vladimir's Seminary Press, 2016.

Kivelson, Valerie, and Robert Greene, eds. *Orthodox Russia: Belief and Practice under the Tsars.* University Park: Pennsylvania State University Press, 2003.

Kizenko, Nadieszda. *The Prodigal Saint: Father John of Kronstadt and the Russian People.* University Park: Pennsylvania State University Press, 2000.

Koellner, Tobias. *Practicing Without Belonging? Entrepreneurship, Morality, and Religion in Contemporary Russia.* Berlin: LIT, 2012.

Kornblatt, Judith. *Doubly Chosen: Jewish Identity, the Soviet Intelligentsia, and the Russian Orthodox Church.* Madison: University of Wisconsin Press, 2004.

Knox, Zoe, and Anastasia Mitrofanova. "The Russian Orthodox Church." In *Eastern Christianity and Politics in the Twenty-First Century*, edited by Lucian Leustean, 38–66. New York: Routledge, 2014.

Krawchuk, Andrii, and Thomas Bremer, eds. *Churches in the Ukrainian Crisis.* New York: Palgrave Macmillan, 2016.

Ladouceur, Paul. *Modern Orthodox Theology.* New York: Bloomsbury, 2019.

Louth, Andrew. *Introducing Eastern Orthodox Theology.* Downers Grove, IL: IVP Academic, 2013.

———. *Modern Orthodox Thinkers: From the Philokalia to the Present.* Downers Grove, IL: IVP Academic, 2015.

Luehrmann, Sonja, ed. *Praying with the Senses: Contemporary Orthodox Christian Spirituality in Practice.* Bloomington: Indiana University Press, 2018.

McGuckin, John Anthony, ed. *The Encyclopedia of Eastern Orthodox Christianity.* Oxford: Wiley-Blackwell, 2011.

McGuckin, John Anthony. *The Eastern Orthodox Church: A New History.* New Haven: Yale University Press, 2020.

———. *The Orthodox Church: An Introduction to Its History, Doctrine, and Spiritual Culture.* Oxford: Wiley-Blackwell, 2011.

———. *The Path of Christianity: The First Thousand Years.* Downers Grove, IL: IVP Academic, 2017.

———. *Standing in God's Holy Fire: The Byzantine Tradition.* London: Darton, Longman and Todd, 2001.

Men, Alexander. *Christianity for the Twenty-First Century: The Prophetic Writings of Alexander Men.* Edited by Elizabeth Roberts and Ann Shukman. New York: Continuum, 1996.

Meyendorff, John. *St. Gregory Palamas and Orthodox Spirituality.* Crestwood, NY: St. Vladimir's Seminary Press, 1974.

Michelson, Patrick, and Judith Deutsch Kornblatt, eds. *Thinking Orthodox in Modern Russia: Culture, History, Context.* Madison: University of Wisconsin Press, 2014.

Oleksa, Michael. *Orthodox Alaska: A Theology of Mission.* Crestwood, NY: St. Vladimir's Seminary Press, 1992.

Papkova, Irina. *The Orthodox Church and Russian Politics.* New York: Oxford University Press, 2011.

Parry, Ken, ed. The Blackwell Companion to Eastern Christianity. Malden, MA: Blackwell, 2007.

———, et al., eds. The Blackwell Dictionary of Eastern Christianity. Malden, MA: Blackwell, 2001.

Pattison, George, Randall Poole, and Carolyn Emerson, eds. *Oxford Handbook of Russian Religious Thought.* Oxford: Oxford University Press, 2020.

Perrie, Maureen, ed. *The Cambridge History of Russia.* Vol. 1, *From Early Rus' to 1689.* Cambridge: Cambridge University Press, 2006.

Plekon, Michael, ed. *Tradition Alive: On the Church and the Christian Life in Our Time.* Lanham, MD: Rowan and Littlefield, 2003.

Poole, Randall, and Paul Werth, eds. *Religious Freedom in Modern Russia.* Pittsburgh: University of Pittsburgh Press, 2018.

Pyman, Avril. *Pavel Florensky, A Quiet Genius: The Tragic and Extraordinary Life of Russia's Unknown da Vinci.* New York: Continuum, 2010.

Richters, Katja. *The Post-Soviet Russian Orthodox Church: Politics, Culture and Greater Russia.* New York: Routledge, 2012.

Robson, Roy. *Solovki: The Story of Russia Told through Its Most Remarkable Islands.* New Haven: Yale University Press, 2004.

Rock, Stella. *Popular Religion in Russian: "Double Belief" and the Making of an Academic Myth.* London: Routledge, 2009.

Rosenthal, Bernice, and Martha Bohachevsky-Chomiak, eds. *A Revolution of the Spirit: Crisis of Value in Russia, 1890–1924.* New York: Fordham University Press, 1990.

Schmemann, Alexander. *For the Life of the World: Sacraments and Orthodoxy.* Crestwood, NY: St. Vladimir's Seminary Press, 1995.

———, ed. *Ultimate Questions: An Anthology of Modern Russian Religious Thought.* Crestwood, NY: St. Vladimir's Seminary Press, 1977.

Shevzov, Vera. "Iconic Piety in Russia." In *A People's History of Christianity.* Vol. 6, *Modern Christianity to 1900,* edited by Amanda Porterfield, 178–208. Minneapolis: Fortress Press, 2007.

———. *Russian Orthodoxy on the Eve of Revolution.* Oxford: Oxford University Press, 2004.

———. "Scripting the Gaze: Liturgy, Homilies and the Kazan Icon of the Mather of God in Late Imperial Russia." In *Sacred Stories: Religion and Spirituality in Modern Russia,* edited by M. Steinberg and H. Coleman, 61–92. Bloomington: Indiana University Press, 2007.

Shukman, Ann. "Metropolitan Sergi Stragorodsky: The Case of the Representative Individual." *Religion, State and Society* 34, no. 1 (March 2006): 51–61.

Siecienski, A. Edward. *Orthodox Christianity: A Very Short Introduction.* Oxford: Oxford University Press, 2019.

Skobtsova, Mother Maria. *Mother Maria Skobtsova: Essential Writings.* Translated by Richard Pevear and Larissa Volokhonsky. Maryknoll, NY: Orbis, 2003.

Smith, Douglas. *Rasputin: Faith, Power, and the Twilight of the Romanovs.* New York: Picador, 2017.

Smolkin, Victoria. *A Sacred Space Is Never Empty: A History of Soviet Atheism.* Princeton: Princeton University Press, 2018.

Solovyov, Vladimir S. *A Solovyov Anthology.* Edited by S. L. Frank. New York: Saint Austin, 2001.

Steinberg, Mark, and Catherine Wanner, eds. *Religion, Morality, and Community in Post-Soviet Societies.* Bloomington: Indiana University Press, 2008.

Steinberg, Mark, and Heather Coleman, eds. *Sacred Stories: Religion and Spirituality in Modern Russia.* Bloomington: Indiana University Press, 2007.

Tolstaya, Katya, ed. *Orthodox Paradoxes: Heterogeneities and Complexities in Contemporary Russian Orthodoxy.* Leiden: Brill, 2014.

Tsurikov, Vladimir, ed. *Metropolitan Antonii (Khrapovitskii): Archpastor of the Russian Diaspora.* Jordanville, NY: Foundations of Russian History, 2014.

Tocheva, Detelina. *Intimate Divisions: Street-Level Orthodoxy in Post-Soviet Russia.* Berlin: LIT, 2017.

Valliere, Paul. *Modern Russian Theology: Bukharev, Soloviev, Bulgakov.* Grand Rapids: Eerdmans, 2000.

Wanner, Catherine. *Communities of the Converted: Ukrainians and Global Evangelism.* Ithaca: Cornell University Press, 2007.

———, ed. *State Secularism and Lived Religion in Soviet Russia and Ukraine.* New York: Oxford University Press, 2012.

Ware, Kallistos. *The Orthodox Way.* Crestwood, NY: St. Vladimir's Seminary Press, 1995.

Ware, Timothy. *The Orthodox Church.* London: Penguin, 2015.

Wawrzonek, Michał. *Religion and Politics in Ukraine: The Orthodox and Greek Catholic Churches as Elements of Ukraine's Political System.* Newcastle: Cambridge Scholars, 2014.

Werth, Paul. *The Tsar's Foreign Faiths. Toleration and Fate of Religious Freedom in Imperial Russia.* Oxford: Oxford University Press, 2014.

Williams, Rowan. *Dostoevsky: Language, Faith and Fiction.* Waco, TX: Baylor University Press, 2008.

Witte, John, Jr., and Frank Alexander, eds. *The Teachings of Modern Orthodox Christianity on Law, Politics, and Human Nature.* New York: Columbia University Press, 2007.

Wolf, Koenraad De. *Dissident for Life: Alexander Ogorodnikov and the Struggle for Religious Freedom in Russia.* Grand Rapids: Eerdmans, 2013.

Wybrew, Hugh. *Orthodox Liturgy: The Development of the Eucharist Liturgy in the Byzantine Rite.* London: SPCK, 2013.

Zenkovsky, Serge, ed. *Medieval Russia's Epics, Chronicles, and Tales.* New York: Penguin, 1974.

Zernov, Nicholas. *The Russian Religious Renaissance of the Twentieth Century.* London: Darton, Longman and Todd, 1963.

Zhuk, Sergei. *Russia's Lost Reformation: Peasants, Millennialism, and Radical Sects in Southern Russia and Ukraine, 1830–1917.* Baltimore: Johns Hopkins University Press, 2004.

Znamenski, Andrei. *Shamanism and Christianity: Native Encounters with Russian Orthodox Missions in Siberia and Alaska, 1820–1917.* Westport, CT: Greenwood, 1999.

Index